Relationship-Centered Practices in Early Childhood

Relationship-Centered Practices in Early Childhood

Working with Families, Infants, & Young Children at Risk

by

Gail L. Ensher, Ed.D.
Syracuse University
New York

and

David A. Clark, M.D.
Children's Hospital at Albany Medical Center
New York

with invited contributors

·P A U L·H·
BROOKES
PUBLISHING Cº ®

Baltimore • London • Sydney

Paul H. Brookes Publishing Co.
Post Office Box 10624
Baltimore, Maryland 21285-0624
USA

www.brookespublishing.com

Typeset by Integrated Publishing Solutions, Grand Rapids, Michigan.
Manufactured in the United States of America by
Sheridan Books, Inc., Chelsea, Michigan.

The information provided in this book is in no way meant to substitute for a qualified health care professional's advice or expert opinion. Readers should consult a qualified health care professional if they are interested in more information. This book is sold without warranties of any kind, express or implied, and the publisher and authors disclaim any liability, loss, or damage caused by the contents of this book.

The individuals described in this book are composites or real people whose situations are masked and are based on the authors' experiences. Poems and parent quotes are used with permission; as applicable, names and identifying details have been changed to protect confidentiality.

As applicable, the photographs that appear throughout the book and on the cover are used by permission of the individuals pictured or their parents or guardians.

Library of Congress Cataloging-in-Publication Data

Ensher, Gail L.
  Relationship-centered practices in early childhood : working with families, infants, and young children at risk / Gail L. Ensher and David A. Clark with invited contributors.
    p.   cm.
  Includes index.
  ISBN-13: 978-1-59857-059-5 (pbk.)
  ISBN-10: 1-59857-059-5
  1. Families. 2. Communication in families. 3. Child rearing. 4. Parent and child. 5. Family social work. 6. Parents of children with disabilities—Services for. I. Clark, David A. (David Albert) II. Title.
HQ519.E57   2011
362.7'2532–dc23   2011017980

British Library Cataloguing in Publication data are available from the British Library.

2015   2014   2013   2012   2011

10   9   8   7   6   5   4   3   2   1

Contents

About the Authors

Gail L. Ensher, Ed.D., Professor of Education, Teaching and Leadership Program, School of Education, Syracuse University, 155 Huntington Hall, Syracuse, New York 13244

In addition to her work as Professor of Education, Gail L. Ensher is Coordinator of two master's degree programs in the School of Education at Syracuse University: Early Childhood Special Education and the Inclusive Program on Severe Disabilities. She received her doctorate in special education from Boston University in 1971. Prior to receiving her doctoral degree, she taught for 3 years in Hanover, New Hampshire, and Quincy, Massachusetts. She later assumed a position on the faculty at the Pennsylvania State University in State College prior to taking a position on the faculty at Syracuse University. For many years, Dr. Ensher has been actively involved in teaching, writing and research, and community service related to families and young children who are at risk and have developmental disabilities. At Syracuse University, she teaches courses at the undergraduate and graduate levels about methods and curricula in early childhood special education, families of young children with special needs, the assessment of infants and young children, and the theoretical foundations of early childhood special education. She has extensive experience in clinical work with infants, young children, and their families and continues to train graduate students in this area of expertise. She has authored play-based assessments for infants and toddlers as well as books for professionals—most recently *Families, Infants, and Young Children at Risk: Pathways to Best Practice* (Paul H. Brookes Publishing Co., 2009). In addition, Dr. Ensher coauthored with Dr. David A. Clark the first and second editions of *Newborns at Risk: Medical Care and Psychoeducational Intervention* (Aspen Publishers, 1986, 1994).

Dr. Ensher is a single mother of two daughters adopted from Calcutta, India—Kimberly and Lindsey—28 and 24 years of age, respectively, at the time of publication.

David A. Clark, M.D., Professor and Martha Lepow Chairman of Pediatrics, Professor of Obstetrics and Gynecology, Albany Medical College, Director, Children's Hospital at Albany Medical Center, 43 New Scotland Avenue, Albany, New York 12208

David A. Clark is a pediatrician and neonatologist who trained at North Carolina Memorial Hospital, University of North Carolina at Chapel Hill, and completed a Neonatology Fellowship at Rainbow Babies and Children's Hospital, Case Western Reserve University in Cleveland, Ohio, and State University of New York, Upstate Medical Center in Syracuse. Dr. Clark's certifications include Diplomate, American Board of Pediatrics; the American Board of Pediatrics, Sub-Board of Neonatal-Perinatal Medicine; and the Neonatal Resuscitation Program, Regional Instructor. Dr. Clark is a member of 25 professional societies, including the American Academy of Pediatrics—Fellow, Section on Perinatal Pediatrics, Section on Gastroenterology and Nutrition, Section on Transport Medicine, and Critical Care Section; the Society of Pediatric Research; American College of Nutrition; American Pediatric Society; and the New York Academy of Sciences. Dr. Clark's curriculum vita includes a total of 103 peer-reviewed publications; 4 books; more than 200 abstracts; and numerous invited chapters, reviews, and presentations.

Dr. Clark is the father of three daughters and a grandfather of six, including William David (WD), who tragically died during Hurricane Katrina at the age of 4 years.

Contributors

Melissa M. Doyle, Ph.D., M.S.W.
Assistant Professor of Pediatrics
Clinical Director of Behavioral
  Pediatrics
Department of Pediatrics
Albany Medical College
43 New Scotland Avenue
Albany, New York 12208

Marilyn A. Fisher, M.D., M.S.
Associate Professor of Pediatrics
Core Faculty, Alden March Bioethics
  Institute
Albany Medical College
Children's Hospital at Albany Medical
  Center
43 New Scotland Avenue, MC-101
Albany, New York 12208

Laura A. Jenkins, M.S.
Clinical Coordinator
Special Programs Inc./Little Lukes
159 West 1st Street
Oswego, New York 13126

Robin J. Streever, M.S.
School of Education
Syracuse University
Post Office Box 365
Jordan, New York 13080

Mary Beth Sullivan, M.S.
Speech-Language Pathologist
Special Programs Inc./Little Lukes
Margaret L. Williams Developmental
  Evaluation Center
215 Bassett Street
Syracuse, New York 13210

Preface

Relationships are the cornerstone for working with families, infants, and young children at risk. Our work offers many rewards, presents many challenges, and crosses all of our respective disciplines in the medical, educational, and clinical fields. With a rapidly changing world of technology, demographics, and cultures in the United States, early intervention services and training programs for educational and the health-related professions now emphasize more than ever the importance of working with families. Still, professionals in the field and students in training often find themselves falling short in terms of the requisite knowledge and experience in practical application and problem-solving strategies essential to this area of expertise. *Relationship-Centered Practices in Early Childhood: Working with Families, Infants, and Young Children at Risk*, a companion text for *Families, Infants, and Young Children at Risk: Pathways to Best Practice*, co-authored by Ensher, Clark, and Songer (2009), has grown out of a need to address these concerns. This book is designed to provide new visions for working with families, coupled with research-based, practical suggestions to nurture healthy relationships with families across a continuum of cultural, economic, and educational situations and event-based contexts. Better preparing and enhancing the abilities of professionals and students to serve young children and their families in natural environments is the primary agenda of this book.

Audience

Like its companion work, *Relationship-Centered Practices in Early Childhood* has been written for professionals across multiple disciplines, graduate students in educational, medical, and clinical preparation programs, and families. The book is centered on key educational, developmental, cultural, and psychosocial issues and challenges that individuals in the helping professions face every day in their work with families and young children with established disabilities and with children at risk for later developmental delays.

This comprehensive book discusses working with families in a variety of settings, including medical facilities such as neonatal intensive care nurseries, educational and clinical programs, homes, neighborhoods, and communities. Teachers, nurses, physicians, clinical personnel (e.g., speech, physical, and occupational therapists), social workers, marriage and family therapists, and psychologists will find essential information in this work to aid them in building and nurturing relationships that are vital to best practice. Topics addressed include

- The needs of training programs, as reflected in historical traditions
- The challenges of working together on teams with family members and other professionals and best environments to facilitate relationships
- The essential role of family relationships in the early years
- High-risk pregnancies and early detection
- Teen parenting
- Substance abuse and child abuse and neglect
- The changing context of American families in terms of membership, culture, and language
- Families living with and learning about their children with disabilities
- Dealing with family crisis in human-made and natural disasters

Goals and Focus

After reading this book, professionals and students in training should be able to answer the following questions:

1. Why are relationships with family members and young children vitally important?
2. Based on evidence from research, what is the foundation for developing and nurturing relationships that is most essential for working with families across diverse contexts?
3. What are the experiences that are most critical to facilitate adult-to-adult and child-to-adult healthy relationships and emotional well-being?
4. How can relationship-based learning be best infused into diverse family situations, events, dynamics, structures, and cultural contexts?
5. What are the implications of what is known about relationship-centered learning for work with other professionals?
6. What is the foundation of relationship-centered learning that is generic to positive interactions between caregivers and their children, and how can we best facilitate such learning?
7. What are the likely challenges in our work with families and other professionals and potential strategies for problem-solving?
8. What are some of the indicators of "successful" relationships and best practices with families and young children?

Organization

Relationship-Centered Practices in Early Childhood is organized into four major sections and includes features intended to enhance reader learning and understanding. Each chapter begins with a set of *chapter highlights* and illustrations or *voices from the field* that exemplify the content and focus. Each chapter closes with a section on *beneficial outcomes* for crystallizing and summarizing essential points of information as well as *questions for discussion* to facilitate reflection and translation of knowledge into best practice. The book is organized around four primary themes to offer the reader a blueprint for understanding and learning.

Part I: Laying the Foundation discusses relationships as the foundation of working with families, continuing needs and challenges of current training and professional practices, a framework for best practice that is grounded in systems theory, and practical approaches to create environments for building partnerships with families. It includes strategies for problem-solving and for working with professionals across disciplines, agencies, and families, who may not share the same perspectives on early intervention and medical treatment.

Part II: Beginnings focuses on new research about the early years, brain development, and the critical connections of building relationships; issues for families attempting to have children at later ages; new horizons in the medical community concerning prevention and genetic counseling with families; continuing challenges of working with teen parents; ongoing issues of working with families with preterm infants; and, finally, the dramatic changes in the culture of American families and the implications of those changes for service delivery.

Part III: Peaks and Valleys Along the Way addresses work with families facing a variety of different scenarios and event-changing situations. Topics include having a child with disabilities; forming relationships with brothers and sisters in families with children who have disabilities; developing supportive relationships with families following the death of a child; developing relationships with families struggling with the ills of child abuse and neglect and/or substance abuse; homelessness and children in America; and, finally, the responsibilities of working with children and adults who have lost family members through natural disasters such as hurricanes or as a result of war or military service.

Part IV: Emerging and Finding the Way Again offers suggestions for resolution to family crisis. This last section encompasses processes for partnerships and collaboration despite differences in priorities, ways to help families build self-sustaining strategies for acceptance, and moving forward. We revisit some ideas for professionals working together, with a few final thoughts about working in hospital and clinical settings, home environments, and school-based and educational settings and supporting families in their local communities. We propose an agenda for the future and, finally, discuss the benefits and power of nurturing relationships with families.

We (the authors) have a breadth and wealth of experience with many families over the years in a variety of settings. We have been involved in providing direct service to children and their caregivers regarding medical treatment, educational programming, and offering guidance as best we could, attempting to nurture relationships to sustain and support families along their pathways when we were no longer with them. It is this experience and the gifts of these encounters that have led us to the imperative of writing this work with the hope that it may have a meaningful and sustaining impact on students in training, other professionals, families, and young children in the years ahead.

Acknowledgments

Books and their respective chapters bear the names of those primarily responsible for the written word. However, those of us engaged in such efforts know very well that the conception, development, and delivery of these works extend far beyond identified authorship. In recognition of this fact, we are deeply indebted to the following people who have touched our lives, shaped our thinking, and thus made this book possible:

- Children and grandchildren in our own families and children whom we have known over the years and their families
- Students who have challenged us, worked with us, and taught us lessons that we otherwise would not have realized
- Special people without whose devoted hours and expertise this manuscript would not have been completed: Janis Keehan, Rachael Zubal-Ruggieri, and Jillian Teresa Scanlon

A Dedication to Nan Songer

To many of us who knew Nan, she was an inspiration.
To countless families and young children, she was a shining beacon of hope.
To members of her family and coworkers, she was a pillar of strength,
through the worst and the best of times.
For those of us who knew and loved her,
we are so grateful that Nan crossed our paths,
warmly touching our lives in immeasurable ways.
This book, written by her co-authors of Pathways to Best Practice,
is dedicated in loving memory to Nan.

Nancy S. Songer
1951–2008

Introduction

Relationships as Foreground

Gail L. Ensher and David A. Clark

Family- and relationship-centered practices constitute one of the basic tenets of the Individuals with Disabilities Education Improvement Act (IDEA) of 2004 (PL 108-446) on behalf of infants and young children who have disabilities or are at risk and their families. Those in the educational, medical, and clinical fields now share a more familiar language and ideology in terms of working with families of young children; however, this mandate is translated into practice across disciplines in very different ways.

In large part, providers' perspectives have arisen from the responsibilities and substance of what they do as they work with families and children, as well as the traditions of their own training backgrounds (O'Neil, Ideishi, Nixon-Cave, & Kohrt, 2008; Raver, 2005). That said, the helping professions share a common ground of historical practice—that is, a largely "deficit" orientation, which gradually has moved toward a more contemporary perspective of competence, driven by legislation and a call for family centeredness (IDEA, 2004). This dynamic continuum between "fixing what is wrong" versus building on the strengths of children and families persists, and perhaps necessarily so. A paramount challenge facing professionals is the development and nurturing of relationships, which can sustain families beyond their time of involvement with providers. An ever-present reality is that families do need different things from service providers. Furthermore, the question remains: As professionals, what do we do and say when solutions are unclear, hardships seem to defy words, and sorrow rocks the foundations of our faith and training? Moreover, once we have made decisions about our different pathways with families, how do we know that our practices are grounded in a solid base of research evidence (Dunst, Trivette, & Hamby, 2007; Singer, Ethridge, & Aldana, 2007; Turnbull, Summers, Lee, & Kyzar, 2007; Warren & Brady, 2007)?

TRADITIONS: HISTORY AT A GLANCE

Stories of families having negative experiences with professionals are not new, nor are they limited to a particular field. Families are sometimes given the news of their infant's disability carelessly. Families of diverse cultures sometimes lack access to services. Families struggling with issues of child neglect, abuse, and violence may encounter barriers seemingly insurmountable. In all of these cases, families are in need of assistance, but how that assistance is delivered makes a world of difference to them. Individuals in need of services are sometimes perceived as different and are treated differently, sometimes even devalued. This has long-lasting repercussions for families and often leads them to feel disempowered in decision-making processes.

Over the past 2 decades, many researchers and scholars have revisited the concept of help-giving services for families (Dunst, 2000; Dunst, Trivette, & Deal, 1988). Inevitably, there are questions and dilemmas. For instance, how do physicians best counsel families about aggressive treatment for their newborn with a condition or degree of prematurity known to be incompatible with life? How do teachers best counsel families about strategies for guiding their preschool child's challenging behavior at home as well as at school? How do doctors best counsel families living below the poverty line about the advisability of in vitro fertilization and multiple gestations, when the parents already have two or three other children younger than age 5? How do teachers work with families who prefer to keep their young child with special needs at home rather than take advantage of preschool services? How do both teachers and physicians best serve preschool children with multiple health care needs within the context of typical educational programs? There are no easy answers to such questions.

What *is* clear, however, is that guidelines for working with families have changed. The following are just a few of the recent and emerging efforts on behalf of families with infants and young children with special needs:

- Families must be involved as full partners in almost every aspect of the services they receive.

- Children must be served within the natural context of their family.

- Preservice and in-service programs for physicians, educators, and clinical personnel must address the concept of family-centered practice in the 21st century (American Academy of Pediatrics, Task Force on the Family, 2003; American Academy of Pediatrics, Task Force on the Future of Pediatric Education II, 2000; Ensher, Clark, & Songer, 2009).

- Services must be coordinated, collaborative, flexible, and accessible to families in communities (American Academy of Pediatrics, Council on Children with Disabilities, 2006; American Academy of Pediatrics, Council on Community Pediatrics, 2009; American Academy of Pediatrics Medical Home Initiatives for Children with Special Needs Project Advisory Committee, 2004; McAllister, Presler, & Cooley, 2007).

- Educators and pediatricians are increasingly recognizing the need to provide counsel to parents on family-related issues, including concerns about domestic violence, substance abuse, and child neglect and abuse (American Academy of Pediatrics, Task Force on the Family, 2003). More and more, topics such as the impact of poverty, raising children in families with same-sex parents, financial access to care, the effects of depression in families, the impact of discord and divorce, the importance of fathering, the risks of single parenthood, and transcultural aspects of perinatal health care are appearing in pediatric, nursing, developmental, psychological, and educational journals.

- All disciplines are charged with making explanations to families that are clear, jargon free, and consistent.

- Educators, physicians, and clinical personnel are increasingly focused on strength-based strategies and services in working with families (Ensher et al., 2009).

- As professionals work in teams, which is mandated by IDEA 2004, families are recognized as an essential part of the collaborative process. Furthermore, as parents struggle to raise their children in an increasingly complex and challenging world, members of professional teams, in particular educators and physicians, are in a unique position to support them. It is providers' responsibility to search for innovative and evidence-based ways to accomplish this primary goal in the decades ahead.

A NEW AGENDA: NURTURING RELATIONSHIPS WITH FAMILIES IN NATURAL CONTEXTS

The requirements for building nurturing relationships and family-centered practices are challenging but not insurmountable, and their accomplishment across disciplines will demand new ways of working with both parents and young children. Such changes are clearly laid out in a report by the Task Force on the Family, in which the American Academy of Pediatrics stated the following:

> Medical education traditionally has not provided adequate education about families and the family unit. There is a need to improve the quality of such education. Growth and development of the individual, the effect of culture on childhood and adolescence, family planning, marriage, family development, and family functioning all are subjects of anticipatory guidance and are clearly within the realm of the practice of family pediatrics. Pediatricians must learn more about the family context of child health, but questions persist about how and by whom it is to be taught. Pronouncements about the family often polarize discussion, and objective information is sometimes lost. Reliable and useful research-based information on families and child development must be made available to pediatricians and pediatric educators. (2003, p. 1564)

Ideologically, few would dispute the critical importance of forming and nurturing relationships within a family-centered context. Definition and implementation, on the other hand, raise a host of issues and questions that are not easily addressed. For example, as Dunst and colleagues noted,

The terms *family-centered care, family-centered practices,* and *family-centered services* have been used interchangeably to refer to an approach to working with families that honors and respects their values and choices and which includes the provision of supports necessary to strengthen family functioning. A family-centered approach is characterized by practices that treat families with dignity and respect; information sharing so families can make informed decisions; family choice regarding their involvement in and provision of services; and parent/professional collaborations and partnerships as the context for family-program relations. . . . The foundations for family-centered practices are value and belief statements about how professional help givers should interact with family members as part of family involvement in human services, education, health care, and other kinds of helpgiving programs and organizations. . . . Family-centered practices have become a practice-of-choice in early childhood intervention programs, . . . family support programs, . . . programs serving persons with mental retardation and developmental disabilities, . . . hospitals, . . . medical practices, . . . and other pediatric programs and settings. . . . Family-centered care is now recognized as a key component of a broad-based approach to working with children and their families. (2007, p. 370)

The long-standing mandate for developing individual family service plans (IFSPs) for infants and toddlers from birth through 2 years of age with families and the new concept of the medical home in pediatrics for children with disabilities and special health care needs (Antonelli, Stille, & Antonelli, 2008) reflect the genuine recognition of the importance of early intervention. In their discerning article, Dunst and colleagues (2007) highlighted central issues that bring to the forefront some of the key aspects of definition, need, training, strategy, efficient and effective implementation, monitoring, research evidence, and cost—all that must be considered for the future development of family-centered practices. Foundational to these efforts will be the creation of processes for nurturing quality relationships with families and their young children that will keep pace with the ever-increasing complexities of society, more sophisticated technologies, changing family and program demographics, growing family responsibilities, and new environmental and sociocultural risks that threaten children and families. Professionals will need to learn more about the construct of resilience, what resilience means to individual family members (Luthar, Cicchetti, & Becker, 2000; Walsh, 2003), and what matters most to families in the long term.

The fields of pediatrics, education, and psychology and the clinical disciplines have rich histories and traditions in training, policy, and research that offer much for the understanding of future practice with families and young children who are experiencing hardship, risks, and special needs (Shonkoff & Phillips, 2000). However, developing relationships must be the foundation of everything providers do in their respective professions. This dimension of building relationships is the most difficult to teach and evaluate; it is the most critical to children's well-being and yet it continues to be the most elusive. For this reason, nurturing relationships is at the heart of this book.

REFERENCES

American Academy of Pediatrics, Council on Children with Disabilities, Section on Developmental Behavioral Pediatrics, Bright Futures Steering Committee and Medical Home Initiatives for Children with Special Needs Project Advisory Committee. (2006). Identifying infants and young children with developmental disorders in the medical home: An algorithm for developmental surveillance and screening. *Pediatrics, 118*(1), 405–420.

American Academy of Pediatrics, Council on Community Pediatrics. (2009). The role of preschool home-visiting programs in improving children's developmental health outcomes. *Pediatrics, 123,* 598–603.

American Academy of Pediatrics Medical Home Initiatives for Children with Special Needs Project Advisory Committee. (2004). Policy statement: Organizational principles to guide and define the child health care system and/or improve the health of all children. *Pediatrics, 113*(Suppl. 5), 1545–1547.

American Academy of Pediatrics, Task Force on the Family. (2003). Family pediatrics: Report of the Task Force on the Family. *Pediatrics, 111*(6), 1541–1571.

American Academy of Pediatrics, Task Force on the Future of Pediatric Education II. (2000). The future of pediatric education II: Organizing pediatric education to meet the needs of infants, children, adolescents, and young adults in the 21st century. *Pediatrics, 105*(1), 163–212.

Antonelli, R.C., Stille, C.J., & Antonelli, D.M. (2008). Care coordination for children and youth with special health care needs: A descriptive multisite study of activities, personnel costs, and outcomes. *Pediatrics, 122*(1), e209–e216.

Dunst, C.J. (2000). Revisiting "rethinking early intervention." *Topics in Early Childhood Special Education, 20*(2), 95–104.

Dunst, C.J., Trivette, C.M., & Deal, A.G. (1988). *Enabling and empowering families: Principles and guidelines for practice.* Cambridge, MA: Brookline Books.

Dunst, C.J., Trivette, C.M., & Hamby, D.W. (2007). Meta-analysis of family-centered helpgiving practices research. *Mental Retardation and Developmental Disabilities Research Reviews, 13,* 370–378.

Ensher, G.L., Clark, D.A., & Songer, N.S. (2009). *Families, infants, and young children at risk: Pathways to best practice.* Baltimore: Paul H. Brookes Publishing Co.

Individuals with Disabilities Education Improvement Act (IDEA) of 2004, PL 108-446, 20 U.S.C. §§ 1400 *et seq.*

Luthar, S.S., Cicchetti, D, & Becker, B. (2000). The construct of resilience: A critical evaluation and guidelines for future work. *Child Development, 71*(3), 543–562.

McAllister, J.W., Presler, E., & Cooley, W.C. (2007). Practice-based care coordination: A medical home essential. *Pediatrics, 120*(3), e723–e733.

O'Neil, M.E., Ideishi, R.I., Nixon-Cave, K., & Kohrt, A. (2008). Care coordination between medical and early intervention services: Family and provider perspectives. *Families, Systems, & Health, 26*(2), 119–134.

Raver, S.A. (2005). Using family-based practices for young children with special needs in preschool programs. *Childhood Education, 82*(1), 9–13.

Shonkoff, J.P., & Phillips, D.A. (Eds.). (2000). *From neurons to neighborhoods: The science of early childhood development.* Washington, DC: National Academies Press.

Singer, G.H.S., Ethridge, B.L., & Aldana, S.I. (2007). Primary and secondary effects of parenting and stress management interventions for parents of children with developmental disabilities: A meta-analysis. *Mental Retardation and Developmental Disabilities Research Reviews, 13,* 357–369.

Turnbull, A.P., Summers, J.A., Lee, S.H., & Kyzar, K. (2007). Conceptualization and measurement of family outcomes associated with families of individuals with intellectual disabilities. *Mental Retardation and Developmental Disabilities Research Reviews, 13,* 346–356.

Walsh, F. (2003). Family resilience: A framework for clinical practice. *Family Process, 42*(1), 1–18.

Warren, S.F., & Brady, N.C. (2007). The role of maternal responsivity in the development of children with intellectual disabilities. *Mental Retardation and Developmental Disabilities Research Reviews, 13,* 330–338.

I

Laying the Foundation

1

A Framework for Best Practice

Gail L. Ensher and David A. Clark

CHAPTER HIGHLIGHTS

At the conclusion of this chapter, the reader will

- Understand family systems theory as the context for working with parents/caregivers and their infants and young children

- Understand relationship-centered practices with families within the framework of systems theory and scaffolding for gathering information

- Appreciate differences among families, their capacity for change, and the implications of diversity for nurturing relationships with family members

- Understand how personal perspectives play a role in interactions, both as deterrents and as facilitators

- Understand what it means to value what families bring to relationships and the potential beneficial outcomes of relationships

If You Would . . .

You ask me how you can bridge the future of my children.
You ask me how you can form a partnership with my family.
You can start by looking at me as important.
Look past the things you think you see.

You can start by looking deeper than
   my social rank in life.
You can start by taking a closer look at
   me.
When you look at me . . .
What are you *really* thinking?

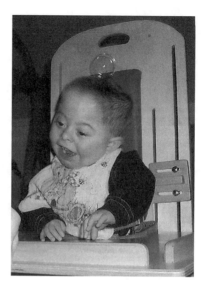

Do you see my hair in need of washing
or my clothes in need of repair?
Do you wonder why I am nervous and
   unsure,
as you look down at me with that con-
   descending stare?

If you step outside your own education,
put down that pen you hold.
Take my hand and walk with me,
if you would be so bold.

Learn of my own tragic childhood,
or perhaps just take a peek.
Learn what I did just yesterday,
or what happened to me last week.

Take the time to listen,
take the time to see.
Put down your misconceptions,
if you would reach inside of me.

We all come through life
on both sides of the tracks,
with secrets and temptations
and burdens on our backs.

You made better choices,
and life's road led you to me.
That road leads backwards and for-
   wards
as far as you can see.

If you want to bridge the future,
then step inside my mind;
for the secret of the future
is in healing what's behind.

Treat me with some dignity,
and if you would erase my frown,
try looking up to me,
instead of looking down.

You can unleash the bonds of mistrust,
one tangle at a time.
You could reach within my walls,
if you would brush long past the grime.

My walls are dark and cold.
My heart is encased in stone.
But you could guide me to the light,
if you would leave your own baggage at
   home.

The message of this poem
is as clear as it can be . . .
If you wish to help my child,
then start by helping me.

—*Virginia Buffett, mother of a son with
autism, 2008*

DEVELOPING RELATIONSHIPS WITH FAMILIES: A FRAMEWORK GROUNDED IN SYSTEMS THEORY

The poem written by Virginia, the mother of a son with autism, dramatically illustrates the essence of working with parents and their children within the context of a family systems framework. Virginia is a single mother who was severely abused as a very young child. Inevitably, she brought that history to the challenges of raising a son diagnosed with autism. Although this family, by self-report, is low income and has worked through numerous issues from the past, as referenced in her poem, Virginia has used her writing talents for the benefit of others and has chosen to return to the pursuit of higher education. By all standards, she is a resilient parent who has survived. At the same time, Virginia shows that families bring with them their own special lenses through which they enter relationships with others, and those lenses color the nature of those relationships and the ways in which families perceive others. These are the liabilities and the strengths that we share as professionals, as parents, and as caregivers.

Writing about families, professionals, and exceptionality, Turnbull, Turnbull, Erwin, and Soodak stated the concept in another way:

> Whatever happens to one of the family members happens to all of them. The metaphor we use to describe the family systems perspective is a mobile. If you put one part of a mobile into action, you will create motion in all of the other parts. That is how it is with families, too: the characteristics of family members . . . their ways of interacting with each other . . . the functions they perform for each other . . . and how they move through various stages of their lives. (2006, p. 3)

Many scholars and researchers have conceptualized family systems and their respective dimensions (Olson, 2000; Turnbull et al., 2006; Weldum, Songer, & Ensher, 2009). Such frameworks are helpful in understanding the impact of many variables on families, including region and location of residence, family characteristics, cultural and ethnic backgrounds, transitions, and different stressors throughout life cycle processes. Although stereotyping always needs to be avoided, examining family dimensions can shed light on some of the reasons that family members respond in particular ways, their genuine limitations and risks, community resources, and other qualities that may heighten or hinder the strength and potential of family members.

First Stage: Getting Started

Scaffolding and simplifying questions during the initial stages of getting to know families, nurturing long-term relationships, and transitioning during the final phases of partnerships make up a framework for developing relationships within the context of a family systems approach. As professionals begin to work with and establish relationships with families, the following questions can serve as a blueprint for guiding them:

- Why do families come to you? How do families view their concerns, their priorities, and their strengths? Who should be involved in addressing the family's essential questions and needs?

- Are families living where they have safe and easy access to friends, other families, and resources such as medical facilities? Are families located in urban or rural neighborhoods?

- How do caregivers define their family? Who is living in the home? Do family members have extended family nearby and regular, positive communication with that extended family?

- Do family members use the same language spoken by professionals, and if not, do they want interpreters and/or need help with technical language?

- What resources do families have, such as living conditions, food, money for medications, and materials for learning, such as books?

- How do cultural background, age, and educational level affect relationships within and outside of the family?

- If the family is facing the diagnosis of a medical condition or developmental disability for their infant or young child, what are their initial perceptions?

- What, if any, health or mental health issues are family members facing, and what services have they already received? Have such services been beneficial from their perspective?

- What information is needed and *wanted* by family members as they proceed with referral or admission processes?

These issues are merely starting points, edges and corners to a puzzle that will continue to be filled in over time. The first phase may include only a one-time meeting, or it may last several weeks. Whatever the amount of time, this phase is critical to families. They often retain lasting impressions of initial meetings, and these impressions can deeply affect the nature of future relationships.

Second Stage: Continuing

Should families qualify for services and desire them, professionals must be prepared to move to the second stage by nurturing more in-depth relationships with families. Traditionally, this stage involves services that are given to individuals. However, within a framework of establishing partnerships with family members, this stage focuses on decision-making processes and examining the stages that family members move through as they enter relationships with professionals. Accordingly, professionals might consider the following:

- What formal and informal supports are important to caregivers in highlighting their strengths and facilitating positive, sustaining relationships among family members?

- How can professionals and family members *together* develop and maintain open communication?

- What ongoing information do families want from professionals so that family members are a genuine part of the decision-making processes that affect them?

- If differences in perspective arise, how can family members and professionals *together* resolve them?

- What situational and life cycle stressors are affecting family members, and what practical interventions might offer relief and facilitate positive courses of action?

This phase may look very different from family to family, and depending on the nature of a family's challenges and resources it may last several weeks, months, or even years. In most cases, there are no quick fixes for children or their families. Parents need to be considered equal partners in the process because ultimately professionals are short-term key participants. And ultimately what providers leave families with in terms of knowledge and relationship-building must sustain them throughout later stages of helping themselves and their children.

Third Stage and Transitions

As families move into the final phases of partnerships with professionals (who may become families' closest collaborators, or even friends), they often do so with much hesitation and fear of the unknown. Therefore, it is imperative that caregivers develop the self-assurance and resilience to carry what they have learned into new efforts and relationships. If help-giving has diminished caregivers' self-efficacy and ability to problem-solve when faced with new challenges, it will have failed. Indeed, the evidence of effective interventions will best be seen as families transition into new phases of their lives and develop healthy relationships among themselves and with others. Thus in this final phase, as families move forward and prepare to depart from existing supports and programs, professionals might keep in mind the following questions:

- What information will prepare families to establish new relationships with future partner professionals?
- What transition processes can be developed to meet family members' unique circumstances?
- What supports, formal and informal, will be most sustaining for family members as they meet new challenges?

With strong relationships as a foundation, families can be more confident and better able to meet current and new challenges. Such resilience was displayed by Virginia, who struggled with a tragic past but was also able to embark on more positive ventures for her son and herself.

AN EVER-CHANGING WORLD: WORKING WITH FAMILIES IN DIFFERENT SETTINGS, WITH DIFFERENT CHALLENGES

Change and the unexpected touch every dimension of our lives each day. Ensher, Clark, and Songer wrote the following:

> A decade ago, we would not have thought it possible to save babies at 23 weeks of gestation. A decade ago, we would not have thought it possible to have reduced the vertical transmission rate of HIV from mother to newborn to approximately 1%. A decade ago, we were markedly less diverse in our schools and communities than

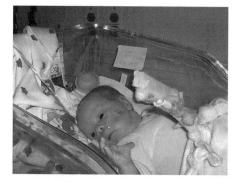

we are today. A decade ago, more than 50% of the mothers in our communities were not working, and the vast majority of children younger than 5 years were not in caregiving situations outside of the home. A decade ago, many mothers were not waiting until their 30s to start their families, with multiple births now a common occurrence in our neonatal intensive care nurseries. A decade ago, we would not have thought that more than 50,000 U.S. women wishing to conceive would be requiring in vitro fertilization. A decade ago, families were less fragmented than they are today. A decade ago, the world was a less violent, less fearful place to live.

Thus, as we look to the decade ahead, our biggest challenge will be keeping abreast of this ever-changing, uncertain world for both young children and their families. Very likely in the decade ahead, the technologies for saving newborns will become even more sophisticated and refined. Very likely in the decade ahead, the social issues in the United States across diverse cultures and ethnic groups with different languages will continue to grow.

Very likely in the decade ahead, teen pregnancies . . . will remain on our radar screen to be resolved, especially among adolescents younger than 16 years of age. Very likely in the decade ahead, this country will continue to struggle with mental health concerns for young children and their families. (2009, p. 358)

This is a snapshot of the backdrop for working with contemporary families and young children in the United States, who are constantly developing and changing. The knowledge specific to our disciplines also is never constant, and the issues facing those in the helping fields are interconnected and complex.

As children develop, so do families as they experience a range of stages and emotions throughout life. There will be periods of joy; there will be sadness beyond belief and perhaps chronic sorrow; there will be periods of leveling off, acceptance, recovery, and resolution. All of these states—fluid as they are—exist within families of every size, income level, cultural and ethnic background, and educational and vocational background. This is the richness, but at the same time the challenge, of what professionals do.

LEARNING WITH FAMILIES: A PROCESS

Providers must keep in mind that as much as they wish to help others, ultimately families *must* take responsibility for their own lives, make their own decisions, and learn to walk alone. This statement does not imply that, for example, families do not need the expert knowledge of the physician who treats the preterm infant in the neonatal intensive care unit. Rather, it is the responsibility of medical and social services staff to partner with families to enable them to take home that premature infant and assume full responsibility of care as parents. Both parties must assume an equal part. This is a process, not unlike a toddler's learning to walk. The following analogy illustrates this point.

 A 21-month-old, who was born prematurely and weighed 4 pounds 12 ounces at birth, was very reluctant to take steps on her own when she was learning to walk. Over and over, her mother would place her on the carpet; the child would stand, but not move. After months of this persistent behavior and the mother's having to continue carrying the child, the mother shared her frustration with a friend, a wise and experienced physical therapist who understood the child's need for support and the mother's need for nurturing.

The physical therapist suggested that the mother do the following: Allow the toddler to hold one end of a tether (a dish towel), while the mother held on to the other end. Initially, the mother was to keep the tether taut so that the toddler would feel completely supported as she stood. Over several days the mother gradually relaxed the tether, and eventually (although without realizing it), her daughter began to *walk independently.*

And so it is with families! For some families the process of working with professionals is short term, and they will be able to take over responsibilities almost effortlessly. For other family members who are living with lifelong issues, such as a child with a severe disability or a chronic illness, or an addiction themselves, the issues are ongoing and require more intensive, sustained supports. In each case, part of the learning curve for families (with the support of professionals) is discerning how to problem-solve in the midst of the challenges they face.

Although professionals come to families and young children with a variety of perspectives, backgrounds, and training, there are important commonalities for emerging reflective best practice. Among these are the following components.

- Thinking within one's own frame of reference and mastering information specific to a particular discipline, that is, competently learning the tools of one's own profession
- Understanding family dynamics and the potential impact of different variables
- Understanding the strengths, limitations, and biases one brings to the dynamics of interacting with other adults and young children
- Practicing the skills of relationship building along with the skills of one's profession

These skills do not develop in a linear fashion or in isolation; they are constantly changing with new information, legislation, technology, and research in our fields. In addition, they require a growing sensitivity to the dynamics of society and particular events that shape the worlds within which professionals and families interact.

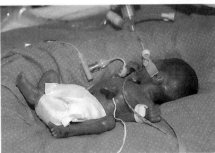

KNOWING ONE'S OWN BACKGROUND AND PERSONAL LENSES

Providers' personal lenses are an important part of who they are, and these lenses offer important cues and opportunities for learning as they interact with others. Lenses characterize one's uniqueness, and they partially define one's passion and the impetus to pursue certain professions. They can facilitate providers' perspectives on complex situations, ground their understanding in empathy, and help them offer alternatives for families in the midst of crisis.

Professionals must understand their own backgrounds and biases to work with families in beneficial ways. Accordingly, best practice requires that professionals do the following:

- Constantly examine how their interactions are affecting family members
- Learn from less-than-optimal situations and change their own behavior accordingly
- Be accessible to families and offer information in jargon-free language
- Problem-solve alternative solutions to issues themselves, with team members, and with families
- Remain open to families' potential for growth, setting aside preconceived ideas
- Communicate a trust in families to change on behalf of themselves and their children, reinforce positive steps, and let those steps become self-fulfilling prophecies for families
- Know their comfort zones and, as necessary, share boundaries with families
- Share ethical guidelines that they must follow, such as a physician's need to provide life-saving medical treatment for an infant, or a teacher's or clinician's obligation to report suspected or confirmed instances of child abuse or neglect
- Always view the child within the context of the family system

These practices do not mean that everyone will always agree, however, differences can be more easily resolved if there exists a foundation of sincerity and authenticity. Honesty will go a long way in developing and nurturing relationships with families.

The balance between maintaining a comfortable distance and expressing caring is a delicate one for professionals to maintain with families, who often are hurting, in crisis, and desperately seeking assistance. Providers diminish their professional obligations to families if they leave them unable to advocate and problem-solve for themselves and their children. Success in relationships with families is best realized when families are *enabled*. Throughout the process of helping families move to a more productive place in their lives, stressors can arise for professionals as well as families. Team members must be responsive to the needs of their own colleagues.

PROBLEM-SOLVING ALTERNATIVES

The helping professions, including medicine, education, and the clinical fields, traditionally have been responsible for sharing information about diagnoses, prognoses, programming, expenses, prevention, and a host of other issues important for families facing complex situations and decisions. In sharing such information, however, professionals often overwhelm families with details that they may not understand or find useful. Those who, for example, work with families in neonatal intensive care units or in clinical settings where developmental diagnoses are given to parents can testify to this.

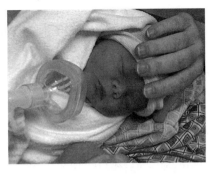

The issues that may arise while working with families are many, and the solutions are far from simple. Often, the various agencies and professionals involved do not work cohesively together, causing further confusion and frustration for families. Messages to families are sometimes conflicting or, at best, do not offer a coherent blueprint of how they might resolve concerns or take next steps. One helpful strategy to address fragmentation is the assignment of a point person or family service coordinator, which has been adopted by health departments funding early intervention (Songer & Menapace, 2007).

With professionals supporting relationships (Percy, Stadtler, & Sands, 2002), families can accomplish best outcomes if given alternative choices, adaptations, and a flexibility that enhances their freedom to make decisions (Dunst, Trivette, & Deal, 1988). During the course of such processes, it is essential that families assume responsibility for their own behavior. Dunst et al. stated the principle in this way:

> Noncontingent help giving, perhaps more than any other aspect of helping relationships, sets the occasion for increased passivity and dependence (Skinner, 1978).
>
> *If the help does not require the recipient to acquire effective behavior and thus renders the person helpless or dependent, the immediate needs of the person may be met, but the ability to teach and foster effective behavior are diminished.* (1988, p. 37)

Writing about the use of T. Berry Brazelton's Touchpoints approach "to promote parental self-competence in low-income, minority, pregnant, and parenting teen mothers" (p. 180), Percy and McIntyre reached a similar conclusion, based on the findings from a small pilot project:

> The significant difference in parenting self-confidence after attending the child development course also supports the importance of a relational/developmental approach with teen parents. Not only did the teens indicate they had gained knowledge about child rearing (the traditional goal of a child development class) but they also increased their level of comfort as parents and valuing of their own parental abilities. . . .
>
> Healthcare providers, teachers, and childcare workers all impact the lives of teen parents. Understanding the needs of teen mothers to feel valued and supported is critical to their ability to parent their own children. This understanding can provide the impetus for professionals to shift their approach to working with teen parents. Instead of viewing this population as problematic, childcare profes-

sionals must recognize the opportunity for these mothers to transcend their own difficult past through the process of parenting their own children. Nurturing and supporting these mothers is crucial to encouraging hope and success in their future. Touchpoints provides a guide for changing the professional relationship with families from a deficit model to a positive supportive model. (2001, p. 185)

The tenet of self-efficacy that underlies opportunities for families to make their own best choices is an important concept to keep in mind because "family-centered practices have empowerment type effects (e.g., strengthened efficacy beliefs), and parents who feel empowered about their parenting capabilities are more likely to provide their children development-enhancing learning opportunities" (Dunst, Trivette, & Hamby, 2007, p. 376). This notion is not specific to any particular discipline or professional field in developing and nurturing relationships with families. Indeed, Dunst et al. (2007) stated that

> Family-centered practices and care are now used widely in many different kinds of programs and organizations working with young children and their families, and especially children with special health care needs and identified disabilities and their families. . . . (p. 376)

To summarize, families must be *active* in decision-making processes throughout the course of their relationships with professionals, *offered opportunities* for problem-solving the *options and pathways* that *they* want (Head & Abbeduto, 2007), and *assume responsibility* for their own behavior and the alternatives that they have chosen. Research conducted by Dunst and colleagues, as noted previously, indicates that such families are more likely to develop a greater sense of well-being, ownership, and competency.

LEARNING TO VALUE WHAT FAMILIES BRING

"Where can you make the BIGGEST difference?" is a question posed by Nan Songer (2008) and many who work with families of infants and young children. Among Songer's (2008) list of *Ten Things to Remember* when working with families are the following:

- Learning occurs in the context of a relationship.
- Teach positive alternatives, don't just limit undesirable behavior.
- Problems are opportunities.
- When something isn't working, CHANGE IT!
- Together is better. Ask for support from others, colleagues, parents, and the kids.

Songer also noted,

> The only way we can predict a family's growth around their child with a disability is to contribute to their knowledge and acknowledge their expertise. They are the constant in their child's life, and we are only support players. Our greatest legacy is to leave behind a family that better understands their child and a family that knows they are the magic. (1998)

Others have echoed similar beliefs in the fundamental strengths of families (Brazelton & Sparrow, 2001, 2006; Dunst, 2000). The concept is a simple one to state; it is much more difficult to put into practice.

As discussed in the Introduction, families and professionals enter relationships with deeply engrained perspectives that are difficult to lay aside. Professionals come to families with discipline-based knowledge and expertise to share; families come to professionals often hoping for answers, cures, or (in the least), remediation. Contemporary thought on families and young children does not devalue the wealth of information that professionals offer. However, contemporary thought does require that parents be *equally recognized and valued* as the constant in their children's lives.

BENEFICIAL OUTCOMES

In conclusion, with shared decision making and an equal balance in relationships, beneficial outcomes can be manifold. Goals should be mutually defined, grounded in families' priorities, and based on strengths rather than deficits.

As families face the future, change will be inevitable. Their lives will not be free of pain; there will be no guarantees; and they will face difficult times. However, professionals will have made the biggest difference with families when they send families forward better informed, better able to problem-solve, more resilient in facing the unknown, and better able to build on their own strengths and their children's strengths. And because interactions are multifaceted and reciprocal, professionals will find that they too have changed.

Thinking It Through: Questions for Discussion

1. How would you want families to describe your interactions with them as a professional? Why?
2. What strengths do you, as a professional, bring to your relationships with families? What are your liabilities, and how do you seek to address these?
3. Reflect on your own learning and development as a professional. Describe two or three situations in which you have experienced beneficial outcomes; what implications do those experiences have for building relationships and working in partnership with families?

REFERENCES

Brazelton, T.B., & Sparrow, J.D. (2001). *Touchpoints—three to six: Your child's emotional and behavioral development.* Cambridge, MA: Perseus.

Brazelton, T.B., & Sparrow, J.D. (2006). *Touchpoints—Birth to 3: Your child's emotional and behavioral development* (2nd ed.). Cambridge, MA: Perseus.

Dunst, C.J. (2000). Revisiting "rethinking early intervention." *Topics in Early Childhood Special Education, 20*(2), 95–104.

Dunst, C.J., Trivette, C.M., & Deal, A.G. (1988). *Enabling & empowering families: Principles & guidelines for practice.* Cambridge, MA: Brookline Books.

Dunst, C.J., Trivette, C.M., & Hamby, D.W. (2007). Meta-analysis of family-centered helpgiving practices research. *Mental Retardation and Developmental Disabilities Research Reviews, 13,* 370–378.

Ensher, G.L., Clark, D.A., & Songer, N.S. (Eds.).(2009). Putting it all together. In *Families, infants, and young children at risk: Pathways to best practice* (pp. 353–358). Baltimore: Paul H. Brookes Publishing Co.

Head, L.S., & Abbeduto, L. (2007). Recognizing the role of parents in developmental outcomes: A systems approach to evaluating the child with developmental disabilities. *Mental Retardation and Developmental Disabilities Research Reviews, 13,* 293-301.

Olson, D.H. (2000). Circumplex model of family systems. *Journal of Family Therapy, 22*(2), 144–167.

Percy, M.S., & McIntyre, L. (2001). Using Touchpoints to promote parental self-competence in low-income, minority, pregnant, and parenting teen mothers. *Journal of Pediatric Nursing, 16*(3), 180–186.

Percy, M.S., Stadtler, A., & Sands, D. (2002). Changing the face of pediatric nurse practitioner education. *The American Journal of Maternal/Child Nursing, 27*(4), 222–228.

Songer, N.S. (1998). *Guiding challenging behavior of young children and their families* [PowerPoint slides]. Syracuse, NY: Syracuse University.

Songer, N.S. (2008). *Families of young children with disabilities* [PowerPoint slides]. Syracuse, NY: Syracuse University.

Songer, N.S., & Menapace, T. (2007). *Transition from EI to EPSE.* Syracuse, NY: The Mid-State Central Early Childhood Direction Center, Syracuse University.

Turnbull, A.P., Turnbull, H.R., III, Erwin, E.J., & Soodak, L.C. (2006). *Families, professionals, and exceptionality: Positive outcomes through partnerships and trust* (5th ed.). Upper Saddle River, NJ: Pearson/Merrill Prentice Hall.

Weldum, J.R., Songer, N.S., & Ensher, G.L. (2009). The family as foreground. In G.L. Ensher, D.A. Clark, & N.S. Songer (Eds.), *Families, infants, and young children at risk: Pathways to best practice* (pp. 39–58). Baltimore: Paul H. Brookes Publishing Co.

2

Teamwork and Knowing Enough About the System to Help

Gail L. Ensher and David A. Clark

CHAPTER HIGHLIGHTS

At the conclusion of this chapter, the reader will

- Understand the responsibilities of working on a team that crosses disciplines and areas of expertise
- Understand the implications, benefits, and difficulties of working as a team
- Understand the challenges and responsibilities of working with families within a framework of informal and established program service delivery

In a chapter titled "A Perilous Partnership—Parents and Professionals," Robert Naseef, a psychologist and father of a son with autism, wrote the following:

> The best outcomes for children and families happen when parents and professionals work as partners with mutual respect and shared decision-making power. Parents, by virtue of their bond with their child, are true authorities in their own right, with information to contribute that no one else has access to. Professionals, however, through training and experience, can offer expertise and a broad perspective that parents alone don't have. Each has only partial knowledge, with complete expertise only possible in partnership. Their combined viewpoint should be the basis for decisions, plans, and goals. (2001, p. 220)

WORKING TOGETHER: OUTSIDE AREAS OF EXPERTISE

Many professionals in pediatrics, teaching, and clinical practices ventured into their chosen disciplines because of their desire to help children. To do that well, however, they must first know how to relate to and interact with other adults. The following skills encompass the essential goals necessary to achieve this:

- Understanding one's role and responsibilities on a team
- Knowing how to acknowledge the expertise of others (especially family members) on the team
- Knowing how to separate one's own values and perspectives from those of others
- Understanding how to make accommodations and modify interactions
- Knowing when to respond and when to listen
- Knowing when to ask questions rather than offer advice or recommendations
- Knowing how to discern and reinforce the positives in ambiguous situations
- Understanding which battles to pursue and which to let go
- Understanding how to suspend judgment

Some of these skills are easier to acquire than others, and some are easier to teach than others. Some people may acquire them naturally; for others, acquiring these skills may entail a lifelong journey.

Understanding Team Roles and Responsibilities

Part B and Part C of federal legislation in early childhood require that assessment be a "multidisciplinary effort" (McLean & Crais, 2004, p. 56); that is, it should have "the involvement of two or more disciplines or professions in the provision of integrated and coordinated services, including evaluation and assessment activities" (Individuals with Disabilities Education Act Amendments of 1997). In particular, McLean & Crais noted,

> The disciplines that may be involved in assessing young children with special needs include audiology, early childhood education, early childhood special education, family therapy, medicine, nursing, nutrition, occupational therapy, orientation and mobility, physical therapy, psychology, social work, and speech-language pathology. Not all of these disciplines will necessarily be involved in the assessment of a particular child, although the family should always be central to the assessment team. (2004, p. 56)

The professionals who are on any given team will largely depend on the nature of the child's medical, developmental, and educational needs, as determined by the agency or source of referral. The roles and responsibilities of each team member, based on training and experience, would seem obvious, yet they may not always be clear in the field of early childhood special education, where co-treatment is often provided by several individuals. With parents or caregivers also assuming key team roles, knowing who is responsible for what may become even less clear. Certain disciplines own particular bodies of knowledge and expertise. But there are also issues that are shared by some team members, such as feeding, sensory processing, challenging behavior, diet and nutrition, and sleep patterns. This may lead to conflicting recommendations for families, causing confusion and frustration. To resolve such potential conflicts, Songer (2007) offered some basic guidelines for collaboration and role definition:

- All partners are in agreement about plans and goals, and all share in the decision-making process.
- Partners understand one another's role in the process and show mutual respect for one another's skills and knowledge.
- Communication is honest, open, and clear, and partners share information.
- Partners jointly evaluate progress.

Responding, Listening, and Waiting

Learning when to respond to families and when to simply listen is not an exact science. Such lessons are garnered largely from experience. Professionals, especially when faced with the uncomfortable silence following delivery of sad or difficult news, may tend to rush in with advice in the hope that words will help minimize the pain. In these situations, however, providers need to be mindful of the simple truth that situations are what they are. They must be compassionate and deliver news with understanding and hopefulness, but they should not deny or devalue the salience of a given situation for families. Families need time to grieve, to recover, and to regain hope so that they can move forward. To do so, they need someone to listen and time to work through the implications of the news. Just as children need wait time to process, so do their caregivers.

Songer (2007) raised two essential questions that may elicit different responses, depending on when they are raised:

- What do families need from the professionals who enter their lives?
- What do families say they want from the professionals who enter their lives?

As Naseef pointed out in the quote at the beginning of this chapter regarding "perilous parent–professional partnerships," both dimensions are essential for goal setting, planning, and decision making. Parents do not exclusively possess knowledge, nor do professionals. It is only by joining both sources of information that outcomes become optimal for children. To tailor service delivery (i.e., information, advice, and recommendations), professionals will need to learn about families—their uniqueness, their priorities, their cultural preferences, and their needs. In some instances, this sharing of information will take place at the outset (e.g., if a newborn is admitted to a neonatal intensive care unit), and the situation may dictate that physicians offer information on medical conditions and updates on daily progress. Information sharing should be ongoing throughout the duration of the relationship, and professionals need to remember that the family is the constant in the child's life.

Battles Worth Pursuing

As much as professionals might hope for universal agreement with families, differences of opinion are natural. Some decisions must be made immediately, without deliberation, and sometimes not in accordance with family wishes (e.g., a family's religious preference for not delivering medical treatment to a newborn). In other, less critical situations, consensus can be achieved by establishing respect and rapport, affirming, sharing information, listening empathically, making sensitive suggestions, asking questions, optimizing family participation (Songer, 2007), and accepting differences of opinion.

Discerning and Reaffirming the Positives

Discerning, reaffirming, and focusing on the positives in families' situations is the essence of building meaningful relationships with families. Even when families face adversity, professionals can reset the tone and empower them to draw upon their strengths. For example, when newborns are admitted to neonatal intensive care nurseries, families find themselves in crisis, facing events and de-

cisions that are far from positive. Nevertheless, caregivers play an important role in their infants' health and well-being, as evidenced by research showing that babies who have the benefit of kangaroo care (i.e., skin-to-skin contact with infant wrapped on a father's or mother's chest) with caregivers and whose families visit and interact frequently with them are much more likely to tolerate

feeding, gain weight more quickly, and consequently leave the hospital earlier (Als et al., 2003;
Feldman, Eidelman, Sirota, & Weller, 2002).

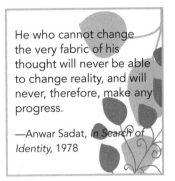

He who cannot change
the very fabric of his
thought will never be able
to change reality, and will
never, therefore, make any
progress.

—Anwar Sadat, *In Search of
Identity,* 1978

Moreover, follow-up clinics, which monitor
the developmental progress of neonatal intensive
care graduates during the first 18 months of life,
repeatedly have witnessed similar scenarios. Critically ill infants with healthy and stimulating home
environments ultimately may show greater developmental progress than children with less remarkable medical histories who have not experienced
such benefits. In particular, healthy, nurturing family relationships make the
critical difference for infants—families hold the magic for children's healthy
growth and development. Over the past decade, health care providers have increasingly recognized the significance of involving families in the design and
development of neonatal intensive care units for the optimal involvement of
families (e.g., more privacy, less noise and light, and more family space) (Johnson, Abraham, & Parrish, 2004).

Flexibility and Accommodations

Songer (1998) expressed this message somewhat differently: "When something
isn't working, CHANGE IT!". As professionals work with families, they quickly
learn that nothing is carved in stone, especially professionally owned agendas.
Considering alternatives can help avoid or minimize confrontations, offer freedom and new pathways to both families and professionals, and demonstrate important problem-solving approaches for families. Families also can be strengthened by drawing on the resources available to them (e.g., informal parent
support groups) (Dunst, Trivette, & Deal, 1988), as opposed to receiving recommendations for goals and objectives that are outside their realm of accessibility
or their community.

Continuing to follow the same pathways can be stagnating or even destruc-
tive for families, especially if they lead to chronic, negative consequences. As difficult as it might be, changing patterns of behavior is an essential part of growth
and building healthy relationships for both children and adults. Consider, for
example, an individual with alcohol addiction who repeatedly drinks despite
knowing the consequences. For a healthier lifestyle, there must be a resetting of
patterns, relationships, and understandings. Likewise, when families are stressed,
it is best for professionals to accept them where they are, build on their priorities, discuss functional outcomes, and share information clearly (Songer, 1998).

Differing Values and Perspectives

As U.S. society has become more heterogeneous, cross-cultural effectiveness has
emerged as an essential skill for all service providers working with families. The
need to be cross-culturally competent is just as critical for neonatal intensive
care nurses, social workers, and physicians in health care environments as it is

 for child care providers, educators, psychologists, physical therapists, occupational therapists, speech-language pathologists, and aides in educational environments. For instance, the health care provider must be aware of families' feelings about the use of surgery and drugs for medical conditions, just as educators must be knowledgeable about families' childrearing beliefs and developmental expectations. All service providers must be sensitive to differences across families in communication style, decision making, and the need or willingness to seek assistance from members outside the family (Lynch & Hanson, 2004).

Service providers must adjust strategies to work effectively with families that may adhere to radically different values, beliefs, and practices. Such adjustments can be frustrating and may necessitate thought and study, but they also offer opportunities for practitioners to be exposed to the richness of human experience, to learn new information, and to grow. The application of individualized, appropriate strategies will result in family members' being nurtured and supported to reach their full potential as individuals (Lynch & Hanson, 2004).

Seeing a situation from another person's perspective is not easy, but it is essential to establishing effective relationships. It is a skill honed through practice and reflection. To refine this skill, one must

- Become an astute observer
- Be willing to learn about another person's background and ideas, and use those as the foundation of growth for families and children
- Be compassionate and responsive
- Be willing to set aside one's priorities and values in the short term and share the territory of expertise with families

In large part, valuing others' perspectives also requires knowing one's own value systems and the ways in which one influences other people. In this regard, Lynch has some instructive words for developing cross-cultural competence, or what might be more broadly termed *cross-family competence:*

Culture is akin to looking through the one-way mirror; everything we see is from our own perspective. It is only when we join the observed on the other side of the mirror that it is possible to see ourselves and others clearly; however, getting to the other side of the glass presents many challenges. Achieving cross-cultural competence requires that we lower our defenses, take risks, and practice behaviors that may feel unfamiliar and uncomfortable. It requires a flexible mind, an open heart, and a willingness to accept alternative perspectives. It may mean setting aside some beliefs that are cherished to make room for others whose value is unknown; it may mean changing what we think, what we say, and how we behave. But there are rewards—the reward of assisting families who need someone who can help them bridge two disparate cultures, as well as the reward of knowing more about ourselves and becoming more effective in all of our interactions. (2004, p. 42)

Acknowledging the Expertise of Others

Closely related to several issues discussed previously is the necessity for professionals to acknowledge others, especially family members, as experts. Despite training and expertise in their respective fields, it is impossible for professionals to know everything. Families have knowledge that they do not. However, it is very difficult for families to feel part of the team if other members fail to include families in the planning process, do not acknowledge or value families' meaningful roles and input, provide misinformation outside of their areas of expertise, and view situations exclusively from one perspective. Discerning solutions will require collaborative efforts on the part of both professionals and family members, all of whom should be acknowledged for their expertise.

The OR Method

We can do what we have always done OR we can. . . Observe (and collect) and Reflect.

—Songer,1998

Suspending Judgment

Providers should also suspend judgment on children and families. Behavior is a form of communication—by their behavior, they are telling professionals something that they need to acknowledge.

More than any other, the ability to suspend judgment requires mastery of all of the skills considered previously. It affirms the fact that every family comes to providers with a need, including a need for all of their beliefs, coping strategies, liabilities, strengths, and priorities to be valued. As Lynch (2004) noted, this ability will necessitate that providers "join the observed on the other side of the mirror" (p. 42) so that they take seriously the mandate to look at situations from multiple perspectives, think through multiple options, resist the tendency to quickly categorize a problem and dictate a remedy, resist drawing premature conclusions and placing the lasting handprint of criticism, and offer genuine opportunities to families.

CREATING RESOURCES FOR FAMILIES

Families of infants and young children seek professional help for many reasons. The reason may be routine, such as for a pediatric visit; or it may be an unexpected crisis, such as the delivery of a preterm infant. Help may be needed because of chronic illness or psychosocial issues, such as substance abuse, or because of intervention by child protective services. Finding services typically is not a problem for families; however, finding services that are appropriate and that are a good match for a particular family is an entirely different matter. Families with no connections to their community, friends, or other family members almost invariably find themselves in difficulty—often with serious consequences. Such scenarios are well documented in research across the plethora of issues that continue to affect families in the United States.

Family Isolation and the Need for Connection

In their book *Early Intervention with Multi-Risk Families: An Integrative Approach,*
Landy and Menna (2006) wrote,

> Some professionals in the field of early childhood intervention have described pro-
> tective factors or strengths as the opposite of risk variables; however, they are not
> simply the *absence* of risk factors but rather, the opposite end of a spectrum. For ex-
> ample, isolation would be seen as a risk factor, whereas the opposite, having a sup-
> portive family network or support system within the community, could act as a pro-
> tective factor. (p. 11)

Numerous articles have made reference to the detrimental effects of isolation
on families, and such effects appear to be compounded by dramatic changes in
family structure and patterns of family life over the past 2 decades (Shonkoff &
Phillips, 2000; Wertlieb, 2003). Johnson, Kastner, and American Academy of Pediatrics Committee/Section on Children with Disabilities (2005) have captured
the essence of these escalating concerns, noting that more and more young children are now living in single-parent families, growing numbers of families are
living in poverty, and there are more families in which the mother or both caregivers are in the workforce. Consequently, there are increases in "social isolation" and "family mobility that often separates families from their extended families and natural support systems" (p. 507). Informal family and community
networks may be compromised, with caregivers having few people to turn to for
guidance and support. The fact that health outcomes for young children typically mirror the quality of family life and family characteristics is now clearly recognized in contemporary pediatric research and practice (Wertlieb, 2003).
Wertlieb laid out the stark realities of families living in the 21st century, with the
"new morbidities" of alcoholism, domestic violence, substance abuse, and mental illness that plague individuals into their adult lives (p. 1572). In a sense, children have problems because society has problems, and families (with the fast
pace and fragmentation of life) have lost vital connections. Commenting further, Wertlieb wrote,

> Among the most substantially documented relationships between a characteristic
> of successful families and health outcomes is *social connectedness* or *social support.*
> This dimension is evident and relevant within the family (e.g., quality of relation-
> ships between and among family members) and in the family's connection to in-
> strumental and emotional resources outside the family. (2003, p. 1576)

Diverse Informal Networks

The value of social supports thus having been well established, what is the context of culturally sensitive, informal community networks that have been correlated with healthy family and child outcomes? To address some of the most pressing issues in contemporary family processes, the scope of professional practices
is being both broadened and complicated (Wertlieb, 2003)—extending well into

nonmedical, nonclinical, and what might be considered noneducational arenas that have major consequences for the developmental and medical well-being of infants and young children.

The process of making meaningful informal connections will differ for families, depending on individual preferences, the nature of the community, the relevance of connections for particular family cultures, parental work and child care schedules, and numerous other considerations. The following is a list of potentially helpful venues for families to make social support and informational connections:

- Health education groups and services
- Parent education groups and services (e.g., for learning about guiding challenging behavior, the importance of reading to a child, expectations for child development, child safety)
- Respite care and/or registered babysitting services
- Parent meetings specific to chronic illnesses (e.g., diabetes), special health care needs (e.g., treatment for leukemia), and developmental disabilities (e.g., trisomy 21)
- Violence prevention centers or shelters
- Local religious communities
- Support groups for family members dealing with anxiety disorders, depression, and other mental health concerns
- Support groups for single-parent families or family members going through separation and divorce
- Play groups for children and families (e.g., Stanley Greenspan's Floortime approach for working with parents and disabled young children)
- Groups to support parents and children coping with painful medical procedures, treatments, and long hospital stays
- Family support groups for learning about financial matters (e.g., Medicaid waivers, insurance)
- Sign language groups or courses/seminars for families about augmentative systems of communication

To achieve an appropriate match between families and support services, Wertlieb (2003) has suggested that pediatricians (as well as other professionals) need to know about household composition, relationships, child care arrangements, familial and extrafamilial social support or conflict, physical and emotional status of all family members, and religious affiliations. Recent initiatives by the American Academy of Pediatrics (i.e., AAP Supervision Guidelines and Bright Futures) and innovations such as Healthy Steps (Zuckerman, Parker, Kaplan-Sanoff, Augustyn, & Barth, 2004) are clearly compatible with the growing realization across disciplines of the need for collaboration to address the issues of "rapid social change, a better understanding of brain development, an increasing emphasis on school readiness, and the growing awareness of the link between parental health and child health" in the United States (Zuckerman et. al., 2004, p. 820).

Established Programs

Established early childhood programs have a long history of providing services to families with infants and young children who are at risk, have chronic or critical illnesses, or have identified disabilities (Bryden & Ensher, 2009). The effectiveness of such interventions with infants, young children, and their families has been well documented (Bailey et al., 2005). What has yet to be determined are those variables that cause some families to experience less favorable outcomes than others as a result of services. For example, reporting on the 36-month outcomes of a sample of 5,668 children drawn from 20 states in the United States [i.e., the National Early Intervention Longitudinal Study (NEILS)], Bailey and his colleagues indicated that

> At the end of early intervention, near their child's third birthday, families of infants and toddlers with disabilities generally describe themselves as competent and confident in their ability to support their child, work with professionals, and gain access to formal and informal supports. These findings, in conjunction with the methodologic strengths of this study, provide important evidence that Part C programs have supported most families in their caregiving responsibilities, at least as perceived by parents at the conclusion of services.
>
> Areas of needed improvement may include . . . especially experimental research, to determine the program models and variables that are most likely to enhance positive family outcomes. (2005, p. 1351)

In their discussion of "programs of promise," Bryden and Ensher (2009) summarized several "themes of effective programs." The authors indicate that from among "different agendas, different goals, and very different approaches to the rich and myriad efforts in early childhood special education," effective programs do the following:

- Recognize that behavior is communication
- Are consistent
- Are monitored and interpreted along multiple dimensions
- Build on fundamental, developmental strengths of families and children
- Facilitate decision making in partnership with families
- Survey and use accessible, community resources
- Are adaptable to settings, communities, and individuals, including different cultures and ethnic groups
- Are centered on relationships (pp. 345–348)

The recent call for the mapping of community assets (i.e., "social capital"; Pan, Littlefield, Valladolid, Tapping, & West, 2005), the need for community-based medical resources that are collaborative and accessible to families (National Committee for Quality Assurance, 2008), efforts to integrate Healthy Steps into residency training programs (Niederman, Schwartz, Connell, & Silverman, 2007, p. e596), and the search for "innovative psychosocial intervention programs" in primary care pediatrics to "reduce family needs and promote child health" (Farmer, Marien, Clark, Sherman, & Selva, 2004, p. 355) are reflective of efforts to address family issues within the context of coordinated, community medical services. Farmer and colleagues (2004) stated the priorities in this way: "Primary care providers have the potential to be a key resource for children with chronic health conditions and their families, especially in collaboration with medical specialists, psychologists, educators, and other team members (Perrin, 1999)" (p. 356).

As Farmer and colleagues (2004) further pointed out, however, there are lingering barriers to accomplishing this goal, including the continued "lack of training in chronic care management," "insufficient time to address nonmedical and family needs," "poor reimbursement," and minimal time for coordinated or collaborative efforts (p. 356). Although there are numerous established programs that provide a variety of educational, clinical, and medical services to families, finding services that match families' needs in terms of finances, work schedules, personnel, range of services, transportation, culture, primary language spoken, and so forth is a challenge that requires professionals to share information.

The question is, then, how can professionals assist families in finding appropriate levels of support and beneficial established programs? Starting with family members themselves is the best place to begin. Once an infant, a child, or a family member has been referred for services, the following steps need to be taken:

- Meet with family members.
- Ask family members what they need and want.
- Map affordable community resources.
- Provide family members with program information, including telephone numbers, addresses, and names of key staff.
- Suggest onsite visits to speak with staff and service providers.
- Ensure that families have transportation to visit programs.
- Ask family members whether they want someone to accompany them on visits.
- Have the family make onsite visits with their child.
- In partnership with the family, facilitate the family's decision.

ALL IN THE COMMUNITY: COMMON CHALLENGES

Coordination and collaboration have become hallmarks of service delivery to children and families in the 21st century. Collaborative efforts have become especially important in light of the complex medical, developmental, clinical, and educational needs of many families and the multiple services from which they might benefit. Yet, coordination among multiple agencies and multiple professionals often is difficult. Baglin wrote the following:

> Interagency coordination is an institutional process, yet it is influenced by personal attitudes and agency loyalties. To be effective, interagency coordination must be ongoing and include operationalized agreements that lead to solutions for difficult and persistent problems. Professionals involved in interagency activities de-

signed to improve service delivery cannot operate independently but must seek to work together as a team. (2009, pp. 42–43)

Baglin (2009) cited several barriers to collaboration between and within agencies, including differing missions and priorities, issues of control, differing eligibility requirements, and differing organizational and management systems linked to funding (e.g., nonprofit agencies versus private agencies or foundations) (p. 56). An example of such barriers is reflected in the variations in funding and service delivery systems in New York State, where the Health Department assumes primary responsibility for services provided to infants, toddlers, and families, and the State Education Department is the major funding agency for preschool children. The pervasive disconnect between these two funding sources not infrequently has resulted in program gaps in service delivery for children. These issues have tended to surface during transitions from one program to another, such as when moving from infant-toddler services to preschool services or from kindergarten to the early primary grades. Even in systems without such funding differences, families frequently have commented that they felt lost or abandoned as their children moved from the protected, nurturing environments of preschool programs to more formal educational facilities.

From Agency to Agency, Adult to Adult

When families' needs are lost amid administrative trivia and professional politics, everyone loses. It would be naïve to assume that such politics do not exist. Unfortunately, this dimension pervades almost every facet of professional work in the educational, medical, and clinical fields. Professionals need to resist engaging in such interactions, which serve only to create division, thwart communication, and stifle processes of best practice. When negative situations do arise, they are best dealt with in a straightforward manner and by using alternative, positive courses of action. At the risk of sounding trite and simplistic, communication truly is the best vehicle for the resolution of issues.

Many of the strategies for collaborating and developing relationships discussed in previous sections of this chapter will help in resolving these barriers. Groups or child care councils have been established for the specific purpose of coordination and collaboration across agencies, medical facilities, educational programs, and age groups. The Medical Home initiative, supported by the American Academy of Pediatrics (AAP), is one such effort, designed with the specific goal of integrating health and related systems of care for children with special health care needs and children with disabilities (AAP Council on Children with Disabilities, 2005). In a 2005 policy statement, the AAP Council on Children with Disabilities noted the following recommendations for successful models of care coordination:

1. Primary care physicians, medical subspecialists and surgical specialists, physician's staff, families, community agencies, educators, early intervention profes-

sionals, allied health professionals, tertiary care centers, state Title V agencies, and insurers should work cooperatively to develop care coordination models that take into consideration the continuum of health, education, and social services needed to improve the quality of care for children with special health care needs.

2. Families of children with special health care needs should have the opportunity to lead the care coordination team and/or be proactive participants.

3. Primary care physicians caring for children with special health care needs should facilitate access to community-based services through the use of the medical home strategies. The AAP National Center of Medical Home Initiatives for Children with Special Needs (www.medicalhomeinfo.org) is a resource that can assist the pediatrician.

4. The primary care physician's role in care coordination should be flexible to meet the dynamic needs of the child and family. The primary care physician, a member of the physician's staff, a family member, or another member of the child's medical home may be designated the leader of the care coordination team.

5. Successful provision of care coordination is contingent on adequate reimbursement for efforts. Health care professionals should be reimbursed by third-party payers for the time spent on care coordination and care plan development and oversight [which are mostly unfunded at present].

6. Research efforts should continue to develop new approaches in care coordination and to investigate the outcomes and benefits of care coordination, especially within the context of the medical home.

7. Interdisciplinary training opportunities in the medical home philosophy and care coordination are available through the National Center of Medical Home Initiatives for Children with Special Needs. Medical students and residents in training should incorporate care coordination skills so that they are better prepared to coordinate care when they begin community practice.

8. Barriers to care coordination should be addressed and overcome. These barriers for the family often include cultural/language status, educational level, economic situation, and transportation resources. (p. 1242)

In the educational arena, a team member (including medical staff) can be designated to serve as family service coordinator. This individual might be from the discipline most closely aligned with the child's major area of programmatic need, or as noted previously, one of the family members might lead the group. Whatever the decision concerning leadership, it is important that one person assume responsibility for coordination so that a family's point of entry into the professional services system is known by all of the key team members.

FAMILIES WHO DECLINE SERVICES

Some families decline services on behalf of themselves and/or their children. Some of their reasons are valid; others are difficult to understand. Parents may decide to forego educational and therapeutic programs for their child on a full-time basis because they believe it is more important for their child to have time at home and to develop closer relationships with family members. There are parents who decide not to attend all of the professional meetings associated with their child's programs, and to spend more time fulfilling their roles as mothers and fathers. These reasons have merit, and such decisions need to be respected without making families feel guilty. There are other instances, however, in which parental decisions are clearly not in the child's best interests, medically or educationally. For example, a caregiver may attempt to discharge a child from the hospital when the child requires medical treatment, or refuse to agree to a medical procedure for a child who may not survive or who may suffer developmental delays without it. In these cases, professionals—after discussing the situation with the family—need to intervene.

There are instances in which families refuse services because they get caught up in controversial issues (e.g., the much publicized misconception that there is a relationship between immunizations and the onset of childhood autism) or because they are fearful, are protective of their children, or perhaps do not wish to have unfamiliar people in their home. Such situations need to be addressed on an individual basis, with the advantages and disadvantages weighed carefully by professionals. Ultimately, services are most effective if family members are fully supportive and actively participating in the services being offered. This is more likely to be the case if families are given appropriate options for frequency and type of services.

BENEFICIAL OUTCOMES

Several beneficial outcomes emerge from successful teamwork and appropriate services for young children. The following are hallmarks of best practice for working with families and professionals.

Professionalism

- Trust, safety, and confidentiality in relationships
- Respect for others' knowledge and experience
- Willingness to problem-solve with others
- Willingness to ask for advice and guidance
- Willingness to share control

Team Role and Function

- Open communication
- Sensitivity to the mutual needs of families and professionals
- Sound documentation
- Reflective practices
- A solid base of knowledge and information
- Willingness to research and learn more

Family Issues

- Respect and appreciation for family differences
- An openness to input from others
- Knowledge about diverse ethnic and cultural backgrounds, especially in relationship to perceptions of disability
- Flexibility
- A commitment to collaboration

Thinking It Through: Questions for Discussion

1. How might professionals and/or family members handle instances of poor attitudes or incompetence among colleagues?

2. What are some positive approaches for resolving persistent control issues among professionals and agencies?

3. How might professionals resolve the disparity between best practice in evaluating infants and young children and less than optimal, established policies for evaluation?

4. How might teams develop an approach to communicate with and better serve families of different cultures?

5. When family members are locked in self-destructive patterns, what are some short- and long-term approaches for helping them reset their patterns and access their own strengths?

REFERENCES

Als, H., Gilkerson, L., Duffy, F.H., McAnulty, G.B., Buehler, D.M., Vandenberg, K., et al. (2003). A three-center, controlled trial of individualized developmental care for very low birth weight preterm infants: Medical, neurodevelopmental, parenting, and caregiving effects. *Journal of Developmental & Behavioral Pediatrics, 24*(6), 399–409.

American Academy of Pediatrics Council on Children with Disabilities. (2005). Policy statement: Care coordination in the medical home: Integrating health and related systems of care for children with special health care needs. *Pediatrics, 116*(5), 1238–1244.

Baglin, C.A. (2009). Providing leadership and support for interagency collaborative efforts. In J.M. Taylor, J. McGowan, & T. Linder (Eds.), *The program administrator's guide to early childhood special education: Leadership, development, and supervision* (pp. 41–61). Baltimore: Paul H. Brookes Publishing Co.

Bailey, D.B., Hebbeler, K., Spiker, D., Scarborough, A., Mallik, S., & Nelson, L. (2005). Thirty-six-month outcomes for families of children who have disabilities and participated in early intervention. *Pediatrics, 116*(6), 1346–1352.

Bryden, D.A., & Ensher, G.L. (2009). Home and school programs for infants and young children with special needs. In G.L. Ensher, D.A. Clark, & N.S. Songer (Eds.), *Families, infants, and young children at risk: Pathways to best practice* (pp. 335–352). Baltimore: Paul H. Brookes Publishing Co.

Dunst, C., Trivette, C., & Deal, A. (1988). *Enabling and empowering families: Principles and guidelines for practice.* Cambridge, MA: Brookline Books.

Farmer, J.E., Marien, W.E., Clark, M.J., Sherman, A., & Selva, T.J. (2004). Primary care support for children with chronic health conditions: Identifying and predicting unmet family needs. *Pediatrics, 29*(5), 355–367.

Feldman, R., Eidelman, A.I., Sirota, L., & Weller, A. (2002). Comparison of skin-to-skin (kangaroo) and traditional care: Parenting outcomes and preterm infant development. *Pediatrics, 110*(1), 16–26.

Individuals with Disabilities Education Act Amendments of 1997, PL 105-17, 20 U.S.C 1400 *et seq.*

Johnson, B.H., Abraham, M.R., & Parrish, R.N. (2004). Designing the neonatal intensive care unit for optimal family involvement. In R.D. White (Ed.), The sensory environment of the NICU: Scientific and design-related aspects. *Clinics in Perinatology, 31*(2), 353–382.

Johnson, D.P., Kastner, T.A., & American Academy of Pediatrics Committee/Section on Children with Disabilities. (2005). Helping families raise children with special health care needs at home. *Pediatrics, 115*(2), 507–511.

Landy, S., & Menna, R. (2006). *Early intervention with multi-risk families: An integrative approach.* Baltimore: Paul H. Brookes Publishing Co.

Lynch, E.W. (2004). Developing cross-cultural competence. In E.W. Lynch & M.J. Hanson, *Developing cross-cultural competence: A guide for working with children and their families* (3rd ed.) (pp. 41–80). Baltimore: Paul H. Brookes Publishing Co.

Lynch, E.W., & Hanson, M.J. (2004). *Developing cross-cultural competence: A guide for working with children and their families* (3rd ed.). Baltimore: Paul H. Brookes Publishing Co.

McLean, M., & Crais, E.R. (2004). Procedural considerations in assessing infants and preschoolers with disabilities. In M. McLean, M. Wolery, & D.B. Bailey, Jr., *Assessing infants and preschoolers with special needs* (pp. 45–70). Upper Saddle River, NJ: Pearson/Merrill Prentice Hall.

Naseef, R.A. (2001). *Special children, challenged parents: The struggles and rewards of raising a child with a disability* (Rev. ed.). Baltimore: Paul H. Brookes Publishing Co.

National Committee for Quality Assurance (NCQA). (2008). Standards and guidelines for physician-practice connections—Patient-Centered Medical Home (PPC-PCMH). Washington, DC: Physician Practice Connections.

Niederman, L.G., Schwartz, A., Connell, K.J., & Silverman, K. (2007). Healthy Steps for young children program in pediatric residency training: Impact on primary care outcomes. *Pediatrics, 120*(3), e596–e603.

Pan, R.J., Littlefield, D., Valladolid, S.G., Tapping, P.J., & West, D.C. (2005). Building healthier communities for children and families: Applying asset-based community development to community pediatrics. *Pediatrics, 115*(4), 1185–1187.

Sadat, A. (1978). *In search of identity.* New York: HarperCollins.

Shonkoff, J.P., & Phillips, D.A. (Eds.) (2000). *From neurons to neighborhoods: The science of early childhood development.* Washington, DC: National Academies Press.

Songer, N.S. (1998). *The home visitor–family relationship* [PowerPoint slides]. Syracuse, NY: Syracuse University.

Songer, N.S. (2007). *Key elements of collaboration and working with families* [PowerPoint presentation]. Syracuse, NY: Syracuse University.

Wertlieb, D. (2003). Converging trends in family research and pediatrics: Recent findings for the American Academy of Pediatrics Task Force on the Family. *Pediatrics, 111*(6), 1572–1587.

Zuckerman, B., Parker, S., Kaplan-Sanoff, M., Augustyn, M., & Barth, M.C. (2004). Healthy Steps: A case study of innovation in pediatric practice. *Pediatrics, 114*(3), 820–826.

II

Beginnings

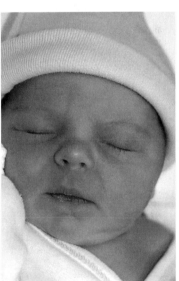

3

The Early Years and Brain Development

The Critical Connections of Building Relationships

Marilyn A. Fisher

CHAPTER HIGHLIGHTS

After reading Chapter 3, the reader will

- Be familiar with typical developmental milestones in early childhood

- Recognize some risk factors for atypical development in the early years

- Understand ways in which environments may give rise to adverse outcomes

- Understand ways in which environments can support and enhance developmental outcomes for infants and young children

- Understand ways that positive family interactions can facilitate developmental outcomes for infants and young children

SETH'S STORY

Mark and Mary were eagerly anticipating the birth of their second child. Mary had taken good care of herself throughout the pregnancy, and the baby was active and growing well. Two days before her due date, Mary developed profuse vaginal bleeding and was rushed to the hospital. There the fetus was determined to be in severe distress, and an emergency cesarean section was performed with Mary under general anesthesia. Mark was not allowed to remain in the room when their baby boy, Seth, was delivered. Doctors told Mark later that the infant needed intense resuscitation, including CPR and placement of a breathing tube. The infant was rushed to the neonatal intensive care unit (NICU) at the university hospital 50 miles away before Mary had a chance to wake up and see him.

Time in the NICU

Over the next several days, the NICU staff determined that Seth had suffered from asphyxia, low levels of oxygen and blood flow to his vital tissues. At first, the health care professionals told Mark and Mary that Seth was very unstable. The oxygen levels in his bloodstream would drop to dangerously low levels in response to minor stimulation, such as a diaper change. The doctors and nurses discouraged Mark and Mary from holding or touching Seth during that vulnerable time.

Although all of Seth's tissues had suffered an insult, their functions eventually returned to normal, with the exception of his brain function. Seth had seizures that required anticonvulsant medications to provide some degree of control. He still had some breakthrough seizures, and the medications seemed to make him excessively sleepy.

He was uncoordinated when feeding, and Mary's plan to breastfeed her infant seemed doomed. He had decreased alertness, and did not appear to know that his parents or 3-year-old brother were present. Initially he did not establish eye contact with his family. He had decreased muscle tone and could not move his arms or legs spontaneously, and had little to no head control. However, as he became more stable, he was able to tolerate handling.

At this point, Mark and Mary received encouragement from the health care professionals to begin to interact with their infant. At first, he was able to tolerate only their quietly talking, singing, or reading a book to him. Later, he allowed a finger to be placed in his palm; sometimes he would try to wrap his little fingers around it. Gradually, he tolerated gentle stroking of his skin. Due to his adverse responses to excess stimulation and the presence of his breathing tube and multiple intravenous lines (which entered his body through his scalp and umbilical cord), he was not quite stable enough to be held on Mark's or Mary's lap. However, he was stable enough to be held in a modified way. With the nurses' help, Mark and Mary were able to slip their hands under Seth through the portholes of the incubator, cradling him gently in that position without removing him from the heated environment or creating any adverse stress for him.

Mark and Mary were taught how to interpret Seth's behavior to determine whether or not he was ready for the stimulation of touch and social interaction. They also were taught to interpret Seth's agitation, excess movement, and oxygen desaturations in response to too much stimulation. They truly became experts in determining the appropriate levels of stimulation to maximize their infant's development and in minimizing the negative effects of that stimulation. Eventually, Seth became stable enough to be held on his parents' lap, and his 3-year-old brother was able to help his parents hold his little brother.

After several weeks, Seth started to develop increased tone and contractures, making him unable to extend his elbows or knees fully. He still was not able to feed by mouth, and had decreased alertness.

An Interdisciplinary Team to Help

Fortunately, an interdisciplinary team had been assembled to help Seth and his family to achieve the best outcomes possible. The team included physicians who specialized in newborn medicine (neonatologists), physicians who specialized in the function of the brain and nerves (neurologists), and neurodevelopmental physicians who were knowledgeable about early child development. A physician with expertise in the function of hormones in the body (i.e., an endocrinologist) was involved to help correct low levels of certain hormones that are produced by the brain. A nutritionist ensured that Seth's nutrition was optimal for him. A lactation specialist helped to maximize Seth's success at breastfeeding, using optimal positioning of both mother and infant during nursing. When Seth became tired and frustrated at trying to get Mary's milk to let down, he was able to receive Mary's pumped breast milk via an innovative method called the *supplemental nursing system*. In this system, Mary's pumped breast milk was made more easily available to Seth via a tiny tube taped to Mary's nipple. Using this technique, he got more immediate positive reinforcement because he would receive some milk with the first suck, without having to wait for milk let down. Mary also received training on techniques for successfully feeding an infant who does not nurse well. Seth received feedings from a tube entering his nose and extending to his stomach only as a last resort.

In addition to the team of professionals noted previously, occupational and speech therapists helped Seth with the tasks of daily living, especially feeding by mouth. A physical therapist addressed the early contractures of his joints with range-of-motion activities. Seth's parents and nurses were also involved in these therapies. Later, the therapists, along with orthopedic surgeons, developed wrist and ankle splints for Seth in an attempt to prevent further contractures and to facilitate more functional use of his hands and feet.

Coming Home

After Seth's discharge from the hospital, his pediatrician followed Seth's development very closely, along with the neurodevelopmental physician. The pediatricians also orchestrated appointments to his various consulting physicians and services, collated the information obtained in those appointments, and called regular interdisciplinary meetings to discuss Seth's progress. Seth's family was an integral part of the team, and information about Seth's challenges, his successes, and plans to encourage further progress were discussed regularly among all team members.

Early Intervention

During his toddler years Seth was enrolled in early intervention, where a variety of therapists and teachers were integral to the development of his educational and therapy program. In particular, they focused on his language skills and neuromotor abilities. His parents were actively involved in the majority of these sessions, learning from his teachers and clinicians techniques and strategies to continue to work on at home.

Going to School and Graduation

Upon reaching school age, Seth was evaluated for placement in school. His classes were selected to offer him the optimal benefits of social interaction with other students and also allow him to continue his therapies and instruction. Seth's parents met with his teachers on a regular basis, and they and Seth's brother continued to reinforce these skills and abilities at home. Mark, Mary, and Seth's older brother looked on proudly when Seth graduated from his local high school.

A Beneficial Outcome

Seth was a young man faced with some disabilities, but he had had a lifetime of nurturing, an academic program of the highest quality with appropriate adaptations along the way, a cultivated desire to help others, an awareness of resources available to him to maintain his independence, and the sure knowledge that he was loved. Thus, in large part because of the lifelong nurturing environment and relationships provided by his family, a child with obvious neurological and intellectual special needs was able to achieve abilities that he might otherwise not have realized.

NORMAL BRAIN DEVELOPMENT IN THE EARLY YEARS

Normal child development in the early years is a reflection of the complex interface between the maturing brain/neurological system and the child's immediate environment. As a child's brain matures with the passage of time, he is able to perform progressively more intricate tasks and activities. There are, of course, variations across diverse home environments, communities, countries, cultures, and inherited native abilities. At the same time, there is a sequence of major milestones in multiple areas of development that are expected with age and increasing opportunities. Fundamental to all of these correlated developments are the nurturing relationships with others—family members, friends, and eventually the wider context of persons initially unfamiliar to the child.

Infants' and young children's emerging behaviors and learning offer a remarkable reflection of ever-changing neurological processes. One example is major motor milestones. For example, like all skills that evidence progressive brain development, gross motor abilities follow a specific pattern, from achievement of head control to achievement of trunk control leading to sitting, standing, and then locomotion. At birth, the head–to–body weight ratio is proportionately greater than it ever will be throughout life. It requires significant muscle strength as well as desire for an infant to meaningfully move his or her head. An infant from birth to 2 months can lift his or her head only momentarily from the prone (i.e., lying on belly) position. By approximately 2 months, the infant should be able to raise his or her head to a 45-degree angle for a sustained period of time.

From birth to 3 months, an infant can be placed in a sitting position, with his or her back rounded, hips bent and turned out for added support, and someone holding the infant in place. By 5–6 months, the infant can soften a forward fall from the sitting position using outstretched arms, and by 8 months typically he or she can sit without support, playing with toys for a sustained period of time.

Simultaneously by 8–12 months, the increasingly more mobile infant can stand while holding on to furniture. At 9–13 months, with improving postural control, the growing toddler can stand unsupported; by 14–15 months, most children can walk independently and stoop from a standing position to retrieve an object dropped on the floor.

Between 2 and 4 years of age, the preschooler typically can walk easily with swinging of the arms, and by 5 years most children can stand on one foot for 10 seconds and play board games on the floor.

Abilities in other developmental domains, such as language, cognitive, social-emotional, and sensory-perceptual, show similar patterns of increasing complexity; at the same time, they reveal behaviors that

are unique to individual children. Between 2 and 7 years of age, the young child, although still in a concrete, egocentric, and illogical stage of thinking, is an adept communicator who has a fairly good understanding of time and space and the past and future, who can act out several sequenced scenarios of pretend play, and who has a widening understanding of the consequences of his or her behavior (see Tables 3.1 and 3.2 for brief summaries of cognitive and fine motor development).

We described (Fisher, 2009) in detail postnatal biochemical brain development that parallels the development just described in the infant and young child:

After birth, the brain maturation that began during fetal life continues. There is further organization, myelination, and growth of the brain. Fatty acids are impor-

tant for the proper myelination and development of the brain, both before and after birth. The quantity and types of fatty acids found in the mother's diet are reflected in the quantity and proportions of these substances found in the mother's breast milk (Xiang et al., 2005). The long-chain polyunsaturated fatty acid, docosahexaenoic acid (DHA), ingested in foods by the mother during gestation and by the infant after birth, is deposited in developing brain tissue and in the developing retina. DHA is deposited in increasing quantities in the brain from approximately 20 weeks of gestation until at least 24 months after a full-term delivery. DHA has been found by some researchers to be associated with improved infant neurodevelopment and vision (Jensen et al., 2005) and may be associated with improved memory and learning in young children (Heinemann & Bauer, 2006). (pp. 63–64)

Relating to issues of the impact of environment, Shonkoff and Phillips wrote:

The brain is the ultimate organ of adaptation. It takes in information and orchestrates complex behavioral repertoires that allow human beings to act in sometimes marvelous, sometimes terrible ways. Most of what people think of as the "self"—what we think, what we remember, what we can do, how we feel—is acquired by the brain from the experiences that occur after birth. Some of this information is acquired during critical or sensitive periods of development, when the brain appears uniquely ready to take in certain kinds of information, while other information can be acquired across broad swaths of development that can extend into adulthood. This spectrum of possibilities is well captured by coinciding evidence of both the remarkably rapid brain development that characterizes the early childhood period

and the brain's lifelong capacity for growth and change. (2000, p. 182)

Critical to the development of psychosocial skills are the nurturing relationships of the infant and young child with adults and peers in the immediate environment. Like other domains of development, psychosocial skills follow a fairly predictable pattern of behavior that parallels brain development. For instance, at 5–8 months, the infant recognizes others as either familiar persons or strangers, and exhibits separation anxiety when away from his or her parents. At 6–8 months, the infant recognizes him- or herself in the mirror. At 7–8 months, the infant prefers to receive care from his or her mother, even when others are available. At 9–12 months, an infant will interact differently with other children than with adults, and by 12 months, the emerging toddler will respond to emotions expressed by his or her parents. The toddler will begin to prefer inter-

Table 3.1.   A brief on cognitive development in the infant and young child

Age	Skill
3–6 months	Focuses on object performing an action
3–6 months	Shows understanding of object permanence
8–9 months	Uses objects in play
9–12 months	Recognizes the effect he or she exerts on the environment
9–12 months	Emulates an adult using a toy or tool
9–12 months	Differentiates play based on a toy's function
12–15 months	Problem-solves by trial and error
12–15 months	Uses simple pretend play directed at him- or herself
12–18 months	Uses simple pretend play on animate and inanimate objects
18–21 months	Uses imagination in playing with nonrealistic toys
2–4 years	Uses words as symbols for people, places, things
3–4 years	Pretends, role plays
3–5 years	Performs complex role imitation; makes two dolls interact
4–7 years	Exhibits beginnings of logical thinking; still egocentric
5+ years playing	Directs actions and interactions of three dolls; organizes other children in role
7–11 years	Understands space, time, future, past, and concept of eternity. Demonstrates concrete thinking; has difficulty with more abstract thinking. Takes into account how different actions will affect different outcomes. Can consider different physical characteristics simultaneously. Understands that number or mass of objects does not change simply because of alteration in their arrangement. Able to understand relationships among objects. Able to give instructions and tell simple stories.

Table 3.2.   Fine motor skills in the infant and young child

Age	Skill
Birth to 1 month	Is unable to release objects from grasp
Birth to 2 months	Visually regards an object
1–3 months	Swipes hands at object
1–4 months	Involuntarily releases objects from grasp
2–6 months	Inspects hands, reaches for objects
2–7 months	Grasps object using palm and fourth and fifth fingers only
3–3½ months	Clasps hands together
4 months	Moves hands in unison
4–4½ months	Opens fist in anticipation of contact with object
4–8 months	Transfers objects from hand to hand
4–9 months	Uses all fingers to rake up an object
5–12 months	Shows progressive forearm voluntary supination
6 months	From prone position, reaches with one hand while supporting upper body with other forearm
7 months	From prone position, reaches with one hand while supporting upper body with other extended arm
7–9 months	Voluntarily releases objects from grasp
9–10 months	Uses pincer grasp to pick up small objects
10–14 months	Releases object from grasp by finger extension into container
12 months	Uses refined pincer grasp with fingertip
12–15 months	Releases object from grasp into container using both finger and wrist extension with greater accuracy
12–18 months	Holds crayon in fist with thumb up
24 months	Holds crayon with fingers, thumb directed downward, with blunt end of crayon abutting the palm; draws vertical line
3 years	Draws horizontal line; holds writing instrument with three fingers; uses movements of wrist and forearm to draw; solves simple puzzles; stacks nine blocks; begins early scissor use
4 years	Draws a cross, uses a fork
5 years	Uses finger movements to move writing instrument on the paper; uses a blunt knife; draws diagonal line
6 years	Shows isolated finger use; coordinates both hands together; shows hand–eye coordination; mature enough to use scissors well; ties own shoelaces; buttons; pours; solves complex puzzles
7+ years	Sews, draws in accurate proportion, prints neatly. With passing years, demonstrates improved writing skills by fluidity of strokes, smaller letters, smaller space between letters/words, increased writing speeds

actions with other children, and at 15–18 months will share toys with his or her parents. Although the toddler will briefly explore away from them, he or she will always return to their side.

By 18–24 months, a child typically is aware of actions that meet with adult approval or disapproval. During this stage, time spent with groups of children consists mostly of solitary activity and watching other children play and interact. As development progresses, group time will come to involve longer sequences during which a child will interact with peers. The skills of taking turns and sharing toys eventually develop beyond 24 months of age, preparing the young child for entry into the broader context of preschool environments outside of the home setting.

THE IMPACT OF BIRTH HISTORY AND ADVERSE ENVIRONMENTS

As illustrated in Seth's story, birth history has a major impact on children's neurological and developmental outcomes. Improved medical technology over the past several decades has saved the lives of countless premature infants, infants with perinatal asphyxia, and newborns with congenital malformations, chromosomal abnormalities, infections, metabolic disorders, and those with other life-threatening or life-altering conditions (Shonkoff & Marshall, 2000). Although infants who might not have lived previously are now surviving, they may have residual developmental delays (Hack, Taylor, Klein, & Mercuri-Minich, 2000).

As known from classic research studies (Kagan, Klein, Finley, Rogoff, & Nolan, 1979), as well as from more recent research (Als, 1997; Als, Duffy, et al., 2004; Als, Gilkerson, et al., 2003; Landry, Smith, & Swank, 2006; Warren & Brady, 2007), environmental factors are significant contributors to developmental outcomes, even in the face of adversity. In this regard, Als wrote more than a decade ago:

> It appears that development in the extrauterine environment leads to different and potentially maladaptive developmental trajectories. Understanding the neurodevelopmental expectations of the fetal infant is increasingly providing a basis for modification of traditionally delivered newborn intensive care, which appears to inadvertently increase the stress and challenge to the vulnerable preterm nervous system. Furthermore, understanding the neurodevelopmental expectation of the fetal infant is increasingly leading to the abandonment of first-generation skill teaching and task-oriented intervention approaches in the NICU for the sake of a process-oriented, relationship-based, individualized, developmentally focused framework of care delivery. (1997, p. 48)

In another, related context of defining "the neurorelationship framework" for infant and child mental health, early intervention, and interdisciplinary practice, Lillas and Turnbull wrote:

> The neurorelational framework is organized according to four global systems—regulation, sensory, relevance, and executive—each representing a collection of related brain functions. The four systems are viewed as being in dynamic, interdependent, and reciprocal relationship with each other, the body, and the world. Each brain develops and lives within a context that has universal and unique properties, shaping the expression of individual behavior. . . . The dynamic and reciprocal nature of brains enmeshed in relationships remind us that the parent's brain is also not isolated but is continually affected by the child. . . . the four systems of the brain are embedded in a context, and conversely, that context shapes and is represented within the four systems. (2009, p. 32)

Clearly, as a result of the impact of his birth history, Seth experienced neurological impairment that was severe, that ultimately resulted in a diagnosis of cerebral palsy, and that carried lifelong developmental and functional consequences. From his earliest days in the neonatal intensive care unit through his early intervention, preschool, and school-age years, Seth required special feeding techniques, therapies, adapted methods, and curricula to address his needs.

His family required an interdisciplinary approach involving neonatologists; neurologists; developmentalists; nutritionists; speech, occupational, and physical therapists; educators; and other specialists working to best serve Seth's needs. Lillas and Turnbull suggested that

> In terms of intervention, parents can play an important role. In particular, involving them in the following strategies can be beneficial:
> - Use states of arousal as a way to guide interactive regulation.
> - Use the child's sensory preferences for alerting, comfort, relaxation, and state recovery.
> - Reinforce that the child should make conscious links to the visceral (body) self.
> - Have parents as well as older children utilize relaxation techniques to address their own levels of stress.
>
> In addition, all practitioners can consider the following possible strategies for assessment and intervention:
> - Observe the infant's communication of visceral cues and the parents' reading of these cues.
> - Support the parents' learning to read the nonverbal cues of states of arousal.
> - Support the parents' understanding of the meaning of stress and stress recovery.
> - Collaborate with occupational therapists to help identify triggers and preferences.
> - Teach how to regulate arousal and create shared joy by incorporating sensory preferences and identifying sensory triggers.
> - Teach relaxation techniques, such as deep breathing, to parents and older children. (2009, p. 190)

With the support and guidance of interdisciplinary team members, Seth's parents' responsiveness to his needs from infancy throughout his preschool and school years and the nurturing relationships they offered were fundamental to maximizing his developmental potential (Warren & Brady, 2007). To be sure, Seth continued to face performance and learning challenges that were not reversible, given the initial neurological insult and impairment at birth. His achievements, however, exemplify the potential that may be realized through best practice on the part of both parents and professionals.

BENEFICIAL OUTCOMES: A CAUTION AND A PROMISE

As this chapter draws to a close, professionals are left with a caution and a promise. Relative to the early years and brain development, a wealth of research clearly points to the multiple, naturally occurring biological and environmental insults that may affect the trajectories of lifelong development, learning, and behavior from conception onward. Some of these insults will be permanent; others will be more malleable and responsive to intervention. Evidence-based research in the field of neonatal brain dysfunction can lead to concern about functional outcomes. As Shonkoff and Phillips (2000) noted, however, it is unwise to assume a perspective of "unwarranted pessimism" that "the die has been cast by the time the child enters school" (p. 216). Instead, despite the enormity of the task of exploration and yet uncharted waters of research on early environments and intervention, it is crucial that professionals recognize that "what happens early" during the period of brain development really matters (Shonkoff & Phillips, 2000). It is incumbent upon providers to tenaciously seek to help affected children during the formative period of brain development to achieve their full potential, using the power of strong interpersonal relationships.

Thinking It Through: Questions for Discussion

1.   An infant is born at 24 weeks of gestation, has a Grade IV intraventricular hemorrhage involving his cerebral cortex, but survives to experience severe problems with feeding. What specialists need to be brought in to assist the parents to facilitate a successful hospital discharge?

2.   A late preterm infant is born at 35 weeks of gestation, weighing 5 pounds, 2 ounces. She remains in the hospital for 2 weeks because of feeding issues and jaundice that is resolved within the first 3 days, then she is discharged to home. At home she is very slow to gain weight, still weighing only 13 pounds and a few ounces at 12 months. The first-time parents are very concerned about her inconsistent eating patterns. What should the parents do? How do they obtain help and advice for their daughter, who has now been diagnosed with failure to thrive?

3.   A family enrolls their child in a local Head Start program at 3 years of age. They have no concerns about their young son's development, but within a month the teaching and social services staff become concerned about apparent delays in speech and language development and the child's aggressive interactions with other children. These issues are raised with the family, who continue to maintain that their son is fine, just a little active. Child Protective Services has been intermittently involved with the family regarding their two other children. What should the Head Start staff do in garnering services to assist this family and support their child?

REFERENCES

Als, H. (1997). Earliest intervention for preterm infants in the newborn intensive care unit. In M.J. Guralnick (Ed.), *The effectiveness of early intervention* (pp. 47–76). Baltimore: Paul H. Brookes Publishing Co.

Als, H., Duffy, F.H., McAnulty, G.B., Rivkin, M.J., Vajapeyam, S., Mulkern, R.V., et al. (2004). Early experience alters brain function and structure. *Pediatrics, 113*(4), 846–858.

Als, H., Gilkerson, L., Duffy, F.H., McAnulty, G.B., Buehler, D.M., Vandenberg, K., et al. (2003). A three-center, controlled trial of individualized developmental care for very low birth weight preterm infants: Medical, neurodevelopmental, parenting, and caregiving effects. *Journal of Developmental & Behavioral Pediatrics, 24*(6), 399–409.

Fisher, M.A. (2008). Neonatal neurology. In G.L. Ensher, D.A. Clark, & N.S. Songer (Eds.), *Families, infants, and young children at risk: Pathways to best practice* (pp. 61–91). Baltimore: Paul H. Brookes Publishing Co.

Hack, M., Taylor, G., Klein, N., & Mercuri-Minich, N. (2000). Functional limitations and special health care needs of 10- to 14-year-old children weighing less than 750 grams at birth. *Pediatrics, 106*(3), 554–560.

Kagan, J., Klein, R.E., Finley, G.E., Rogoff, B., & Nolan, E. (1979). A cross-cultural study of cognitive development. *Monographs of the Society for Research in Child Development, 44*(5, Serial No. 180).

Landry, S.H., Smith, K.E., & Swank, P.R. (2006). Responsive parenting: Establishing early foundations for social, communication, and independent problem-solving skills. *Developmental Psychology, 42,* 627–642.

Lillas, C., & Turnbull, J. (2009). *Infant/child mental health, early intervention, and relationship-based therapies: A neurorelational framework for interdisciplinary practice.* New York: W.W. Norton & Co.

Shonkoff, J.P., & Marshall, P.C. (2000). The biology of developmental vulnerability. In J.P. Shonkoff & S.J. Meisels (Eds.), *Handbook of early child intervention* (2nd ed., pp. 35–53). New York: Cambridge University Press.

Shonkoff, J.P., & Phillips, D.A. (Eds.). (2000). *From neurons to neighborhoods: The science of early childhood development.* Washington, DC: National Academies Press.

Warren, S.F., & Brady, N.C. (2007). The role of maternal responsivity in the development of children with intellectual disabilities. *Mental Retardation and Developmental Disabilities Research Reviews, 13,* 330–338.

4

Cultural Conceptions of Motherhood and Pregnancy in the 21st Century

Melissa M. Doyle

CHAPTER HIGHLIGHTS

At the conclusion of this chapter, the reader will

- Understand the traditionally accepted, cultural conceptions of motherhood in the United States

- Given social and economic changes in the United States, understand some of the conflicting and difficult choices for women balancing careers and rearing children

- Recognize the role that helping professionals can have when providing support to women and their families who choose a less traditional path to motherhood

- Understand the options and issues for women surrounding genetic counseling, adoption, and Assistive Reproductive Technology (ART)

Few roles in U.S. culture have been imbued with as much conflict and expectation as motherhood. Women have greater opportunities for educational achievement and career advancement than at any other time in history. Unlike in previous generations, women are now permitted and often expected to pursue opportunities for education, training, and career achievement. Yet society also expects women to pursue motherhood, which can limit or conflict with other opportunities. Career advancement often requires a single-minded focus and a commitment of long hours and several years. Delaying pregnancy until one's late 30s and 40s to establish a career can result in difficulty conceiving without medical intervention. The abundance of educational and professional possibilities available for women may be accompanied by stress, challenges, and even censure from other women who have made different choices.

 ### C.S., AGE 37 YEARS

I wanted to go right on to college; it was the chance that my mother didn't have because she got married early and then had kids, and certainly no one ever bothered to ask my grandmother if she even wanted an education.

And yet the whole time I was in school, I was struck with a certain sense of urgency to find someone and settle down. My family would always be cheering every advancement I made, and then in the same sentence ask if I was seeing anyone, considering settling down and having kids. It was almost as if, if I didn't, I would be stuck forever with a career, which I wanted. I just didn't want to have to choose one or the other.

Our culture offers a suggested timeline for motherhood. Pregnancy, it is generally believed, should occur after college or job training, with an established partner, yet be completed by one's mid-30s in order for one to be prepared for middle adulthood. Families who vary from these norms often encounter surprise or even censure. Adolescents who are expectant or new mothers, for example, rarely hear "congratulations" or good wishes. Rather, they often hear warnings about how their educational and career options will be limited, warnings that are often delivered with frustration that the young women have failed to appreciate all the opportunities available to them. Single mothers or families who seek to have children later in life may encounter concerns about how their energy may waver or how they may lose out on some of their own opportunities when choosing to parent in mid-life.

The evolution of the supermom identity is a direct result of efforts to balance the desire to have a career with the desire to pursue motherhood. While it is wonderful for women to know that one option does not preclude their ability to also choose the other, we often fail to identify the costs of attempting to balance both career and motherhood. In addition, those around them may not wholeheartedly support their desire to do both. Those who choose to parent early in adulthood, while also beginning careers, may be viewed as compromising the position that women should be equally considered for executive-level positions. Women who choose to pursue a career first often receive warnings about the rapidly diminishing chances of achieving a healthy pregnancy as one grows older. Regardless of one's choices, it is clear that it is difficult to achieve a balance between parenting and a career, and attempting this balance can result in significant challenges and sacrifices.

K.S., AGE 28 YEARS

I knew that I wanted to be both: be a partner in the firm and yet have a child. I felt that I had to keep my desire a secret while interviewing for fear that I would not be viewed as a good candidate. Now with a baby, I am always torn between conflicting obligations, feeling like wherever I am, I am doing a poor job and letting someone else down. The pressure to prove myself never ends.

CULTURAL CONCEPTIONS OF MOTHERHOOD

The role of motherhood in many cultures is implicitly tied to social adulthood and female identity. Although many would disagree that this view objectifies a woman's worth and value to the culture and family, it does persist. It is impossible to determine to what extent the value placed on this role as part of women's identity has been socialized into young girls (Hammons, 2008). The pretend behaviors observed in young girls who play house and spend time with dolls underscores this point. Despite cultural awareness, growing acceptance of different life choices, and support for women's academic achievement, many people still feel compelled to inquire of adult women when they are planning to have children.

Motherhood at a life stage that U.S. culture would consider early or late can challenge people's perceptions of adult life. Although society may support the view that women can make any choices at any point in their lives, society also has identified normative tasks for late adolescence as well as for middle adulthood. Parenting either in adolescence or in one's middle age challenges society's view of the tasks of that life stage. Both adolescent mothers and older mothers may equally feel social censure for a nontraditional choice, but there are pressures and demands unique to each of those positions.

MOTHERHOOD IN ADOLESCENCE

In past generations, the need for family laborers, high infant mortality rates, and shorter life expectancy necessitated early marriage and parenting. Modern culture, however, has extended the age range for adolescence through one's 20s. It is normative to delay or extend one's college years, remain living with one's parents beyond the completion of college, and remain financially dependent on them into adulthood. Adolescents have available contraception and increased educational and occupational options. Early parenting is no longer expected and often results in social stigma.

Although every facet of development holds critical tasks, poor choices in adolescence can lead to serious emotional, physical, and financial consequences. Ideally, one emerges into adulthood with a cohesive sense of self, a focus on future goals, and the capacity to work toward their achievement. The hallmark characteristics of adolescence—an egocentric view of the world, impulsive decisions, sudden mood shifts, an evolving capacity for future planning and goal setting—fit poorly with the needs of a demanding infant. Pregnant or parenting adolescents must rapidly assimilate additional responsibilities and concerns that are often in conflict with their own needs and desires, as well as with those of their peers.

Adolescent mothers often reside with some constellation of their primary or extended family. Although this arrangement may offer a young mother support and modeling for parenting, it can also lead to role confusion as she seeks to develop a differentiated role and identify as a mother while surrounded by more experienced mothers (Savio Beers & Hollo, 2009). Despite this potential conflict, it has been suggested that motherhood may be a role of choice for some young women, particularly those who may see few options for education or careers in their communities. In this role, which may have been modeled for them by family members or neighbors, they may have greater autonomy and certainly a clear role and purpose (Merrick, 1995).

Researchers have long pointed to the negative consequences of adolescent pregnancy and parenting, including poor educational, economic, and occupational outcomes for these young women (Sadler et al., 2007; Savio Beers & Hollo, 2009; Suner, Nakamura, & Caulfield, 2003). However, socioeconomic factors—including poverty—have been shown to have a tremendous impact on these outcomes as well. Certainly there is a direct link between the impact of poverty on the poorer health of adolescents prior to pregnancy, poor prenatal care, and the resulting high incidence of preterm birth and low birth weight (Merrick, 1995). Rather than a single factor, it is more likely a constellation of these factors that contributes to the greater likelihood of teenage mothers having lower graduation rates, living in impoverished conditions, and having children who are inadequately prepared for classroom learning (Suner et al., 2003). These poor outcomes markedly increase in severity for every subsequent pregnancy during adolescence (Sadler et al., 2007).

Studies of community support services and school-based services for teenage mothers have shown significant improvement in school attendance, improved social support, and avoidance of subsequent pregnancies, while ensuring quality care and developing supports for infants (Sadler et al., 2007). Abstinence-only programs have a demonstrated impact on the decision to delay sexual activity, yet they have also led to decreased use of contraception and testing for sexually transmitted diseases once sexual activity begins (Santelli, Lindberg, Finer, & Singh, 2007). Other group intervention programs for teenage parents claim impressive results (Barlow & Coren, 2001; Sadler et al., 2007; Woods et al., 2003). However, as these programs often target varying outcomes and have to follow teenagers for several years, success can be difficult to define and measure. In 2005, Gallagher and colleagues provided an overview of various community demonstration projects funded by the Centers for Disease Control and Prevention (CDC) to determine factors contributing to the success of programs targeting teen pregnancies. Successful programs with data collection were those that had very involved local organizations, focused on issues identified as important by the community, and had high client participation.

These factors identified by the CDC study have been the framework of ecological models of intervention. Suner and colleagues (2003) suggested that a successful intervention must recognize individual, family, and community-based supports in the context of the community culture. Their work, based on Bronfenbrenner's ecological model of development (1979), highlights the importance of recognizing and incorporating cultural values into the model of support. Program development frequently fails to account for this influence, often applying one intervention model universally despite differences in the target population. The work of Suner and colleagues in Hawaii appropriately determined that ignoring the cultural context of youth in their region would undermine the success of their program. Likewise, an intervention for youth in the inner city would fare poorly in the rural portions of the country. Unfortunately, programs that adequately recognize the values and needs of the individual community remain poorly funded and in scarce supply for the level of need nationwide.

MOTHERHOOD LATER IN LIFE

Prior to the availability of assisted reproductive technologies (ART), achieving pregnancy later than mid-adulthood was highly unlikely. It has become much more common, however, for women to begin a family after age 35 and into their 40s. Just as U.S. culture has extended the duration of adolescence, science has allowed women to extend the age of pregnancy, resulting in a middle adulthood that is equally likely to be filled with proms or disposable diapers. The tasks and goals previously associated with middle age—such as having adolescents who are becoming more independent and preparing for college and career—now blur with those of younger adulthood. Pregnancy later in life therefore has unique social complications and concerns.

One's social identity, formed as a result of relationships with others, often serves as a source of pride, shame, or ambivalence. Therefore, parents' social circle and the views of their peers on both early and older parenting highly influence parents' sense of self and their acceptance in the community (Friese, Becker, & Nachtigall, 2008). Friese and colleagues found that although both mothers and fathers undergoing ART felt that their older age affected their personal identity, mothers felt that their age led to a social stigmatization that negatively affected their personal identity. Both parents felt that their age contributed to concerns about their own health and experiences that might not been the case had they parented at a younger age. Mothers often noted being identified as their child's grandmother in interactions with others in play spaces, schools, and restaurants, which led them to feel ashamed. Friese and colleagues noted that in groups of mothers, although the older mothers were new to parenting, they often were the oldest mothers in the group—leading to their feeling excluded from this important social support and group experience. Some mothers, in an effort to appear younger and thus limit the questions others might ask, focused on exercise, healthy eating, and cosmetic changes (Friese et al., 2008).

Although the use of ART offers tremendous benefits to women struggling to achieve a pregnancy, it also poses several challenges to the cultural view of motherhood and parenting. Initial interventions often seek to use genetic material from both members of the couple. When these interventions do not lead to a pregnancy, the next step may be to use donor eggs or a surrogate mother. These medical advances have led to questions about social motherhood, or becoming a mother through these means, versus biological motherhood, referring to women who provide the genetic material or carry the child (Hammons, 2008). Thus, scientific advances, though offering tremendous benefit for many, have also raised complex legal and social questions.

PREVALENCE OF INFERTILITY

Approximately 8% of couples in the United States experience infertility (Levin & Sher, 2000), either primary or secondary, at some point during their childbearing years. Infertility is defined as having at least 12 months of intercourse that does not result in a conception (Kainz, 2001).

Infertility treatment tends to have the greatest impact on the female partner. There are tremendous cultural expectations regarding motherhood as a developmental milestone in adulthood, and women experiencing infertility often feel as though they have failed in a fundamental achievement. The majority of infertility treatments tend to involve women, leading to a greater impact on their health and time, with the possibility that they will again feel responsible if a positive result does not occur (Watkins & Baldo, 2004).

GENETIC TESTING

Advances in scientific research have led to increased availability of genetic screening and testing for women. Such testing may be strongly recommended for women using ART, especially when advanced maternal age is a concern. Adolescent mothers are also referred when genetic concerns are raised by their medical history. Many women describe feelings of ambivalence about genetic testing, desiring the knowledge it offers but not wanting to face the possibility of ending a highly desired pregnancy or incur any harm to a potentially healthy fetus through invasive procedures (Sapp et al., 2010).

H.Y., AGE 38 YEARS

I had been waiting so long to be pregnant; it was horrible to even consider that something could be wrong with the baby. How could I ever consider ending the pregnancy after spending so much time, energy, and money to get pregnant; yet our dream was for a healthy baby. After all of the suffering we had endured, I decided that I really needed to know if we were just facing more of that after the baby was born.

Ambivalence about genetic testing is common, and most women describe feeling torn about how to proceed. The ambivalence frequently occurs at the intersection of one's religious, moral, and intellectual values, which may provide conflicting direction (Sapp et al., 2010). Interestingly, adolescent mothers describe the same struggles and ambivalent feelings as older mothers, despite the differences in age, maturity level, and education (Plaga, Demarco, & Shulman, 2005).

DIFFICULT PREGNANCIES

Expectant parents often look forward to a number of social supports and cultural or religious rituals once their infant arrives, such as having family members file into the hospital room for photos, bringing the mother and newborn home shortly after birth, and celebrating the first visit to the pediatrician. Couples whose infant is born prematurely—perhaps after the parents have endured the rigors of infertility treatment—miss out on many of these anticipated occasions and interactions. Their child cannot be held shortly after birth. Visitors must scrub up, put on a gown, and stand outside an incubator for a glimpse of the tiny, fragile newborn. The mother goes home with empty arms to a room prepared for a child who is not there, and then must return daily to stand outside the incubator. Rather than tracking heights and weights at periodic and expected doctor visits, these parents watch the flickering screens of medical equipment, learn quickly which numbers on the daily laboratory reports are critical, and watch the frequent needle sticks and other invasive medical procedures taking place with their infant. Hodapp and Young (1992) found that mothers of preterm infants experienced reactions similar to mothers of infants with disabilities, including increased feelings of helplessness, crying, and worry. The researchers noted, however, that these feelings diminished within a few months of discharge from the hospital. This improvement was aided by social supports, including positive marital relationships and friendships. Clearly, the birth of a preterm infant results in significant stress for each parent, as well as a future that often entails ongoing involvement with and support from medical, educational, and social resources. These supports and resources may help alleviate the additional stresses for families who have a child with complex medical or cognitive needs, as their self reports on coping and stress often reflect families with typically developing children (Hodapp & Young, 1992).

There remain significant concerns, as well, for parents who give birth to multiple infants. Parents, especially mothers of preterm infants, have noted increased feelings of sadness, worry, and distress after a birth; for mothers of twins and other multiples, studies have found that such feelings often persist through the children's preschool years (i.e., 4 years of age). These feelings are compounded by previously existing mental health problems and/or marital instability

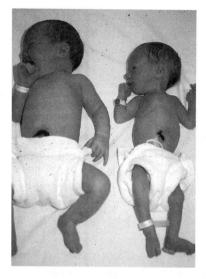

(Klock, 2004). Mothers noted a fear of not being able to provide enough attention to all of their children, leading to feelings of distress and inadequacy. Moreover, in this long-term study Klock reported that mothers of multiples had significant struggles with social isolation and fatigue.

OPTIONS TO ADOPT

Adoption has long been an option for couples with the required financial resources who meet established criteria, which often included being a heterosexual, married, established couple younger than 40 years of age. In the last 3 decades, international possibilities have greatly increased the number of children available for adoption and the opportunities for single and nontraditional couples to adopt. As with traditional adoptions, international adoption can be costly and the process lengthy. What is different is that the criteria for adoptive parents vary by country and the availability of children often changes rapidly, depending on political events or civil unrest in the respective countries. Prospective parents of internationally adopted children may never have the opportunity to meet birth parents, accompany them to prenatal visits, or hold their child shortly after birth. Instead, they may spend hours viewing the few available photos or peering over minutes of video, searching for personality characteristics or trying to discern signs of malnutrition, disease, or developmental delays. For these families, "pregnancy" can take more than months. They may wait years to be approved for adoption and for a child of their choosing to become available. Labor and delivery generally do not occur in a hospital room but rather in an airport or a visa office, often far from home and without the presence of family and friends.

Many internationally adopted children adapt quite well to their new family, home, and culture. However, concerns have arisen over some children who appear to have significant difficulties that manifest during latency and adolescence. Particular issues have been noted for children who resided in institutionalized care prior to adoption, often experiencing little human contact or bonding with caregivers. A small but statistically significant number of these children demonstrate symptoms of attention deficit disorder (ADD) or attention-deficit/hyperactivity disorder (ADHD); some exhibit externalizing behaviors, such as acting out, destructiveness, and oppositional behavior, and internalizing disorders, such as anxiety and depression (Wiik et al., 2010). These findings have been noted using established measures such as the Child Behavioral Checklist (Achenbach, 1991) and, given the appearance of these difficulties years after adoption, likely reflect disadvantages in children's early social and emotional environments (Hawk & McCall, 2010).

Despite all of the dilemmas, international adoption has opened opportunities for individuals or couples who have grown discouraged waiting for an infant from their own country, who are not eligible for domestic adoption, or who feel committed to helping a child escape impoverished circumstances. For many couples, adoption often is considered after unsuccessfully trying to achieve a pregnancy through ART. Although the international adoption process is lengthy and expensive, it can remove much of the pressure involved with infertility treatment. The ongoing perception that one's body is failing, and the sense of shame and depression at not conceiving, are removed. Invasive physical exams and painful medical procedures are also eliminated, leaving the prospective parents (particularly the woman) to refocus on another pathway to parenting.

BENEFICIAL OUTCOMES: COUNSELING AND ADVICE FOR FAMILIES

There are numerous resources for parents at every stage. Pregnant or parenting adolescents, though a diverse group due to economic status, culture, and educational achievement, may share commonalities in developmental maturity and experience. Group interventions that offer supportive counseling and education are often used with adolescents for clinical as well as practical considerations. At this developmental juncture, when peer acceptance and support are critical, a built-in peer group is a tremendous resource. Group interventions permit the greatest amount of information to be disseminated to a larger audience, and given that teenagers often do not reliably attend therapy, a group format provides insurance that the group will always have some participants. Even for those adolescents with family supports, group-based intervention programs are a critical resource for parent education and to advocate school attendance, promote medical care, and ensure that they have adequate financial resources.

Older mothers, those engaged in fertility treatments, or those seeking to parent through adoption have also found support and assistance through group interventions. However, despite the bond of a shared experience, differences in social strata, culture, and education are harder to bridge in these groups.

New opportunities for prospective mothers and their partners to achieve parenthood and have healthy infants will surely arise in the years ahead, thanks to continuing research efforts on hormonal support (i.e., progesterone) to decrease preterm labor, nutritional strategies to improve neonatal and preterm brain growth and function following delivery, the possibility of having grandmothers serve as surrogate mothers for their daughters, and detailed genetic screening prior to conception.

This chapter, covering topics as divergent as teen pregnancy and assisted reproductive technology, may appear to highlight more differences than similarities in the path to pregnancy and motherhood. Despite diverging paths, what remains true and valid is that women embarking on pregnancy and parenting at any time in their lives continue to need support, encouragement, and acceptance. Our ability to provide this critical support, whether as family member, friend, or helping professional, will be greatly affected by recognizing our own cultural expectations regarding motherhood. Awareness of our own bias allows us the opportunity to meet the emotional, social, and educational needs of all mothers, regardless of age, family structure, or path to parenthood.

Thinking It Through:
Questions for Discussion

1. The Internet has given parents greater access to information on medical trials, treatment, and research; consequently, they are becoming more informed health care consumers. Parents are thus often prepared to advocate for their child, but unfortunately they may not recognize the limitations or inaccuracies of information available through public media. This can be a challenge for medical providers, especially when parents are not adequately informed about complications. How can nonmedical professionals encourage the medical community to view parents as resources, and encourage parents to view their physician as an advocate for the child in order to pursue joint decision making, especially when a child is critically ill or when treatment involves risky procedures and possible complications?

2. The rising cost of medical care has led to challenging discussions regarding health care rationing. Uncomfortable questions arise as to whether society should provide the same breadth and depth of medical care to all individuals, regardless of ability to pay, health and cognitive status, or possible treatment outcomes. Advances in ART have allowed infants born early to survive, but with uncertain medical, learning, and behavioral outcomes. Faced with these issues, how do professionals advocate for medical care on behalf of those who cannot advocate for themselves?

3. Economic opportunities or concerns may mean that families move away from extended family and known support networks. ART and changing social perceptions continue to extend the age of conception and birth even further into middle age. Older parents can rely on maturity and possibly a secure financial status to balance their flagging energy reserves. Wisdom, patience, and child care support may be enough to aid a 50-year-old mother of a toddler having a tantrum, yet consider a 70-year-old parent faced with a teenager having an out-of-control party in the basement. What are the societal implications for aging parents whose physical health and perhaps cognitive capacity may not permit them to provide adequate supervision and guidance to teenage children?

REFERENCES

Achenbach, T.M. (1991). *Integrative guide to the 1991 CBCL/4–18 YSR and TRF profiles.* Burlington: University of Vermont, Department of Psychology.

Barlow, J., & Coren, E. (2001). Parent-training programmes for improving maternal psychosocial health. *Cochrane Database System Review 2,* CD002020

Bronfenbrenner, U. (1979). *The ecology of human development: Experiments by nature and design.* Cambridge, MA: Harvard University Press.

Friese, C., Becker, G., & Nachtigall, R.D. (2008). Older motherhood and the changing life course in the era of assisted reproductive technologies. *Journal of Aging Studies, 22,* 65–73.

Gallagher, K., Stanley, A., Shearer, D., & Klemon, L.V. (2005). Challenges in data collection, analysis and distribution of information in community coalition demonstration projects. *Journal of Adolescent Health, 37,* S53–S60.

Hammons, S.A. (2008). Assisted reproductive technologies: Changing conceptions of motherhood? *Affilia: Journal of Women and Social Work, 23,* 270–280.

Hawk, B., & McCall, R.B. (2010). CBCL behavior problems of post-institutionalized international adoptees. *Clinical Child and Family Psychology Review, 13,* 199–211.

Hodapp, R.M., & Young, K.T. (1992). Maternal emotional reactions to the premature infant in the context of the family. *Canadian Journal of Behavioural Science, 24,* 29–41.

Kainz, K. (2001). The role of the psychologist in the evaluation and treatment of infertility. *Women's Health Issues, 11,* 481–485.

Klock, S.C. (2004). Psychological adjustment to twins after infertility. *Best Practice & Research: Clinical Obstetrics and Gynaecology, 18*(4), 645–656.

Levin, J.B., & Sher, T.G. (2000). Psychological treatment of couples undergoing fertility treatment. *Cognitive and Behavioral Practice, 7,* 207–212.

Merrick, E.N. (1995). Adolescent childbearing as career "choice": Perspective from an ecological context. *Journal of Counseling and Development, 73,* 288–295.

Plaga, S.L., Demarco, K., & Shulman, L.P. (2005). Prenatal diagnostic decision-making in adolescents. *Journal of Pediatric and Adolescent Gynecology, 18,* 97–100.

Sadler, L.S., Swartz, M.K., Ryan-Krause, P., Seitz, V., Meadows-Oliver, M., Grey, M., et al. (2007). Promising outcomes in teen mothers enrolled in a school-based parent support program and child care center. *Journal of School Health, 77*(3), 121–130.

Santelli, J.S., Lindberg, L.D., Finer, L.B., & Singh, S. (2007). Explaining recent declines in adolescent pregnancy in the United States: The contribution of abstinence and improved contraceptive use. *American Journal of Public Health, 97*(1), 150–156.

Sapp, J.C., Hull, S.C., Duffer, S., Zornetzer, S., Sutton, E., Marteau, T.M., et al. (2010). Ambivalence toward undergoing invasive prenatal testing: An exploration of its origins. *Prenatal Diagnosis, 30*(1), 77–82.

Savio Beers, L.A., & Hollo, R.D. (2009). Approaching the adolescent-headed family: A review of teen parenting. *Current Problems in Pediatric Adolescent Health Care, 39,* 216–233.

Suner, J., Nakamura, S., & Caulfield, R. (2003). Kids having kids: Models of intervention. *Early Childhood Education Journal, 31*(1), 71–74.

Watkins, K.J., & Baldo, T.D. (2004). The infertility experience: Biopsychosocial effects and suggestions for counselors. *Journal of Counseling and Development, 82,* 394–402.

Wiik, K.L., Loman, M.M., Van Ryzin, M.J., Armstrong, J.M., Essex, M.J., Pollak, S.D., et al. (2010). Behavioral and emotional symptoms of post-institutionalized children in middle childhood. *Journal of Child Psychology and Psychiatry, 52,* 56–63.

Woods, E.R., Obeidallah-Davis, D., Sherry, M.K., Ettinger, S.L., Simms, E.U., Dixon, R.R., et al. (2003). The parenting project for teen mothers: The impact of a nurturing curriculum on adolescent parenting skills and life hassles. *Ambulatory Pediatrics, 3,* 240–245.

5

Born Too Early

David A. Clark and Gail L. Ensher

CHAPTER HIGHLIGHTS

At the conclusion of this chapter, the reader will

- Understand the perceptions of family members whose newborns are born prematurely

- Understand the challenges families face when newborns are hospitalized for extended periods of time

- Understand families' challenges in learning to care for their newborn in the hospital and at home

- Be familiar with communication strategies that are helpful to families with newborns in the hospital, close to discharge, and post-discharge at home

With about 2 minutes left in the procedure, the anesthe-
siologist kept telling me, "Okay, she's almost born now;
they're getting her; she's almost ready; she's almost out;
she's almost out." That time seemed to take an hour; yet
it was only a matter of minutes before she was born. I
hoped and prayed that she was not dead. As things
turned out, Jennifer was born and she started to cry immediately. She sounded like a battery-operated doll—a little tiny voice.
Then the doctors brought her over to me. I looked and I could not believe
my eyes. There lay this tiny creature with a fur-like covering; all her veins
were showing through her skin. Everything was in the proper place. She had
all her limbs, toes, and fingers. She was so tiny. It was a real shock. In fact, I
was looking at a fetus! (Ensher & Clark, 1986, p. 287)

The rate of premature births in the United States stands at 12.3%, totaling
nearly 500,000 newborns per year (Batshaw, Pellegrino, & Roizen, 2007; Ensher,
Clark, & Songer, 2009). This figure represents a substantial increase from 7.6%
a little over a decade ago, with babies between 23 and 25 weeks' gestation now
surviving as a result of highly sophisticated technologies. With these infants requiring extended hospital stays, an increasing body of research is now focusing
on family-based intervention "to enhance infant–parent relationships" in neonatal intensive care units (NICUs) (Browne & Talmi, 2005, p. 667).

When infants are born early, families face many unexpected challenges:
trauma over unanticipated events, fear of the unknown, juggling of responsibilities at home while visiting the hospital, potentially staggering expenses, difficult-
to-answer questions from other family members and friends, little or no sleep,
worry over feeding and weight gain, and doubts about the infant's health and
development. None of these concerns has an easy answer. For many families
these issues will linger for months, sometimes years, as they observe, seek information, and nurture their infant.

FACING THE EXPECTED AND UNEXPECTED

From the day that I learned I was pregnant, I knew that
there was something wrong with my baby. I told Bill constantly that something was not right and something
should be done. Everyone thought that it was just a feeling and that everything would be fine once I had the
baby. Finally, when I was about 7 months along, I went to
my doctor. He could not find a heartbeat and had not felt
any life. I was hysterical. I told the doctor that he needed to find out if the
baby inside me was dead or alive because I refused to deliver a dead baby.
At that point, he did find the baby's heartbeat, which made me feel a little
better. Yet, I still had a sense that something was not right. I could not get
rid of that worry.

Meanwhile, I started to feel life, very faint flutters and a faint kick now and then. That was all! A week before I delivered the baby, my obstetrician sent me for a second sonogram. The day before I had the baby I went in for the results, and the doctor told me that he was going to put off my delivery for another month. At that point, I knew that he was wrong because I was very sure about when I had gotten pregnant. The doctor did not listen to me. Within 24 hours, I delivered Joey. (Ensher & Clark, 1986, pp. 286–287)

All families are different when expecting a new baby. Some parents, especially mothers, know instinctively that there is something wrong with their pregnancy, even months in advance; for others, the early delivery of their newborn comes as a complete surprise. In either case, physicians, nurses, social workers, family service coordinators, prospective early intervention teachers, and other professionals need to focus on those times during which they can make a positive difference: before birth and during delivery, while the infant is hospitalized, and when the family takes their infant home.

Before Birth and Delivery

 It was ironic that so many people came in to consult with me on breast-feeding, on caring for twins, on my physical care; but no one talked with me about those feelings that were the most painful. I needed someone at that time who had gone through the same kind of situation, who could comfort me and let me know that what I was feeling was not abnormal, that it was okay for me to cry for Anna [who was markedly smaller than her twin sister, Margaret, and who was born with a serious heart defect in need of surgical repair]. (Ensher & Clark, 1986, p. 288)

Many of the difficulties families face arise because of a crisis for which they have had little or no time to prepare. Families often recount horrific stories about circumstances surrounding the deliveries of their preterm infants or newborns with identified impairments, and professionals must look at how these situations might have been dealt with differently. It is imperative to recognize that parents in crisis not infrequently hear selectively and that they interpret and understand information differently. Information should be repeated, rephrased, perhaps written down, and reviewed several times.

When mothers such as Pam (mother of Joey, described previously) recognize symptoms of difficulty in their pregnancy, they should not hesitate to ask for a second opinion or further tests so that their pregnancy can be monitored more closely, especially if they have experienced previous complications or high-risk pregnancies. If it appears that a mother will deliver early, she can now be transported in advance to a center that offers newborn intensive care (if labor is not too far advanced). Such practices have greatly reduced morbidity and mortality rates, and medical staff can provide information that may better prepare families for what to expect with a premature infant. With the arrival of a preterm newborn or an infant with impairments, close collaboration between obstetricians and neonatologists is advantageous for families, who will need time to grieve, ask questions, and learn about these unanticipated events.

Experiences in the Neonatal Intensive Care Unit

The nurse handed us a booklet about the neonatal intensive care unit. Pictures prepared us for what we were soon to see. However, little helped us emotionally to deal with the stress of having our baby in a neonatal ICU. Entering the hospital was like visiting a strange and frightening world.
(Ensher & Clark, 1986, p. 290)

A neonatal intensive care unit is a frightening place to most parents, who often find themselves in a state of emotional shock. Almost without exception, families with newborns in neonatal intensive care nurseries are terrified and find the weeks and months that follow extremely difficult. Also, parents may be torn between attending to children who may be at home and to the hospitalized infants. Although neonatal units now have more family space, privacy remains an issue; there is often little room for siblings (if they are allowed at all), for visiting grandparents, for nursing, or even for talking and grieving. Not infrequently in Level 3 and 4 units (the most technologically advanced to manage and treat the most critically ill infants; the latter are typically designated as regional perinatal centers), families may be miles from home, needing to travel long distances for each visit. This is the backdrop to each new day—the unknown, coupled with often conflicting information about an infant's condition and fear of what the future might bring.

Brian was sedated, given antibiotics to ward off infection, kept in an incubator, and essentially left to heal himself. The nurses were marvelous, loving toward the babies and so patient with us, the families. We kept in touch by phone and were happy, yet apprehensive, when he was moved out of the ICU. We knew Brian was being transferred because he was improving. Yet, until we could visit him in his new surroundings and become accustomed to them, we felt very uneasy. At home, so many miles away from him, we needed the comfort of being able to envision him in his surroundings. The unknown worried us.
(Ensher & Clark, 1986, p. 290)

The time that Rebecca was in the nursery was filled with many fears of her being handicapped. It was all such a delicate balance. She needed to have the right oxygen level; that was being monitored and measured. Too much oxygen could be harmful. She needed to have the right blood sugar level; in the beginning she could not regulate that very well. Again, that condition was being monitored. It was scary, relying on all of these machines. Temperature was another problem. She was kept warm by a heating system, at first in an open crib and later in the Isolette [incubator]. This had to be checked. Exactly 2 weeks after the baby was born, Pat lost his job. I was still on leave of absence from my job. This situation added tremendously to our stress. For those who are familiar with the *Holmes Stress Scale*, we were getting pretty high in our score of traumatic life events (Ensher & Clark, 1986, p. 291)

For those first 28 days, she was cared for totally—fed, changed, dressed, warmed, administered medication—by someone else. I went in to visit her, but she did not seem like my child. (Ensher & Clark, 1986, p. 291)

Such scenarios show that there is much that health care professionals can do for families. Involving parents in the nurturing care of their infant to the extent possible has been strongly encouraged in growing numbers of intensive care nurseries over the past decade (Als et al., 2003; Browne & Talmi, 2005; Goldberg-Hamblin, Singer, Singer, & Denney, 2007; Melnyk, Crean, Feinstein, & Fairbanks, 2008; Melnyk et al., 2006; Teti et al., 2009). While this participation does not resolve all of the concerns families face, it does help facilitate the healing process and enable family members to feel needed. Attachment to a newborn who looks so fragile and so different from typical infants takes time for mothers and fathers, but it is crucial for long-term development. Much research has documented heightened depression, anxiety, and stress among parents, especially mothers, of newborns admitted to neonatal intensive care nurseries (Allen et al., 2004; Shaw et al., 2006; Talmi & Harmon, 2003). Health care professionals increasingly recognize that they can do much to support families in developing these earliest relationships with their newborn—offering guidance as to how to touch their infant, encouraging skin-to-skin contact with kangaroo care (Browne, 2003), and teaching ways to talk to their infant and how to read his or her behavioral cues. NICUs that employ primary nursing care may have an added advantage in facilitating nurturing relationships between newborns and families because they may know more intimately the behavioral responses and unique patterns of infants to whom they have been consistently assigned. More-

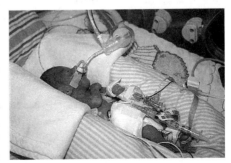

over, the nurses themselves form relationships with parents at a critical time in the newborns' medical care.

When families have newborns in neonatal intensive care nurseries, communication understandably is a continuing concern. Primary care nurses can serve important roles, lending consistency to a seemingly chaotic and changing world of hospital staff. Although attending physicians vary widely in personality and their approach to speaking with families, they and other medical staff must offer information (especially regarding the status of an infant's medical condition) as consistently as possible so parents do not receive conflicting messages. Holding regular nursery team meetings for professionals in primary, decision-making roles can be a useful strategy for achieving more uniform communication across large and often diverse teams of health care professionals associated with intensive care units.

Such teams need to draw upon the expertise and regular feedback of the attending neonatologists, head and primary care nurses, social workers, pediatric physical and/or occupational therapists assigned to the nursery, developmental psychologists assigned to developmental follow-up clinical visits, public health nurses assigned to work with families once infants are discharged, and Early Childhood Direction Centers educators associated with Child Find or facilities that are familiar with early intervention services in the catchment area. Such groups have the capacity for sharing medical and psychosocial information relevant to nursery infants at any given time and for coordinating feedback provided to families.

Physicians, nurses, social workers, and other health care professionals offer important support for families, yet we have known many parents who have suggested that they needed something more. In particular, nursery discussion groups or buddy programs (Preyde & Ardal, 2003), headed by families of infants who have left the hospital as well as those with infants not yet discharged, can provide critical information and an emotional outlet. Although each child follows his or her own medical and developmental trajectory, the experiences of other families who have survived these traumatic events and resumed fulfilling lives can be an enormous strength to those still in the midst of the unknown.

Finally, despite high expectations and the longing to have their infant at home, families repeatedly have commented that the transition from hospital to home is traumatic. There are concerns about bringing home a newborn who often weighs no more than 4 pounds and a few ounces and still requires very special care. Public health nurses assigned to families and infants at the time of discharge can provide an important resource, but their presence in the home is another individual from outside, whose visits may be awkward and are painful reminders of difficult times. Moreover, a severely premature infant's arrival home often resembles a world far from normalcy. There will be frequent visits to the doctor for weight checks and other special needs for an extended period of time. If early intervention services have been planned with the family prior to hospital discharge, the family service coordinator and other professionals such as itinerant teachers and physical, occupational, and speech therapists can help parents and caregivers learn appropriate early learning activities, routines, and interactions with their infant during the first weeks and months at home.

HOME AT LAST!

 After a while, we honestly felt as if we had entered "no man's land." We never got more than 4 hours sleep. I remember getting up one day when Linda had gone to work, starting to get dressed, and putting on my suit to go to work. I had no job and had to take care of the baby, yet almost went out the door. I remember hearing the baby [Rebecca] and saying to myself, "My God, what are you doing?" I was confused, disoriented, did not even know what day it was. (Ensher & Clark, 1986, p. 295)

 Things started to smooth out a bit during the middle months. My anger seemed to diminish, although at times it seemed ever present. I still had concerns about whether we were taking proper care of the baby. I felt as if I did not have enough time to do the reading that I wanted to do, take care of Rebecca, and continue my work. I remember the La Leche counselor saying that it is difficult for people with jobs because they feel that if they are doing their work successfully, they are not giving all they could to their children. If they are doing the most they can with mothering, they feel as if they are cheating their employer. It is difficult to come to a balance, and I was having trouble with that. (Ensher & Clark, 1986, p. 299)

 It should have been a glorious day, the day that Anna came home from the hospital with us, but I had a great deal of apprehension. The doctors had reassured us that she would not lapse into a crisis condition, that if she were to develop a problem with her heart we would have a period of days rather than minutes or hours of warning to get her checked. This was reassuring insofar as her physical condition; however, I soon discovered that the absence of a relationship was a genuine problem for me.

   We could not go anywhere as a family unit without exposing Anna. It was bitterly cold during those days, and I could not take her out unless it was for a doctor's appointment or an urgent situation. After a while, the lengthy feedings caused me great agitation. At times, I simply wanted to say to Anna, "Why can't you just be normal?" (Ensher & Clark, 1986, p. 295)

I could see the frustration setting in with Pam, thinking about bringing Joey home. He was very used to being in the hospital, in his crib, with someone holding him only when he ate. He was not comfortable being rocked. Joey really got to her. I tried to talk with Pam, thinking that we ought to let Joey be by himself.

Then the nightmare came true. They told us that we could bring our son home, as long as he was on oxygen. With all that equipment in the house—the oxygen tent, the heart monitor, the oxygen tanks—I was afraid of the whole set-up. (Ensher & Clark, 1986, p. 296)

Juggling Many Agendas

Although families find themselves beginning to resolve some of the issues that they have lived with during months of hospitalization and after their infant's arrival at home, they continue to juggle work and home matters, perhaps other children, a newborn who may be difficult to care for, and lingering doubts and uncertainties about the infant's health and development. Time is tight, and parents often long for peace of mind, relaxation, and sleep. Because of the risk of infection, families may be homebound for a period, and any subsequent hospitalizations only serve to reinforce concerns about an infant's health. Physicians, public health nurses, early childhood intervention educators, and other professionals can provide information on key issues such as feeding, ways to calm and soothe the infant, and finding qualified respite care workers to offer critical breaks from routines; they can also listen to family questions and worrisome concerns. Although professionals cannot fix the myriad problems facing parents and caregivers, they *can* be important reservoirs for comfort when families are exhausted, feeling guilty, and reaching the end of their reserves.

Doubts and Questions

We still did not know if she was going to have any problems as far as her health or development. It was a wait-and-see time. That was hard and made us very tense. In fact, it was quite a while until we felt confident that she [Jennifer] was going to be fine. We told ourselves and other people that she did not have problems, but inside we had a lot of doubts. (Ensher & Clark, 1986, p. 294)

When Brian was 9 weeks old, both the public health nurse who had been visiting weekly and I noticed how stiff his muscles were becoming and how he was arching his head. Brian's GP suggested that again we see a specialist 120 miles away. He did not warn us that Brian might be hospitalized. Therefore, we were totally unprepared for this event.

Every 3 weeks, we drove the 120 miles to see a specialist and physical therapist. We found dealing with the doctor a very frustrating experience. He was an extremely busy person and always pressed for time.

Once while Brian was in the hospital, we overheard him speaking to students about cerebral palsy in regard to Brian. It was 2 weeks before we could question him about that comment at our regularly scheduled appointment. Naturally, in those weeks we imagined the worst and worried incessantly. The doctor gave us no prognosis for the future. (Ensher & Clark, 1986, p. 294)

 In total, Anna did not look like a baby; she did not act nearly her age in comparison with Margaret. I was not able to nurse her, as I did Margaret and Peter. Finally, it came as a shock to me one day that I could not say to Anna, very naturally 'I love you.' This realization occurred sometime in April [when Anna was 10 months old], when I began to analyze some of my feelings. The recollection that kept coming back to me was an experience that I had as a child—watching a litter of pups, which had been born to our family dog. There appeared to be too many pups for the number of working nipples. I remember finding one little pup tucked under the mother's leg each time the puppies nursed. This puppy was not attached to a nipple, and seemed to grow weaker and weaker.

I recall being angry with the mother dog, questioning why wasn't she watching out for this little one; why wasn't she taking special care since it was so weak? Thinking back to this experience, it suddenly occurred to me that this was how I was feeling about Anna. In a sense, she was my "runt of the litter"! (Ensher & Clark, 1986, p. 299)

It is difficult for parents to think about placing their infant under a year of age in an early intervention program. Relatives, other children, and friends ask questions that are difficult, if not impossible, to answer and are painful to consider: Is the baby going to be normal? When is she going to start to walk? Why does he cry all the time? Why do people come to play with her and not me? Why can't my friends come to visit? Although there are no guarantees, as professionals interact with families and begin to develop relationships, it is important to keep hope and motivation high, focusing on strengths rather than deficits as much as possible.

Home- and school-based early intervention programs can offer families direction in the areas of feeding, handling, and developmental activities, but families often need much more support and periodic breaks from daily caring

for their infant. Most centers are unable to meet the time and care requirements of some children with extraordinary special needs. Appropriate respite arrangements, other than early childhood centers and costly individual medical care facilities, rarely are open to parents with infants who are difficult to care for. Collaboration among professionals from diverse disciplines who can problem-solve on behalf of families may help address unmet needs. Assistance may not alter the ultimate course of events; however, it may help families deal more creatively with their circumstances and enhance their potential as teachers and primary caregivers.

The Other Children

Given legislation and a central focus on interactions and relationships within the context of the *entire family*, researchers and professionals are now recognizing the fact that the birth of a preterm infant affects all members of the family (Kresak, Gallagher, & Rhodes, 2009). With Urie Bronfenbrenner's (1979) concept of "the ecology of human development" in mind and the broad influence that one member of a family has on others, it is easy to understand how the birth of a premature infant (especially one born extremely early) might have a strong impact on siblings. As Munch and Levick wrote,

> The birth of a premature or critically ill newborn creates a crisis for the family, . . . as most of the family's energy is focused on the well-being of the infant. Similarly, the NICU staff engages in the minute-to-minute challenge of life-threatening events faced by the neonate. Thus, both parent and staff efforts are primarily aimed at the NICU baby who needs their attention and care. This is as it should be. There are, however, other members of the family—the siblings—who desperately need attention and care, but who may be overlooked—not intentionally, but because of the very nature of the crisis. In the midst of the chaos, commotion, and disorganization, there is often little time or energy for parents and caregivers to focus on what is happening in the daily lives of siblings (2001, p. 58).

Prior to discharge from the hospital, visiting privileges for siblings of preterm newborns can afford them opportunities to see the new baby, to ask questions, to understand on a simple level why Mom and Dad leave home to visit the hospital, to understand that they have not been abandoned with the arrival of this newest family member, and to be reassured that they too are special despite the disruption in family routines. Similarly, after the newborn's discharge from the hospital, including siblings in caretaking and play activities with early intervention professionals can lessen the feeling that all of the attention is focused on the new baby. In the long term, the well-being of all family members, including siblings, will be determined by the family's cohesion, feelings of competence, and adequate social support in parenting a new baby with special health care needs. In many respects, addressing the needs of siblings of infants born too early parallels the experiences of siblings of children with other chronic illnesses and pediatric medical conditions (Sharpe & Rossiter, 2002).

SETTLING IN AND A FEW FINAL WORDS

End of the First Year

With discharge from the hospital and a few months at home with their newborn, families settle in to routines, become familiar with patterns of their infant's behavior, learn how to manage caring for their infant and other children, learn how to meet any continuing developmental and medical needs, and develop new relationships with professionals as necessary. For some parents, anxieties begin to subside as they note their infant's progress. Other families are not so fortunate. In the following pages, two families speak about their infants' needs, their own perceptions, and their continuing concerns—concerns that needed to be addressed by professionals.

We have been pretty fortunate since we have had a great deal of support from our family and friends when we needed it the most. We also have made some new friends, who helped us to understand and deal with all of Wayne's problems. Without them, it would have been very difficult for us. There have been some disappointments and irritations along the way.

For example, when Wayne started school at an early childhood center, he was evaluated as physically handicapped. That term bothered both Gary and me. Our son was, and still is, slow in some ways. We were told that being labeled physically handicapped did not mean anything. It was just a label. Still to us, it was much more than that. We went along with the decision, only because we wanted him to get the help he needed. (Ensher & Clark, 1986, pp. 298–299)

Regardless of how inevitable it seems, the awareness that a child has an impairment or a disability is *always* painful for parents. In many respects, the labeling of a condition means that parents' greatest fears from their infant's NICU days have been realized. Moreover, families are forced to accept these circumstances in order to obtain the services for their child. Professionals need to be sensitive about parents' emotional response to this and to their feelings of loss. Most children thrive with the benefit of early intervention and appropriate services, and with time the changes witnessed by families help to mitigate the sense of loss of what might have been. For many parents, however, thoughts of what was imagined and hoped for linger and probably resurface with every transition or setback their child experiences.

Although children like Wayne respond well to programs and services, there are families in catastrophic circumstances whose needs will probably never be entirely met by communities and professionals. Such was the case with Joey's family, who struggled through 12 long months following their NICU experience, with repeated hospitalizations and doctor visits, only to lose their son's battle to hypertension and other complex health issues. His mother's words express this sorrow.

By this time, Joey was 9 months old, and things were not getting any easier. We took a trip to Rochester and spent the day with a pediatric pulmonary specialist. He examined Joey and looked at his x-rays. The doctors had not one bit of advice to offer, except to say that if Joey's pulmonary hypertension did not improve very soon, he would not live to see his second birthday. I was glad that they were so blunt. Again, all of the deep feelings that both my husband and I had since the day Joey arrived home came back. We knew deep down inside that somehow our son would never see his second birthday. (Ensher & Clark, 1986, p. 300)

Joey's parents did not face their son's imminent death alone. When he passed away shortly after his first birthday, they had strong family support and hospital staff who listened, helped them grieve their loss, and did not try to minimize their pain by suggesting that they could have other children.

SOME ADVICE FROM FAMILIES

Parents have shared many suggestions with us over the years, and their advice continues to reinforce the need for professionals to maintain open communication with families. This advice may not alter the final course of events for a particular family. Heeding it can do much, however, to change the trajectory of perceptions and relationships, which may enhance families' ability to nurture and parent their children in more creative and insightful ways. Following are the words of some mothers and fathers who have experienced a baby born too early.

I regret that we were not more demanding of Brian's first physician. We knew he was overworked and therefore did not want to bother him. Had we been a bit more firm, asked more questions, and not hesitated to disturb him, we would have been better informed and perhaps saved ourselves a lot of worry.

One thing that has helped me over the past 2 years has been talking about Brian's handicap. Everyone I could corner heard Brian's story from beginning to end. The more I talked about it, the more comfortable I became with the fact that he had a handicap. It is very therapeutic for me to share my fears and concerns, even when they seemed trivial or silly. This was especially true with family and close friends. (Ensher & Clark, 1986, p. 301)

Ask doctors, nurses, and others to suggest groups that you can talk to so that you can see what other people have gone through and know that you are not alone. Other people have had some of the same feelings, same fears, and concerns. Learn about how they have coped with them . . . .go and get all the information and support that you can. Talk with other parents. If you are able to give them suggestions, that may make you feel good too. Find ways to acknowledge and release your anger and disappointment. In addition, try to examine your expectations, realize that even though term births look ideal, they also are not perfect. (Ensher & Clark, 1986, p. 303)

One of my greatest joys was watching what Joey did for other people. He gave so much love to everybody around him. It seemed almost impossible that this tiny baby could bring such happiness to so many people. As an example of that joy, one of the nurses who took care of Joey wrote a poem for his first birthday. It was titled just plain

Joey

Sweet little babe, beautiful boy,
you'll never know the wondrous joy
you've brought our hearts in one small
   year
and all the reasons we hold you dear.

You seem to always understand
just when we need your smile
and when we feel you hold our hands
that makes our lives worthwhile.

Sometimes we feel it isn't fair
that you should suffer so.
But God knows that your way with us
will give us strength to grow.

And so with smiles and happiness
we celebrate today
for the love you give and the love we
   share
will never fade away.

—*C. Lockyer, June 4, 1982 (Ensher &
Clark, 1986, pp. 303–304)*

Clearly, there was much pain in Joey's very short year of life, as with many children with disabilities and health-related problems. On the other hand, as is evident in the poem, Joey brought much joy to those who lived with him, took care of him, and knew and loved him.

BENEFICIAL OUTCOMES

Despite what professionals might think, families do not expect them to have all the answers to their problems. For experts in the health care, clinical, or educational fields, there should be some consolation in that thought. As Murphy wrote so insightfully,

Participating in the lives of special children is frustrating and fascinating. We play many roles in the process, and interwoven are the countless distractions that are part of every life. It is quite a trick to keep from scrambling the roles, to make the quick shift from one to the other—caretaker, teacher, listener, friend. Every individual's situation is unique, and it is a lot of work to keep a healthy balance. Every parent or professional lives, works, and stays vital as long as there is response with spirit and some success to the challenges. If we stop responding we die. We stop responding only if we relinquish the will and the strength to persevere, to make our own decisions, and to abide by our own true conscience. We work with what we have and what we believe. There will be doubt, but doubt will be used as a springboard to more productive reasoning. (1981, p. 195)

In the words of families with whom we have worked and shared the best and most difficult of times, we leave you with the following thoughts:

- Listen to families. They are amazing teachers!
- Encourage families to speak to and support one another. They need each other. Professionals do not have all the answers!
- Focus on the positives and strengths with families—even though they may be difficult to find and often get lost in the chaos of the moment.
- Offer all of the honest information that you have at the moment, but also let families know that there are many unknowns with babies born early. Every day, newborns, with time, are reversing the odds and "best predictions"!
- The ways in which you communicate with families invariably are just as important as what you say.
- Always be open to revisiting information with families. Families may not be able to recall everything said at the moment, and situations do change.

Thinking It Through: Questions for Discussion

1. When families have received conflicting information about their newborn in the NICU, how might other professionals respond to family questions and the key service providers involved to resolve the issue?
2. What strategies might be used to assist families as their infant transitions from hospital to home, especially if the infant has continuing medical and developmental needs?
3. If the medical home model is not yet in place in a family's community, how might professionals help parents coordinate services across diverse agencies and settings?

REFERENCES

Allen, E.C., Manuel, J.C., Legault, C., Naughton, M.J., Pivor, C., & O'Shea, T.M. (2004). Perception of child vulnerability among mothers of former premature infants. *Pediatrics, 113*(2), 267–273.

Als, H., Gilkerson, L., Duffy, F.H., McAnulty, G.B., Buehler, D.M., Vandenberg, K., et al. (2003). Three-center, randomized, controlled trial of individualized developmental care for very low birth weight preterm infants: Medical, neurodevelopmental, parenting, and caregiving effects. *Journal of Developmental and Behavioral Pediatrics, 24*(6), 399–408.

Batshaw, M.L., Pellegrino, L., & Roizen, N.J. (2007). *Children with disabilities* (6th ed.). Baltimore: Paul H. Brookes Publishing Co.

Bronfenbrenner, U. (1979). *The ecology of human development: Experiments by nature and design.* Cambridge, MA: Harvard University Press.

Browne, J.V. (2003, November). New perspectives on premature infants and their parents. *Zero to Three,* 4–12.

Browne, J.V., & Talmi, A. (2005). Family-based intervention to enhance infant-parent relationships in the neonatal intensive care unit. *Journal of Pediatric Psychology, 30*(8), 667–677.

Ensher, G.L., & Clark, D.A. (1986). *Newborns at risk: Medical care and psychoeducational intervention.* Rockville, MD: Aspen.

Ensher, G.L., Clark, D.A., & Songer, N.S. (2009). *Families, infants, and young children at risk: Pathways to best practice.* Baltimore: Paul H. Brookes Publishing Co.

Goldberg-Hamblin, S., Singer, J., Singer, G.H.S., & Denney, M.K. (2007). Early intervention in neonatal nurseries: The promising practice of developmental care. *Infants & Young Children, 20*(2), 163–171.

Kresak, K., Gallagher, P., & Rhodes, C. (2009). Siblings of infants and toddlers with disabilities in early intervention. *Topics in Early Childhood Special Education, 29*(1), 143–154.

Lockyer, C. (1982). *Joey.* Unpublished poem.

Melnyk, B.M., Crean, H.F., Feinstein, N.F., & Fairbanks, E. (2008). Maternal anxiety and depression after a premature infant's discharge from the neonatal intensive care unit: Explanatory effects of the Creating Opportunities for Parent Empowerment Program. *Nursing Research, 57*(6), 383–394.

Melnyk, B.M., Feinstein, N.F., Alpert-Gillis, L., Fairbanks, E., Crean, H.F., Sinkin, R.A., et al. (2006). Reducing premature infants' length of stay and improving parents' mental health outcomes with the Creating Opportunities for Parent Empowerment (COPE) Neonatal Intensive Care Unit Program: A randomized, controlled trial. *Pediatrics, 118,* e1411–e1427.

Munch, S., & Levick, J. (2001, February). "I'm special, too": Promoting sibling adjustment in the neonatal intensive care unit. *Health and Social Work, 26*(1), 58–64.

Murphy, A.T. (1981). *Special children, special parents: Personal issues with handicapped children.* Cambridge, MA: Harvard University Press.

Preyde, M., & Ardal, F. (2003). Effectiveness of a parent "buddy" program for mothers of very preterm infants in a neonatal intensive care unit. *Canadian Medical Association Journal, 168*(8), 969–973.

Sharpe, D., & Rossiter, L. (2002). Siblings of children with a chronic illness: A meta-analysis. *Journal of Pediatric Psychology, 27*(8), 699–710.

Shaw, R.J., DeBlois, T., Ikuta, L., Ginzburg, K., Fleisher, & Koopman, C. (2006). Acute stress disorder among parents of infants in the neonatal intensive care nursery. *Psychosomatics, 47*(3), 206–212.

Talmi, A., & Harmon, R.J. (2003, November). Relationships between preterm infants and their parents: Disruption and development. *Zero to Three,* 13–20.

Teti, D.M., Black, M.M., Viscardi, R., Glass, P., O'Connell, M.A., Baker, L., et al. (2009). Intervention with African American premature infants: Four-month results of an early intervention program. *Journal of Early Intervention, 31*(2), 146–166.

6

Diversity in Context

What Difference Does a Difference Make in a Family?

Gail L. Ensher and David A. Clark

CHAPTER HIGHLIGHTS

At the conclusion of this chapter, the reader will

- Understand the influence of culture and ethnic background on families

- Understand the potential impact of being raised by a single caregiver, same-sex parents, a parent with a disability, or a grandparent

- Understand the potential impact on children of full-time working parents and full-time child care arrangements

- Understand the potential impact on families of living below the poverty line

- Understand the potential impact on infants and young children of being adopted

 Several years ago a 5-year-old returned home, clearly upset by events that had taken place on a brief bus ride to a friend's house following school. The young kindergartener was an adopted child from India, living with her family in a predominantly white suburban community and school district. Two or three third graders who were unknown to the 5-year-old began to make derogatory remarks—referring to her as "black," and devaluing her in ways which she little understood. In response, she tried to explain to the other children that she was "brown" and "Indian." The others refused to listen, continuing to deride her verbally with their remarks. In retelling the story to her mother, she explained: "Mom, I tried to tell them that I was brown, not black, but they did not know what an Indian was!" (Anonymous, 2009)

 As the student teaching supervisor made her way down the hallway of the urban public school, she could hear the all-too-familiar raised voices of the team of kindergarten teachers. Upon her arrival, the supervisor was greeted with a barrage of adult complaints about the behaviors of the "unruly," out-of-control young children. The lead teacher later greeted the supervisor with the revealing exclamation . . . "What else can you expect from street kids!" (Anonymous, 2000)

Farran wrote,

> A pervasive and pernicious environmental state that also is understudied is membership in a minority group (e.g., African Americans) in the United States. Disproportionally more minority families are poorer than majority families, which leads to the assumption that poverty is the primary factor in low birth weights, poor school achievement, and high rates of delinquency for minority children. It is true that African American families are both more likely to be poor for a longer time than Caucasian families (Duncan et al., 1994), but poverty alone is not a sufficient explanation for the effects. (2001, p. 250)

Statistics relating to families in the United States are noteworthy in light of the significant changes that have evolved since the beginning of the 21st century. These statistics have compelling implications for the ways in which infants and young children are raised and educated in this country. For example,

- The official poverty rate in 2008 was 13.2%, up from 12.5% in 2007. This was the first statistically significant annual increase in the poverty rate since 2004, when it increased to 12.7% from 12.5% in 2003 (U.S. Census Bureau, 2010a, p. 13).
- The number of Americans living without health coverage is staggering: 46.3 million people were uninsured in 2008, and communities of color continue

to make up a disproportionate number of the uninsured. In 2008, people of color made up 35% of the U.S. population but 54% of the uninsured. As in previous years, every racial and ethnic group had uninsured rates that were higher than the rate for non-Hispanic white people and higher than the national average (Minority Health Initiatives, 2009, p. 1).

- Although people of color make up 35% of the population, they account for 57% of the 39.8 million people living in poverty (Minority Health Initiatives, 2009, p. 3).

- In the United States, approximately 1.35 million children experience homelessness during a given year. Many of these children—42%—are under the age of 6 (The National Center on Family Homelessness, 2008). Some of them temporarily have a roof over their head but live in a large and impersonal shelter that makes forming routines difficult. Having more than a few simple possessions becomes impossible (Casper & Theilheimer, 2010, p. 41).

- Conservative estimates based on census data suggest there were 293,365 female same-sex households in the United States in 2000 (Simmons & O'Connell, 2003). The Census Bureau and scholars, however, note several challenges in estimating the number of lesbian families. Gates and Ost (2004) suggested that the true count of lesbian families is between 10% (322,701) and 50% (440,047) higher than census figures. Even if statistics on lesbian families with children are partial and inexact, the number of lesbian families is on the rise (Suter, Daas, & Bergen, 2008, pp. 26–27).

- From 1981 to 2001, the total number of cohabiting-couple (or common law) families with children quadrupled, and the total number of single-parent families almost doubled (Liu, Kerr, & Beaujot, 2006). Of children living in single-parent families, about one half entered this situation through divorce or separation, and one third reside in households headed by a never-married single parent. The majority (80%) of single-parent households are headed by women (Wu, Hou, & Schimmele, 2008, pp. 1602–1603).

- The need for cross-cultural understanding also increases with the demographic shifts that occur in the United States. Cohn and Bahrampour (2006) reported,

Nearly half of the children under 5 are racial or ethnic minorities, and the percentage is increasing mainly because the Hispanic population is growing so rapidly, according to a census report released today. . . . They find that one in three Americans is now a member of a minority group and, further, that "immigrant families are becoming more concerned with the quality of their children's early education, aware that it can affect their future academic success." . . . The census report also shows that the number of Hispanic and Asian children younger than 5 years grew by double-digit percentages since 2000, while the number of African American children grew more slowly. . . . Sam Dillon (2007) noted rapid minority growth in schools in the United States. He stated: "The nation's population of minority students has surged to 42% of the public school enrollment, up from 22% three decades ago." (Norton, 2009, p. 1)

Based on these data from multiple sources, it is clear that the makeup of families in the United States is rapidly changing. The first decade of the 21st century has ushered in new definitions of *family;* shifts in families' economic stability, with increasing numbers of working caregivers below the poverty line; new economic, social, and health-related pressures and demands on families; and changing demographics in the United States that require heightened sensitivity to cultural and ethnic populations. This era of change has significant implications for how children are raised and educated, and for how professionals across diverse disciplines work within contemporary circles of community and family.

UNDERSTANDING AND WORKING
WITH FAMILIES FROM DIFFERENT CULTURES

As a teacher, physician, nurse, social worker, clinician, psychologist, or other service provider working with families of infants and young children, what does it mean to be culturally and ethnically sensitive and competent? What are the implications of culture for developing relationships with families? Realistically, one cannot know everything about different ethnic and religious groups. Moreover, it is essential not to stereotype families with regard to patterns of behavior, perceptions, and beliefs. The availability of resources, work and residence location, education, income level, access to health care, extended family members, friends, religious beliefs and individual personalities are among the myriad factors that affect the unique ways in which parents interact with each other, raise their children, and develop relationships with others. Still, having some familiarity with the customs and core beliefs of diverse cultures and ethnic groups and the unique circumstances of particular family constellations (e.g., single-parent families) can help professionals as they enter homes or work with families in schools, hospitals, or other community-based settings. The following information may therefore assist service providers who themselves likely represent diverse backgrounds, training, and belief systems. Professionals need to be sensitive to many elements in the home environment, including

- Language(s) spoken in the home
- Family membership
- Closeness and patterns of interaction among family members
- Caregivers' responsiveness to children's needs
- Patterns of developmentally appropriate stimulation with children

In addition, two constructs are essential to professionals as they work with families. These constructs are not intended to be comprehensive; rather, they are a sampling of contemporary cultural, ethnic, and family diversity that might facilitate the building of relationships between family members and professionals. The first is family themes and traditions; the second, pathways and strategies that are conducive to nurturing relationships.

Family Lenses, Beliefs, and Dominant Traditions

African American Families   It is important to note that in the contemporary United States, African Americans have diverse values, lifestyles, and cultural preferences. The black community is a blending of people from different backgrounds and experiences because it is largely composed of three distinct groups: those born in the United States, those born in the Caribbean, and those born in Africa.

> Most African American families are doing well and thriving, with increasing numbers completing their education, entering the work force, and building strong, adaptive, and regenerative family units. The common bond is family and kinships. . . . Most African Americans are ordinary people who are making it from day to day without fanfare. . . . Despite some gains, however, a disproportionate number of African Americans live in poverty or near poverty. Their circumstances highlight the need for national, state, and local policy changes, which would sustain a quality of life for all. . . . The data also support the need for African Americans to work collectively to implement principles and concepts of enlightened self-development. (Willis, 2004, p. 149)

For decades, African American families have suffered from the negative perceptions of others (Harry, Klingner, & Hart, 2005). In large part, these perceptions are a result of the enormous disadvantages, years of marginalizing, and violence that have plagued the African American community (McNeil, Capage, & Bennett, 2002). For children, assumptions of poor performance, cognitive delays, and behavioral issues may precede their first day in a school setting, and may set in motion a self-fulfilling prophecy of failure (Pianta & Cox, 1999; Pianta & Kraft-Sayre, 2003; Zionts, Zionts, Harrison, & Bellinger, 2003). The patterns of delimiting and discrimination are renewed, generation after generation.

Contemporary studies (Fouts, Roopnarine, & Lamb, 2007; Roopnarine, Fouts, Lamb, & Lewis-Elligan, 2005) of African American families, their social experiences, child–caregiver interactions, and daily routines across different socioeconomic contexts highlight the confounding variables and biases that have pervaded the findings of much research in early childhood to date. In this regard, Fouts and colleagues wrote,

> These results underscore the need to study African American families in a variety of socioeconomic contexts because families in more advantaged circumstances may greatly differ from those who are disadvantaged, especially in terms of reliance on extended kin as caregivers. (2007, p. 655)

Moreover, findings of some contemporary studies run counter to the "widespread stereotypes about poor families," noting these families' sensitivity, warmth, and nurturing relationships in their attempts to parent their infants and young children "responsibly" (Roopnarine et al., 2005, p. 730).

Given the persistent discrimination toward African American families, coupled with the encouraging changes of more recent decades, there is much that professionals need to keep in mind as they work with black families and children. Among them are the following:

- Interventions need to take advantage of the African American heritage of strong family bonds and a commitment to extended family members.

- African American families teach their children self-reliance and socially adept coping skills in order to face hardships and pain that may be encountered (McNeil et al., 2002).

- African American parenting styles may seem more restrictive and authoritarian than those of Caucasian families as a result of the often challenging environments that confront families (McNeil et al., 2002, p. 145).

- Some African American families may distrust professionals and show inconsistent responses to offers for services, due to their own turbulent life experiences.

- The use of health care and medical services may be sporadic among some African American families in light of the widespread incidence of poverty within this ethnic group (especially among the working poor who cannot afford insurance but do not qualify for Medicaid).

- African American families may have a strong network of nonrelative families available within their communities to support both children and parents. This network is especially important to single mothers.

- Given the history of racial discrimination against African Americans, consistency on the part of professionals and valuing family strengths are essential pathways to the development of relationships with African American families across all income and educational levels.

- Due to the strong spiritual beliefs many African American families hold, infants and young children with disabilities or special health care needs often are viewed as blessings—given as gifts from God. For example, speaking about her fragile daughter Melanie, "bird with a broken wing," Beth Harry compassionately wrote,

As I called across the room to Mercedes, the words flowed easily as if they had been forever on the tip of my tongue. I reminded her how much she had loved Melanie and how much that love had been returned. Melanie died in the arms and in the care of someone she loved and trusted. She knew that she was not alone and that

Mercedes was doing everything she could to help her. We had never deserted her. She had known that all her life. We had loved her unreservedly and had shown our love every day of her life. (2010, p. 201)

Hispanic Families According to U.S. Census Bureau figures, the estimated Hispanic population living in the United States as of July 1, 2008, was 46.9 million U.S. citizens, approximately 15% of the nation's total population. There were another 4 million persons living in Puerto Rico (U.S. Census Bureau, 2009). A percentage increase of 3.2% in the Hispanic population between July 1, 2007, and July 1, 2009, made Hispanics the fastest-growing minority group (in part a result of immigration, family size, and frequent adolescent pregnancies). The projected Hispanic population in the United States for July 1, 2050, is estimated to be 132.8 million people (U.S. Census Bureau, 2009).

Commenting about Hispanic parenting practices and cognitive development in young children, De Von Figueroa-Moseley, Ramey, Keltner, and Lanzi (2006) highlighted the diversity within this population, which broadly encompasses Mexican, Puerto Rican, Cuban, Central American, South American, and other Latino national origin subgroups (Chaps & De La Rosa, 2004). De Von Figueroa-Moseley and colleagues noted,

> Much of the existing literature on parenting and child-rearing styles of Latino families has been derived from studies of Mexican American families. Consequently, assumptions concerning normative child-rearing behaviors and practices of Latino families have operated within a Mexican American value system. To achieve a more balanced perspective, the current research is concerned with illuminating the diversity of the members of this community and the effect of this diversity on parental practices and child cognitive developmental outcomes.
>
> Parenting practices or styles, in the universal sense, shape the lives of children. At the minimal level, Latino families do share a common language (Spanish), religion, ideas concerning family, and Latino ancestry that can lead to a common view of Latino families if examined at the surface level. The Latino family in the United States is characterized by enormous diversity. Although it is common to view all Latino families in this country as being similar in values, beliefs, behaviors, resources, and concerns, such sweeping assumptions are seriously erroneous. . . . Far from being homogeneous, the Latino population in the United States represents a heterogeneous group in terms of language, racial composition, socioeconomic status, historical origins, cultural customs and practices, and regions of settlement. (2006, p. 102)

With these cautions in mind, the following might serve as initial guideposts or pathways for establishing relationships with families with Hispanic roots.

- Latino families are committed to the centrality of family and "strong kinship bonds" (De Von Figueroa-Moseley et al., 2006, p. 103).

- Though not shared by all Latino families in most recent decades, there has been a tradition of male role dominance as head of the family, with child-rearing responsibilities largely allocated to mothers or female partners. More recent studies have reported that both African American and Latino fathers are more involved in socializing their young children (Shears, 2007) and protecting and providing for their families (Campos, 2007). Despite the heavy familial orientation, Chaps and De La Rosa (2004) indicated a decrease in marital rates among Hispanic families.

- Similar to African American families, Hispanic families have a strong sense of spirituality and are deeply grounded in church and religious traditions (with the dominant religion in Hispanic families being Catholicism).

- Although there is much variation across population subgroups, Hispanic families are more than twice as likely as non-Hispanic families to live in poverty, and they lag behind non-Hispanic American families in educational attainment (Chaps & De La Rosa, 2004), although there is increasing awareness of the heightened value that Hispanic families place on education (Campos, 2007).

- Overall, Hispanic parents and caregivers have very nurturing relationships with their children (De Von Figureroa-Moseley et al., 2006; Kolobe, 2004; Zuniga, 2004). Parents are sometimes perceived as being indulgent of less mature behaviors in young children.

- Economic and educational levels, specific ethnicity, and life events, as well as length of time living in the United States, may influence family perceptions of disability and the ways in which children learn. Overall, however, many Hispanic families tend to be accepting of the medical and special education services provided—especially those of physicians—although they are not always satisfied with such services as early intervention (Bailey, Hebbeler, Scarborough, Spiker, & Mallik, 2004; Bailey, Skinner, Rodriguez, Gut, & Correa, 1999). Information and decisions may need to be reframed within contexts, but open communication is essential to continued acceptance and use of services (Zuniga, 2004). Religious beliefs may play a central role in some Hispanic families' perceptions of their children with disabilities (Zuniga, 2004). Moreover, there may be variations across different ethnic groups. For example, Reyes-Blanes, Correa, and Bailey pointed out that

> Migration could also alter family demands and the way family members respond to them [family demands] in their new sociocultural environment. . . . These plausible changes could transform the family structure and increase family demands. Early interventionists who understand the impact of these changes can assist the family in redesigning their roles, identifying alternative sources of support, and responding effectively to their demands. (1999, p. 54)

Native American Families   As with Hispanic families, Native American families living in the United States represent much diversity in terms of traditions, languages spoken (including eight different language groupings) (Joe & Malach, 2004), family constellations, and location of residence. According to the U.S. Census Bureau (2010b), as of July 1, 2009, the estimated population of American Indians and Alaska Natives, including those of more than one race, composed 1.6% of the total population, or 5 million individuals.

Some notable features and trends seen within Native American families include the following:

- Similar to African American families, Native American families may be distrustful of outsiders as a result of a history of marginalization (Unger, Soto, & Thomas, 2008) and displacement from their homes.

- Despite advertisements to discourage smoking in the United States, tobacco and other substances such as peyote still play a sacred cultural role among many American Indian tribes (Unger et al., 2008).

- "Custodial grandparenting and kinship care" (Kopera-Frye, 2009, p. 394) are common among families with Native American roots. Moreover, 45% of the children in the custodial care of grandparents are younger than 6 years of age. The number of children in the custodial care of grandparents is due to some extent to "parental substance abuse, divorce, physical and emotional child abuse, teen pregnancies, or abandonment of children by birth parents" (Kopera-Frye, 2009, p. 395). Based on findings from a qualitative study, Kopera-Frye indicated that "grandparents were more likely to seek professional help for their grandchild rather than self, despite experiencing poorer well-being, greater social isolation, and more disrupted relationships with their grandchildren" (p. 396). Kopera-Frye, Wiscott, and Begovic (2003) found that custodial grandparents without legal custody (which poses a problem in securing consent for medical care) worried whether parents would return and were concerned about future caregiving in the face of their own failing health.

- Among 562 federally recognized Native American and Alaskan Native tribes with more than 270 languages (Unger et al., 2008), grandparents are recognized as playing a significant role in the equivalent of 41% of the total U.S. Native American population, accordingly viewed as "key conduits of cultural values and knowledge to their grandchildren" (Kopera-Frye, 2009, p. 399). Pertinent to this point, Kopera-Frye emphasized that

> Understanding the cultural context of caregiving is critical to success in working with ethnically diverse families. Historical and societal interactions have shaped how a family may perceive assistance seeking, trust level of community support, and the professionals working with them, thus affecting the cooperation level in seeking outreach services. (2009, p. 404)

- Health care problems (Berry et al., 2004) and poverty rates (31% of Native American children live below the poverty line, Unger et al., 2008) within Native American populations exceed prevalence rates for Caucasian families in the United States. The Indian Health Service (IHS) is an agency in the U.S. Department of Health and Human Services that provides free services to members of federally recognized tribes (Unger et al., 2008), although there are restrictions for individuals from non–federally recognized tribes.

- Professionals working with Native American families must be aware of the Indian Child Welfare Act (ICWA), mandated by Congress in 1978, which stipulates that should a child be placed for adoption or foster care or parental rights be terminated, "a child should be placed with a member of the child's extended family, other members of the child's tribe, or other Native American families" (Kopera-Frye, 2009, pp. 405–406).

- The belief system of many Native American families of living in harmony with nature and spirituality is very different from the "mainstream U.S. concept and belief in individualism" (Applequist & Bailey, 2000; Pewewardy & Fitzpatrick, 2009, p. 91). Such traditions may place children and parents at odds with the culture of American schools, raising the possibility of philosophical and communication misunderstandings. Moreover, despite the fact that Native American students represent a fairly small segment (1.2%) of students in public schools, they have the "highest rates of disability status" in the United States (Pewewardy & Fitzpatrick, p. 92), and are overrepresented in special education programs, especially in comparison with other ethnic groups (12% and 9%, respectively).

- Many Native American families prefer face-to-face communication rather than email, telephone calls, or letters—an important point for professionals to note. Moreover, nonverbal communication may be considered among Native American people to be just as important as the use of words, and much time is spent listening and observing rather than talking (Unger et al., 2008).

- The concept of *disability*, although well recognized in the Western world, has no parallel in Native American Indian culture (Waldman, Perlman, & Swerdloff, 2004). Native American families tend to view caring for their children with disabilities as a means of continuing their cultural beliefs, and therefore may be reluctant to seek special education services despite their overrepresentation in such programs (Keltner, Crowell, & Taylor, 2005; Pewewardy & Fitzpatrick, 2009). Learning as much as possible about the culture and beliefs of individual families is a critical pathway to nurturing healthy professional partnerships with family members, which may include parents, grandparents, and extended family members. In particular, "communication with American Indian families who have children with disabilities should include respect, reciprocity, inclusivity, thoughtfulness, and planning" (Pewewardy & Fitzpatrick, p. 94), as well as a commitment to spending time on developing relationships with these families.

Middle Eastern Families   Middle Eastern families living in the United States include those with origins in Lebanon, Syria, Israel, Iraq, Palestine, Turkey, Afghanistan, Iran, Egypt, Yemen, Lybia, Tunisia, Jordan, Kuwait, Sudan,

Oman, Qatar, Bahrain, and the United Arab Emirates (Sharifzadeh, 2004). These families represent a growing population in the United States, with approximately 3.5 million Arab Americans living in the country. Understanding some of the heritage of Middle Eastern families living in the United States is especially important in light of the potential for ethnic and cultural discrimination against individuals of Middle Eastern origin.

Concerns about racial discrimination have been especially prominent since the terrorist attacks of September 11, 2001, on the United States and in the face of continuing terrorism threats. Acquiring a genuine understanding of Middle Eastern families, however, is no simple task considering the tremendous diversity of this population throughout the United States in terms of languages, religions and religious sects, family customs, geographic areas of origin, and other culture-specific considerations (Sharifzadeh, 2004).

To build relationships with families of Middle Eastern origin, professionals must understand several core beliefs and customs shared by these diverse cultures. These include the following:

- Religion, both historically and in contemporary times, has been a dominant influence in the lives of many Middle Eastern families (Carteret, 2010). There is close observance of religious holidays.

- Members of Middle Eastern families have a very strong sense of family and kinship with others of Middle Eastern heritage, placing less confidence in those outside their respective ethnic or cultural group (Carteret, 2010).

- Separate roles often are assigned to women and men within Middle Eastern families, with women assuming the primary responsibility for caring for younger children (Sharifzadeh, 2004). Wives may defer to husbands for making health decisions for them and/or their children (Carteret, 2010). Men tend to have the final word in terms of discipline within the home environment.

- Members of Middle Eastern families may be offended by the American tendency to "get things done rather than taking the time to establish a relationship" (Carteret, 2010).

- Middle Eastern families may display a "fatalistic acceptance of disease or death," deferring less to preventive care (Carteret, 2010).

- In contrast to the individualism and independence valued by American parents in raising their children, Middle Eastern families place more emphasis on relationships, interdependence, and time spent with parents.

- The birth of a child with a disability may be accompanied by feelings of "shame and personal defeat" (Sharifzadeh, 2004, p. 404). Families with children with multiple and severe disabilities may tend to isolate themselves from communities. For example, Azar and Badr, in a study of adaptation of mothers of children with intellectual disability in Lebanon, wrote:

> In many Middle Eastern countries, including Lebanon, there is a stigma attached to families who have an intellectually impaired child. These families complain of isolation and lack of community resources that could help them cope with their circumstances to optimize the child's abilities. Health professionals and researchers should be cognizant of factors related to the process of stress adaptation to help families cope with their circumstances. . . . Mothers are the persons most affected by this situation because they are the primary caregivers of the child. (2006, p. 375)

Asian American Families   Like the other ethnic groups considered previously, Asian American families living in the United States represent tremendous diversity. Differences may be reflected in myriad ways, including language, lifestyle and family values, religious beliefs and traditions, emphasis on education, style of interactions and child-rearing practices, perceptions of disability, and use of health care and special education services. Such diversity is not surprising; the Asian American population (Asian American/Pacific Islander) is 10.6 million people, or about 4% of the total U.S. population (Ghosh, 2003). This population comprises several rapidly growing groups (an increase of 110% since 1990): Chinese (24%), Filipino (18%), Asian Indian (16%), Vietnamese (11%), Korean

(10%), Japanese (8%), and other Asian groups (13%) including Burmese, Cambodian, Hmong, Laotian, Thai, and Tongan (Chang, 2009). To cover each of these groups is beyond the scope of this chapter. There are numerous pieces of research and writing on the child-rearing practices and other intervention-related characteristics of Asian American families (Chen & McCollum, 2001; Cho, Singer, & Brenner, 2000; Chow, Jaffee, & Snowden, 2003; Dinh & Nguyen, 2006; Kannan, Carruth, & Skinner, 1999; Lubell, Lofton, & Singer, 2008; Parette, Chuang, & Huer, 2004; Park & Kwon, 2009; Wang, McCart, & Turnbull, 2007).

More broadly, professionals working with Asian American families should be aware of several prominent beliefs and traditions related to child rearing, family structure, and perceptions of disability that might influence the development of relationships with these families.

- Strong kinship ties are valued in Asian American families, 80% of which are headed by married couples. Families are often large, with five or more family members. Chan and Lee (2004) defined marital roles in Asian families as follows:

> Within the immediate family, traditional marital roles have been characterized by the husband serving as the principal provider and family representative in the pub-

lic domain: that is, the father serves as the "secre-
tary of state" or "minister of foreign affairs." . . .
The wife serves as the "minister of the interior"
and is primarily responsible for what happens
inside the house, which includes monitoring
the family's emotional well-being, raising and
educating the children, and taking care of financial matters. (p. 256)

- As children move from infancy into the
  preschool years, greater value is placed on
  meeting higher expectations, conformity,
  discipline, and education (Chan & Lee,
  2004; Park & Kwon, 2009).

- The considerable diversity among families
  with Asian roots is evident in the bimodal economic status of families, i.e.,
  those who are well educated with incomes approaching $50,000 or more and
  those who continue to live below the poverty line and have limited English
  skills.

- Many Asian American families traditionally have been characterized by a tendency to protect their children, restricting interactions with individuals outside of the family structure, although contemporary influences in the United
  States have initiated rapid changes in these tendencies (Chan & Lee, 2004).

- Silence is highly valued among many families of Asian American heritage. Family members may be reluctant to make eye contact with unfamiliar individuals.

- Disability in Asian American families tends to be attributed to one of two
  causes: as punishment for parental sins or mistakes in early parenting, in
  which case there may be feelings of self-blame, guilt, shame, and anger; or as
  a reflection of a divine plan (Cho, Singer, & Brenner, 2000). As a result of
  these beliefs of attribution, prevalent especially among mothers, Asian American families may be reluctant to seek health care or special education services. Moreover, families who place a high value on education may be concerned that a child with a disability will bring shame to the family name.

Chan and Lee (2004) summarized their insightful chapter on Asian American families as follows:

The predominant Asian values pertaining to family, harmony, education, and selected virtues offer fundamental guidelines for living. The family, for example, is
the basic unit of society and the central focus of the individual's life. Harmony is
the keynote of existence. Successful academic achievement is the greatest tribute
one can bestow on one's parents and family. Virtues such as patience, persever-
ance, self-sacrifice, maintenance of inner strength, self-restraint, modesty, and hu-
mility are each considered necessary expressions of dignity that promote group
welfare . . . .[and] have contributed to the profound strength and resiliency
demonstrated by Asian people. (pp. 274–275)

WHO'S LIVING AT HOME?

Culture is one of several dimensions of the ecology of families that strongly affect the development of relationships and that are essential to understanding how family members respond to persons outside their immediate family, how they interpret illness and disabilities, how they access and use professional services and other resources, and how they gain a sense of resilience in their lives. Also integral to the changing landscape of American familes are significant changes in family membership, including greater numbers of families headed by single parents, same-sex couples, and grandparents or other extended family members.

Single Moms/Single Dads

The number of single parents in the United States is on the rise—both single mothers and single fathers (U.S. Census Bureau, 2010a). In 2009 there were 1.7 million father-only family groups with children under 18 years of age, and 9.9 million mother-only groups. Among the father-only groups, 16% were unemployed in March 2009, and 10% of mother-only groups were unemployed. These figures do not include the number of cohabiting, unmarried, adult couples of the opposite sex living with at least one child in the United States (estimated at 2.851 million in 2008) (Wilcox, 2009).

Single parenthood alone does not constitute a negative factor in child outcomes. Many children raised in single-parent families do well in school and become very healthy, well-adjusted adults. On the other hand, the interface of a number of variables that coexist with single parenthood has been well documented in the research for decades (Coles, 2009; Misra, Moller, & Budig, 2007; Sweeney & Bracken, 2000; Thomas-Presswood & Presswood, 2008; Tsushima & Gecas, 2001). The list of associated factors that continue to place mother- and

father-only families at risk is a familiar one, i.e., greater likelihood of living in poverty, substance and child abuse and neglect, stress and depression of caregivers, teen pregnancy, lower academic achievement of children in school, truancy, and health and behavioral issues among children. Moreover, even single-parent families with greater economic and interpersonal resources are affected by the complexities of raising young children in modern society. Time and emotional reserves are not without limits. Children become ill, and employers too often are not understanding about more time off. Quality child care is at a premium in the United States, especially for children with special health care needs and disabilities. Dependent on relatives and friends nearby, who may or may not be willing to offer support, single parents may find themselves in desperate need of a break and some time for themselves. Job security in the 21st century is no certainty. Professionals must consider all of these factors as they develop relationships and work with families.

Two Moms/Two Dads

In the United States, the traditional concept of family—marriage between two individuals of the opposite sex who remain together for a lifetime and raise children—is becoming less and less the dominant model for raising young children. As a result of cohabitation; single-family homes; divorce and separation; and families headed by same-sex couples, the landscape of American families is increasingly characterized by individuals living together for periods of time of unknown duration, i.e., relationships that are not necessarily permanent. Not surprisingly, these family patterns have ushered in a new era of research and practice with families and young children. Regarding families with same-sex parents, Meezan and Rauch (2005) raised the following question:

> Same-sex marriage, barely on the political radar a decade ago, is a reality in America. How will it affect the well-being of children? Some observers worry that legalizing same-sex marriage would send the message that same-sex parenting and opposite-sex parenting are interchangeable, when in fact they may lead to different outcomes for children.
>
> A second important question is how same-sex marriage might affect children who are already being raised by same-sex couples. Meezan and Rauch observed that marriage confers on children three types of benefits that seem likely to carry over to children in same-sex families. First, marriage may increase children's material well-being through such benefits as family leave from work and spousal health insurance eligibility. It may also help ensure financial continuity, should a spouse die or be disabled. Second, same-sex marriage may benefit children by increasing the durability and stability of their parents' relationship. Finally, marriage may bring increased social acceptance of and support for same-sex families, although those benefits might not materialize in communities that meet same-sex marriage with rejection or hostility. (Meezan & Rauch, 2005, p. 97)

Although acquiring accurate data remains an issue, the 2000 Census Bureau estimated 594,000 same-sex households living in the United States, with approximately 27% of such households having children (an estimated 166,000) (Meezan & Rauch, 2005). These figures are undoubtedly conservative at best, and the 2010 census will surely yield greater numbers. By 2008, same-sex marriage

was legal in four states (California, Massachusetts, Iowa, and Connecticut), with a handful of other states recognizing civil union and domestic partnerships (Yen, 2009).

Researchers who have attempted to study same-sex parenting are quick to acknowledge the diversity of couples and that same-sex families represent not just one phenomenon but many phenomena (Meezan & Rauch, 2005). Given these realities, two fundamental questions remain. First, is there evidence that children raised by parents who are gay grow up confused about their gender identity, and/or manifest long-term psychosocial problems? Second, what, if any, are the effects of discrimination against families headed by same-sex couples?

Research has revealed the following, according to Pawelski and colleagues (2006). Addressing the first question, the authors wrote,

> Children born to and raised by lesbian couples seem to develop in ways that are in-distinguishable from children raised by heterosexual parents. Ratings by their mothers and teachers have demonstrated children's competence and the preva-lence of behavioral difficulties to be comparable with population norms. In fact, growing up with parents who are lesbian or gay may confer some advantages to children. They have been described as more tolerant of diversity and more nurtur-ing toward young children than children whose parents are heterosexual. (p. 359)

In conclusion, the authors wrote,

> There is ample evidence to show that children raised by same-gender parents fare as well as those raised by heterosexual parents. More than 25 years of research have documented that there is no relationship between parents' sexual orientation and any measure of a child's emotional, psychosocial, and behavioral adjustment. . . . Conscientious and nurturing adults, whether they are men or women, heterosex-ual or homosexual, can be excellent parents. (p. 361)

Long-term follow-up studies report similar findings in terms of psychosocial out-comes of individuals raised in same-gender families (Golombok & Badger, 2010; Perrin & the AAP Committee on Psychosocial Aspects of Child and Family Health, 2002).

The data on discrimination against families with same-sex couples, how-ever, are less reassuring, and children of these families may meet with bullying and isolation in school. Pawelski and col-leagues pointed out that

> Children whose parents are of the same gender may experience social marginal-ization and become the objects of ridicule and harassment by other children and adults who do not understand or who dis-approve of gay and lesbian parenting. Children experiencing this type of treat-ment may not know how to seek, or where to find, support. Although same-gender

couples are raising children in 96% of the counties in the United States, support services and trusted individuals are not available in all of these areas. (2006, p. 358)

With growing numbers of same-gender parents with children, whether biological or adopted, professionals in school, clinical, and medical settings will need to continue to address the increasingly complex issues of understanding, support, advocacy, and relationship building in order to better serve this new minority of families (Lambert, 2005).

Grandparents as Parents

We noted that having grandparents serve as the primary caregivers for infants and young children is a familiar and accepted practice among several cultural and ethnic groups. Mutchler and Baker (2009) indicated that "estimates suggest that more than 6 million children live with at least one grandparent" (p. 1576). Such co-residence arrangements are especially likely in cases of economic hardship, in mother-only families—which are more vulnerable to the risks of poverty—in families with young children with disabilities and special health care needs, and in families dealing with substance abuse (Fitzgerald, 2001; Fuller-Thomson & Minkler, 2007; Minkler & Fuller-Thomson, 2005; Mutchler & Baker, 2009). Whatever the predisposing factors, "surrogate parenting" by grandparents, with or without parent caregivers living in the home, appears to be a growing trend in the United States (Fitzgerald, 2001, p. 297). As several recent studies and reviews have pointed out, these family arrangements are not without stressors for older grandparents (Hayslip & Kaminski, 2005; Kelch-Oliver, 2008; Leder, Grinstead, & Torres, 2007), and they may constitute an additional phenomenon that needs to be addressed by those in the educational, medical, and clinical fields who are offering services to families.

SPECIAL CONSIDERATIONS

Even in ordinary circumstances, families have always faced challenges in raising their infants and young children, and always will. However, families are facing complex economic and psychosocial circumstances as never before. Among these are dwindling economic resources, with more and more parents out of work and having difficulty supporting their family, chronic illnesses and special health care needs that continue to drain the energy of parents and extended family, inadequate or no health insurance, children with increasingly complex developmental and behavioral problems, more families separating and divorcing under the pressures and demands of daily life, and families torn apart by war or natural disasters.

We would like to touch briefly on several special situations that can dramatically affect the trajectory of families' lives: living below the poverty line, living with two working parents, and living with divorced or separated parents. To be sure, these are not the only important variables affecting families today, and frequently families face a combination of these factors.

Living Below the Poverty Line

We began this chapter with alarming statistics on the growing number of families living below the federal poverty line, as reported by the U.S. Department of Commerce, Economics and Statistics Administration (U.S. Census Bureau, 2009). (As reported in the Federal Register [U.S. Department of Health and Human Services, 2009], official poverty line benchmarks were $18,310 for a family of three; $22,050 for a family of four; $29,530 for a family of six; and $37,010 for a family of eight.) In 2008, the official poverty rate was 13.2%. Single-parent families in particular are affected by poverty, but in reality all families, with and without children, have been affected—even as there are greater numbers of families in which both parents work. We further elaborated on the large numbers of families living without health insurance, a situation that has an indelible, adverse impact on the well-being of infants and young children.

Both Parents Are Working

With greater numbers of families with dual-wage earners who are nevertheless living below the poverty line (in 2008, 5.5%, or 3.3 million), greater numbers of children are receiving care from extended, often older family members, or in home- and center-based child care. The United States has yet to genuinely invest in the lives of its youngest consumers receiving care in centers. Wages for child care workers remain extremely low ($8–$10 per hour), and there is little professional training or staff consistency. Such situations continue to compromise the well-being of infants and preschoolers, both developmentally and psychosocially; at the same time, families are often stretched to the maximum with child care costs that can exceed monthly mortgage payments. Finding appropriate care for children with disabilities or special health care needs is even more difficult, particularly because of the lack of trained caregivers. To date, the United States has no national policy on extended leaves of absence from employment for parents without the risk of dismissal or loss of job beyond allowed leaves of absence.

Divorce and Separation

In *Recent Changes in Family Structure: Implications for Children, Adults, and Society,* Amato wrote,

> Nearly one million children experience divorce every year, and about 40% of all children with married parents will experience divorce before reaching adulthood. The high rate of marital disruption, combined with the increase in nonmarital births, means that about half of all children will reside at least temporarily in single-parent households, usually with their mothers (Amato, 2005).
>
> The research literature is consistent in showing that children who experience divorce, compared with children who grow up with two continuously married parents, have an elevated risk of conduct disorders, psychological problems, low self-esteem, difficulties forming friendships, academic failure, and weak emotional ties to parents, especially fathers (Amato & Keithe, 1991; Amato, 2001). As adults, these children experience more symptoms of psychological distress, have more

troubled marriages, are more likely to see their own marriages end in disruption, and have poorer physical health (Amato & Booth, 1997). (2008, pp. 4–5)

Also addressing the dramatic changes in family patterns, Smock and Manning wrote

> The last few decades have ushered in significant changes in family patterns—in union formation, union dissolution, childbearing, and attitudes about a range of family issues. . . . After a brief period characterized by early marriage and low levels of divorce after World War II (i.e., the Baby Boom), recent decades have been marked by lower levels of childbearing, . . . and cohabitation.
> Although most Americans still marry at some point and the vast majority express strong desires to marry, unmarried cohabitation has dramatically transformed the marriage process. Today, the majority of marriages and remarriages begin as cohabiting relationships. . . . Clearly, cohabitation has become a widely-experienced, even normative, phenomenon in recent decades. (2004, p. 2)

Most studies estimate that marital instability stands at approximately 50%. Such circumstances inevitably have major implications for the children in these families, whenever separation occurs (Kelly, 2003). Moreover, from the considerable mass of research on single-parent families, it is clear that the outcomes for children from fragile families may not be as positive as those from more secure home environments, at least in the short term. With the likelihood that cohabitation will continue to increase, scholars who are studying this trend and professionals who are offering services to families must be aware of the needs and challenges posed by the changing face of American families. In two articles published by the Academy of Pediatrics (Cohen & the AAP Committee on Psychosocial Aspects of Child and Family Health, 2002; Tanner, 2002), Tanner stated that "parental separation and divorce stands as one of the most common and significant risks to the healthy development of children today" (2002, p. 1007).

Ultimately, how children respond in the midst of crises will depend on a number of factors, including the extent of conflict in the family prior to and concurrent with the separation, children's ages, the degree of support from extended family and friends, psychosocial difficulties of either or both parents, living arrangements following the separation, opportunities to visit with one or both parents, changes in educational programs, and changes in lifestyle as a result of economic circumstances. As noted previously, changes in child behavior and school performance are common, and professionals may serve as a critical source of support to either or both parents and to children. The safety of the children is paramount, and "psychologically competent parenting" (Kelly, 2003, p. 247) will be a critical factor in children's well-being (short term and long term) (Lamb, Sternberg, & Thompson, 1997).

Parents with Disabilities

There are extraordinarily capable individuals who themselves have a range of disabilities, who have children by natural birth or adoption, and who raise them very successfully to become healthy, well-adjusted, bright adults. In other situations, limitations experienced by parents with disabilities require significant support from family members and perhaps professionals from the medical, clinical, educational, and legal fields. The problems are complex, as described by Kleinmann and Songer (2009), and frequently require intense, sustained support, depending on the nature of the parent's disability. A writing by Deborah Kent (1999), a parent with a visual impairment, is instructive in this regard in terms of her own perceptions of her blindness versus those of her parents when she gave birth to a seeing daughter. In the concluding paragraph to her chapter entitled *Somewhere a Mockingbird*, she says,

> In recent years a new insight has gradually come to me. Yes, my own loved ones hold the unshakeable belief that blindness is and always will be a problem. Nevertheless these same people have made me welcome. Though they dread blindness as a fate to be avoided at almost any cost, they give me their trust and respect. I don't understand how they live without discomfort amid such contradictions. But I recognize that people can and do reach out, past centuries of prejudice and fear, to forge bonds of love. It is a truth to marvel at, a cause for hope and perhaps some small rejoicing. And somehow it reminds me of the mockingbird that sang so boldly in a place where no one thought it belonged, making a crowd of busy people stand still to listen. (p. 51)

Serving families in which a parent has a disability requires professionals' full vigilance in order to make accurate assessments—taking care not to over- or underestimate areas of need. At a minimum, professionals must make certain that

- The children are safe and are not in harm's way as a result of neglect and/or abuse.
- The children's and parents' basic health care and daily living needs are being met.
- The children are being stimulated and provided with age-appropriate development and learning opportunities.
- Legal issues are addressed by appropriate personnel.
- Services on behalf of the entire family are coordinated.

Kleinmann and Songer wrote,

> Parents with developmental disabilities and their children face a number of challenges that exceed the typical difficulties that any parent might encounter. Fortunately, the prognosis for families with parents with developmental disabilities has improved in recent decades with the advancement of legislation to protect their rights, development of research and training programs, and increased valuing and appreciation of people with special needs. (2009, p. 295)

Through the Looking Glass, the new National Center for Parents with Disabilities and Their Families, was formed to realize these goals on behalf of parents with disabilities (National Institute on Disability and Rehabilitation Research [NIDRR], 2009). Center activities focus on "priority issues facing parents with disabilities and their families; custody and parental evaluations; family roles and personal assistance; para-transit; and intervention with parents with cognitive and intellectual disabilities and their children" (NIDRR, p. 1).

Born Outside the Family: Adopted Children

There are many reasons to believe that infants and young children who are adopted by a family should fare very well, both developmentally and psychosocially. Families adopting children, domestically or internationally, typically have the financial means and resources to do so. Children are very much wanted, and often parents have waited for months or years until the time of arrival and finalization. Once a child has arrived, families usually are well educated about community resources.

Still, there may be unknowns that will challenge families as their children develop. From among the approximately 40,000 internationally adopted children from more than 100 countries (Juffer & van IJzendoorn, 2005), there are multiple cases of "insufficient medical care, malnutrition, maternal separation, and neglect and abuse in orphanages" (p. 1), as well as little to no prenatal care, unknown medical and social histories and genetic backgrounds, and exposure to infection and numerous other environmental hazards. Families adopting domestically may face similar issues, although they may have more knowledge of birth parents' pregnancies, backgrounds, and medical histories. Most interesting are the concluding remarks of Juffer and van IJzendoorn, based on their meta-analyses of children adopted internationally versus those born and adopted in the United States. They wrote,

> In sum, our series of meta-analyses showed that the majority of international adoptees are well-adjusted, although more adoptees are referred to mental health services compared with nonadopted controls. Contrary to common opinion, international adoptees present fewer behavior problems than domestic adoptees, and they have lower rates of mental health referral. Unexpectedly, age at adoption does not appear to be important for the development of behavioral problems. International adoptees with backgrounds of extreme adversity are at risk for more behavior problems, in particular externalizing problems, compared with international adoptees without preadoption adversity. Clinicians should be aware of higher risks for problem behaviors in domestic adoptees and in international adoptees who experienced neglect or maltreatment in the preadoptive period. (p. 10)

Overall, reports indicate that children adopted, both domestically and internationally, have similar and greater risks for disability (12.2% versus 12.7%) than do children within an age range of 5–15 years (5.8%), who are not adopted (Kreider & Cohen, 2009). These rates of disability understandably vary with the countries of origin—likely depending on mothers' accessibility to adequate nutrition prenatally and well-baby medical care following delivery. Moreover, as adopted children grow older and become aware of circumstances surrounding their adoptions (both domestically and internationally), issues of abandonment and questions about biological parents and siblings, the structure of their families (e.g., living in single-parent families), their likeness to adoptive parents, and genetic factors can become significant contributors to the life trajectories of adolescents and adults. Kreider and Cohen pointed out that "health, education, and social service professionals, as well as adoptive and prospective adoptive parents, should be aware of the risk for disabilities among internationally adopted children to devote the resources necessary to addressing them" (p. 1311).

VALUING WHAT DIFFERENCE BRINGS: IMPORTANT PATHWAYS FOR PROFESSIONALS

We began this chapter on differences across and within families with an observation that, based on our experiences and research, the landscape of families in the 21st century has changed dramatically. Moreover, valuing differences in families is essential as professionals offer services to families and nurture relationships with them. To be successful, professionals of all disciplines will need to know when and how to

- Offer suggestions and information
- Expand their knowledge base
- Set aside their lenses to understand others' perspectives
- Take a firm stand on issues and advocate for families, even in the face of differences with colleagues
- Look at the larger context of extended family, community, and other resources
- Listen
- Honor and respect the diversity among families
- Realize that having similar ethnic or cultural roots does not mean that all families will think alike
- Remember that most of the time they are merely a professional touchpoint in families' lives, striving to make a difference that will enable families to realize their potential

Thinking It Through: Questions for Discussion

1. A same-gender family for whom you provide pre-K services is experiencing discrimination by families of other children in the class. How would you resolve these issues?

2. A grandmother is the primary caregiver for a 2-year-old toddler with disabilities. When visiting the home, the early intervention team finds

conditions that are not conducive to the child's development and psychosocial well-being. How should the team raise this issue with the child's mother, who is single and depends on the grandmother for child care?

3. Based on their cultural beliefs, a family has decided not to have a child with suspected disabilities immunized or evaluated. To receive services and attend an inclusive preschool, the child must be both immunized and evaluated. How should the pediatrician and preschool team coordinate their efforts on behalf of the child?

REFERENCES

Amato, P.R. (2008). *Recent changes in family structure: Implications for children, adults, and society.* Fairfax, VA: National Healthy Marriage Resource Center.

Applequist, K.L., & Bailey, D.B., Jr. (2000). Navajo caregivers' perceptions of early intervention services. *Journal of Early Intervention, 23*(1), 47–61.

Azar, M., & Badr, L.K. (2006). The adaptation of mothers of children with intellectual disability in Lebanon. *Journal of Transcultural Nursing, 17*(4), 375–380.

Bailey, D.B., Jr., Hebbeler, K., Scarborough, A., Spiker, D., & Mallik, S. (2004). First experiences with early intervention: A national perspective. *Pediatrics, 113*(4), 887–896.

Bailey, D.B., Jr., Skinner, D., Rodriguez, P., Gut, D., & Correa, V. (1999). Awareness, use, and satisfaction with services for Latino parents of young children with disabilities. *Exceptional Children, 65*(3), 367–381.

Berry, M.F., Reynoso, C., Braceras, J.C., Edley, C., Jr., Kirsanow, P.N., Meeks, E.M., et al. (2004). *Broken promises: Evaluating the Native American health care system.* Washington, DC: U.S. Commission on Civil Rights.

Campos, R. (2007). Considerations for studying father involvement in early childhood among Latino families. *Hispanic Journal of Behavioral Sciences, 30*(2), 133–160.

Carteret, M. (2010). *Cross-cultural communications for healthcare professionals: Healthcare for Middle Eastern patients & families/Dimensions of culture.* Retrieved January 11, 2010, from http://www.dimensionsofculture.com/2010/10/health-care-for-middle-eastern-patients-families/

Casper, V., & Theilheimer, R. (2010). *Early childhood education: Learning together.* New York: McGraw-Hill.

Chan, S., & Lee, E. (2004). Families with Asian roots. In E.W. Lynch & M.J. Hanson (Eds.), *Developing cross-cultural competence: A guide for working with children and their families* (3rd ed.) (pp. 219–298). Baltimore: Paul H. Brookes Publishing Co.

Chang, S.S. (2009, February). *Improving services for Chinese American children—Challenges, resources, and recommendations.* Presentation given at the 2009 convention of the Illinois Speech-Language-Hearing Association.

Chaps, J., & De La Rosa, B. (2004). Latino population growth, socioeconomic and demographic characteristics, and implications for educational attainment. *Education and Urban Society, 36*(2), 130–149.

Chen, Y.J., & McCollum, J.A. (2001). Taiwanese mothers' perceptions of parent-infant interaction with children with Down syndrome. *Journal of Early Intervention, 24*(4), 252–265.

Cho, S.J., Singer, G.H., & Brenner, M. (2000). Adaptation and accommodation to young children with disabilities: A comparison of Korean and Korean American parents. *Topics in Early Childhood Special Education, 20*(4), 236–249.

Chow, J.C.C., Jaffee, K., & Snowden, L. (2003). Racial/ethnic disparities in the use of mental health services in poverty areas. *American Journal of Public Health, 93*(5), 792–797.

Cohen, G.J., & the AAP Committee on Psychosocial Aspects of Child and Family Health. (2002). Helping children and families deal with divorce and separation. *Pediatrics, 110,* 1019–1023.

Coles, R.L. (2009). Just doing what they gotta do: Single Black custodial fathers coping with the stresses and reaping the rewards of parenting. *Journal of Family Issues, 30*(10), 1311–1338.

De Von Figueroa-Moseley, C., Ramey, C.T., Keltner, B., & Lanzi, R.G. (2006). Variations in Latino parenting practices and their effects on child cognitive developmental outcomes. *Hispanic Journal of Behavioral Sciences, 28*(1), 102–114.

Dinh, K.T., & Nguyen, H.H. (2006). The effects of acculturative variables on Asian American parent–child relationships. *Journal of Social and Personal Relationships, 23*(3), 407–426.

Farran, D.C. (2001). Critical periods and early intervention. In D.B. Bailey, Jr., J.T. Bruer, F.J. Symons, & J.W. Lichtman (Eds.), *Critical thinking about critical periods* (pp. 233–266). Baltimore: Paul H. Brookes Publishing Co.

Fitzgerald, M.L. (2001). Grandparent parents: Intergenerational surrogate parenting. *Journal of Holistic Nursing, 19*(3), 297–307.

Fouts, M.N., Roopnarine, J.L., & Lamb, M.E. (2007). Social experiences and daily routines of African American infants in different socioeconomic contexts. *Journal of Family Psychology, 21*(4), 655–664.

Fuller-Thomson, E., & Minkler, M. (2007). Central American grandparents raising grandchildren. *Hispanic Journal of Behavioral Sciences, 29*(1), 5–18.

Ghosh, C. (2003). *Healthy People 2010* and Asian American/Pacific Islanders: Defining a baseline of information. *American Journal of Public Health, 93*(12), 2093–2098.

Golombok, S., & Badger, S. (2010). Children raised in mother-headed families from infancy: A follow-up of children of lesbian and single heterosexual mothers at early adulthood. *Human Reproduction, 25*(1), 150–157.

Harry, B. (2010). *Melanie, bird with a broken wing: A mother's story.* Baltimore: Paul H. Brookes Publishing Co.

Harry, B., Klingner, J.K., & Hart, J. (2005). African American families under fire. *Remedial and Special Education, 26*(2), 101–112.

Hayslip, B., Jr., & Kaminski, P.L. (2005). Grandparents raising their grandchildren: A review of the literature and suggestions for practice. *The Gerontologist, 45*(2), 262–269.

Joe, J.R., & Malach, R.S. (2004). Families with American Indian roots. In E.W. Lynch & M.J. Hanson (Eds.), *Developing cross-cultural competence: A guide for working with children and their families* (3rd ed.) (pp. 109–139). Baltimore: Paul H. Brookes Publishing Co.

Juffer, F., & van IJzendoorn, M.H. (2005). Behavior problems and mental health referrals of international adoptees. *Journal of the American Medical Association, 293*(20). Retrieved January 28, 2010, from http://jama.ama-assn.org/cgi/content/full/293/20/2501

Kannan, S., Carruth, B.R., & Skinner, J. (1999). Infant feeding practices of Anglo American and Asian Indian American mothers. *Journal of the American College of Nutrition, 18*(3), 279–286.

Kelch-Oliver, K. (2008). African American grandparent caregivers: Stresses and implication for counselors. *The Family Journal: Counseling and Therapy for Couples and Families, 16*(1), 43–50.

Kelly, J.B. (2003). Perspectives on children's adjustment following divorce: A view from the United States. *Childhood, 10*(2), 237–254.

Keltner, B.R., Crowell, N.A., & Taylor, W. (2005). Attitudes about disabilities in a Southeastern American Indian tribe. *American Indian Culture and Research Journal, 29*(2), 57–74.

Kent, D. (1999). Somewhere a mockingbird. In M. Waters & R. Jade (Eds.), *Bigger than the sky* (pp. 45–51). London: The Women's Press Ltd.

Kleinmann, A.E., & Songer, N.S. (2009). Parents with developmental disabilities caring for infants and young children. In G.L. Ensher, D.A. Clark, & N.S. Songer (Eds.), *Families, infants, and young children at risk: Pathways to best practice* (pp. 287–296). Baltimore: Paul H. Brookes Publishing Co.

Kolobe, T. (2004). Childrearing practices and developmental expectations for Mexican-American mothers and the developmental status of their infants. *Physical Therapy, 84*(5), 439–453.

Kopera-Frye, K. (2009). Needs and issues of Latino and Native American nonparental relative caregivers: Strengths and challenges within a cultural context. *Family and Consumer Sciences Research Journal, 37*(3), 394–410.

Kopera-Frye, K., Wiscott, R.C., & Begovic, A. (2003). Lessons learned from custodial grandparents involved in a community support group. In B. Hayslip, Jr., & J.H. Patrick (Eds.), *Working with custodial grandparents* (pp. 243–256). New York: Springer.

Kreider, R.M., & Cohen, P.N. (2009). Disability among internationally adopted children in the United States. *Pediatrics, 124*(5), 1311–1318.

Lamb, M.E., Sternberg, K.J., & Thompson, R.A. (1997). The effects of divorce and custody arrangements on children's behavior, development, and adjustment. *Family and Conciliation Courts Review, 35*(4), 394–404.

Lambert, S. (2005). Gay and lesbian families: What we know and where to go from here. *The Family Journal, 13*(1), 43–51.

Leder, S., Grinstead, L.N., & Torres, E. (2007). Grandparents raising grandchildren: Stressors, social support, and health outcomes. *Journal of Family Nursing, 13*(3), 333–352.

Lubell, K.M., Lofton, T., & Singer, H.H. (2008). *Promoting healthy parenting practices across cultural groups: A CDC research brief.* Atlanta, GA: Centers for Disease Control and Prevention, National Center for Injury Prevention and Control.

McNeil, C.B., Capage, L.C., & Bennett, G.M. (2002). Cultural issues in the treatment of young African American children diagnosed with disruptive behavior disorders. *Journal of Pediatric Psychology, 27*(4), 339–350.

Meezan, W., & Rauch, J. (2005). Gay marriage, same-sex parenting, and America's children. *The Future of Children, 15*(2), 97–115.

Minkler, M., & Fuller-Thomson, E. (2005). African American grandparents raising grandchildren: A national study using the Census 2000 American community survey. *The Journal of Gerontology Series B: Psychological Sciences and Social Sciences, 60,* S82–S92.

Minority Health Initiatives (September, 2009). *Health coverage in communities of color: Talking about the new census numbers* (pp. 1–4). Retrieved October 29, 2009, from www.familiesusa .org/assets/pdfs/minority-health-census-sept-2009.pdf

Misra, J., Moller, S., & Budig, M.J. (2007). Work family policies and poverty for partnered and single women in Europe and North America. *Gender & Society, 21*(6), 804–827.

Mutchler, J.E., & Baker, L.A. (2009). The implications of grandparent co-residence for economic hardship among children in mother-only families. *Journal of Family Issues, 30*(11), 1576–1597.

The National Center on Family Homelessness. (2008). *The characteristics and needs of families experiencing homelessness.* Retrieved February 10, 2011, from http://www.familyhomelessness .org/media/147.pdf

National Institute on Disability and Rehabilitation Research (NIDRR) (2009). *The new national center for parents with disabilities and their families.* Retrieved January 27, 2010, from http://www.lookingglass.org/ncpd/index.php

Norton, D.E. (2009). *Multicultural children's literature: Through the eyes of many children* (3rd ed.). Boston: Pearson.

Parette, P., Chuang, S.J.L., & Huer, M.B. (2004). First-generation Chinese American families' attitudes regarding disabilities and educational interventions. *Focus on Autism and Other Developmental Disabilities, 19*(2), 114–123.

Park, J.H., & Kwon, Y.I. (2009). Parental goals and parenting practices of upper-middle class Korean mothers. *Journal of Early Childhood Research, 7*(1), 58–75.

Pawelski, J.G., Perrin, E.C., Foy, J.M., Allen, C.E., Crawford, J.E., Del Monte, M., et al. (2006). The effects of marriage, civil union, and domestic partnership laws on the health and well-being of children. *Pediatrics, 118,* 349–364.

Perrin, E.C., & AAP Committee on Psychosocial Aspects of Child and Family Health. (2002). Technical report: Co-parent or second-parent adoption by same-sex parents. *Pediatrics, 109,* 341–344.

Pewewardy, C., & Fitzpatrick, M. (2009). Working with American Indian students and families: Disabilities, issues, and interventions. *Intervention in School and Clinic, 45*(2), 91–98.

Pianta, R.C., & Cox, M.J. (1999). *The transition to kindergarten.* Baltimore: Paul H. Brookes Publishing Co.

Pianta, R.C., & Kraft-Sayre, M. (2003). *Successful kindergarten transition: Your guide to connecting children, families, and schools.* Baltimore: Paul H. Brookes Publishing Co.

Reyes-Blanes, M.E., Correa, V.I., & Bailey, D.B., Jr. (1999). Perceived needs of and support for Puerto Rican mothers of young children with disabilities. *Topics in Early Childhood Special Education, 19*(1), 54–63.

Roopnarine, J.L., Fouts, H.N., Lamb, M.E., & Lewis-Elligan, T.Y. (2005). Mothers' and fathers' behaviors toward their 3- to 4-month-old infants in lower, middle, and upper socioeconomic African American families. *Developmental Psychology, 41*(5), 723–732.

Sharifzadeh, V.S. (2004). Families with Middle Eastern roots. In E.W. Lynch & M.J. Hanson (Eds.), *Developing cross-cultural competence: A guide for working with children and their families* (3rd ed.) (pp. 373–414). Baltimore: Paul H. Brookes Publishing Co.

Shears, J.K. (2007). Understanding differences in fathering activities across race and ethnicity. *Journal of Early Childhood Research, 5*(3), 245–261.

Smock, P.J., & Manning, W.D. (2004, March). *Living together unmarried in the United States: Demographic perspectives and implications for family policy.* PSC Research Report, #04-555. Ann Arbor: University of Michigan, Institute for Social Research, PSC Population Studies Center.

Suter, E.A., Daas, K.L., & Bergen, K.M. (2008). Negotiating lesbian family identity via symbols and rituals. *Journal of Family Issues, 29*(1), 26–47.

Sweeney, R.B., & Bracken, B.A. (2000). Influence of family structure on children's self-concept development. *Canadian Journal of School Psychology, 16*(1), 39–52.

Tanner, J.L. (2002). Parental separation and divorce: Can we provide an ounce of prevention? *Pediatrics, 110,* 1007–1009.

Thomas-Presswood, T.N., & Presswood, D. (2008). *Meeting the needs of students and families from poverty: A handbook for school and mental health professionals.* Baltimore: Paul H. Brookes Publishing Co.

Tsushima, T., & Gecas, V. (2001). Role taking and socialization in single-parent families. *Journal of Family Issues, 22*(3), 267–288.

Unger, J.B., Soto, C., & Thomas, N. (2008). Translation of health programs for American Indians in the United States. *Evaluation and the Health Professions, 31*(2), 124–144.

U.S. Census Bureau. (2010a, January). Census Bureau reports families with children increasingly face unemployment. *U.S. Census Bureau News.* Retrieved March 20, 2010, from http://www.census.gov/newsroom/releases/archives/families_households/cb10-08.html

U.S. Census Bureau. (2010b). *Facts for features American Indian and Alaska Native heritage month: November 2010.* Retrieved February 10, 2011, from http://www.prnewswire.com/news-releases/census-bureau-news—facts-for-features-american-indian-and-alaska-native-heritage-month-november-2010-106514248.html

U.S. Census Bureau. (2009). *Hispanic fact sheet: Hispanic heritage month 2009.* Retrieved December 29, 2009, from http://www.census.gov/newsroom/releases/pdf/cb09-ff17.pdf

U.S. Department of Commerce, Economics and Statistics Administration, U.S. Census Bureau (2009, September). *Income, poverty, and health insurance coverage in the United States: 2008—Current population reports* (p. 13). Retrieved October 9, 2009, from http://www.census.gov/prod/2009pubs/p60-236.pdf

U.S. Department of Health and Human Services. (2009). Poverty guidelines for Even Start family literacy programs: 2009–2010 income eligibility guidelines. *Federal Register, 74*(14).

Waldman, H.B., Perlman, S.P., & Swerdloff, M. (2004, July). Native American children with disabilities. *Exceptional Parent.* Retrieved January 6, 2010, from http://findarticles.com/p/articles/mi_go2827/is_7_38/ai_n29451267/

Wang, M., McCart, A., & Turnbull, A.P. (2007). Implementing positive behavior support with Chinese American families: Enhancing cultural competence. *Journal of Positive Behavior Interventions, 9*(1), 38–51.

Wilcox, W.B. (2009). *Social indicators of marital health & wellbeing: The state of our unions 2009.* Retrieved January 15, 2010, from http://www.stateofourunions.org/2009/si-fragile_families.php

Willis, W.O. (2004). Families with African American roots. In E.W. Lynch & M.J. Hanson (Eds.), *Developing cross-cultural competence: A guide for working with children and their families* (3rd ed., pp. 141–178). Baltimore: Paul H. Brookes Publishing Co.

Wu, Z., Hou, F., & Schimmele, C.M. (2008). Family structure and children's psychosocial outcomes. *Journal of Family Issues, 29*(12), 1600–1624.

Yen, H. (2009). *Census: 150,000 gay marriages reported.* Retrieved January 19, 2010, from http://www.huffingtonpost.com/2009/09/22/census-gay-marriages-numb_n_294322.html

Zionts, L.T., Zionts, P., Harrison, S., & Bellinger, O. (2003). Urban African American families' perceptions of cultural sensitivity within the special education system. *Focus on Autism and Other Developmental Disabilities, 18*(1), 41–50.

Zuniga, M.E. (2004). Families with Latino roots. In E.W. Lynch & M.J. Hanson (Eds.), *Developing cross-cultural competence: A guide for working with children and their families* (3rd ed., pp. 179–218). Baltimore: Paul H. Brookes Publishing Co.

III

Peaks and Valleys Along the Way

7

Diversity in Context

What Difference Does
a Difference Make for a Child?

Gail L. Ensher and David A. Clark

CHAPTER HIGHLIGHTS

At the conclusion of this chapter, the reader will

- Understand that not all disabilities are equal

- Understand that families perceive and interpret disabilities differently, and that these perceptions may require different responses from professionals

- Understand the implications of severity of disability for families and professionals

- Understand the implications of children's chronic illnesses for families and professionals

My name is William David Pardo, but you can call me WD.

I was born in Metarie, Louisiana, just outside of New Orleans.

I'm a special child, as all children should be.

In fact, I'm extra special because my parents, Jenny and Bill, love me,

even though I was not born perfect; they call me God's gift.

I just happen to be missing a small piece of a chromosome that

must be important, because there are so many things that I have a hard time doing.

I had extra fluid in my brain and had to have a shunt to drain it.

But I can smile.

I could never suck and swallow good enough and had surgery

for a permanent feeding tube into my stomach.

But I can smile.

Despite surgery on my hip, I never did develop enough strength to walk.

But I can smile.

I've had the chance to meet many people who have helped me,

nurses and doctors in intensive care nurseries, teachers, physical therapists, speech therapists, and many others.

I smiled at all of them (when I didn't hurt), and they smiled back at me.

Maybe that's how I got one of my nicknames, Sweet William.

I had to leave sooner than I expected, but I know I was loved

and will be remembered by many, especially Mama and Dada.

Thank you.

This book my Grandpa helped write is dedicated to the thousands of children who are "extra special" like me, and to the many professionals who devote their lives to help us.

SMILE!

William David Pardo (WD)
April 18, 2001–September 1, 2005
David A. Clark, 2008
(Ensher, Clark, & Songer, 2009)

William David Pardo was a very special child, a preschooler with extraordinary special needs who required medical care and early intervention from the time that he left the hospital after his special needs were identified at birth. During his infancy and preschool years, he received special education services along with speech, physical, and occupational therapy on a regular basis. His family, including his grandfather neonatologist/pediatrician, gave WD (the first grandchild) abundant love and special care until his life was cut short at 4 years of age

during the ravages of Hurricane Katrina in the late summer of 2005. Those who knew William David and his family would have to agree that not all disabilities are equal.

THERE ARE DISABILITIES, AND THERE ARE DISABILITIES!

There are, of course, many kinds of disabilities—those evident at birth, those that do not manifest until 18–24 months, and those that do not show themselves until children start school or later. Some disabilities are short term, and with time seem to be less demanding of families; some severely limit family outings and activities, such as those that involve extreme behavior; still others require lifelong commitments from both family members and service providers. To some extent, the severity of an infant's or young child's disabilities does allow professionals to anticipate the services that may be needed by the child and the family. On the other hand, it is important to remember that severity, to some degree, is in the eyes of the beholder. Professionals should not make assumptions about how families view their children and their challenges. Their perceptions should always be grounded in the realities of the present. Situations change over time for families; however, it is important to work with families where they are in order to help them move forward.

More Significant Challenges

Much research over the past 20–30 years has been devoted to understanding the outcomes common in families with children who require intensive intervention. These include high parental stress levels (especially among mothers), depression, social isolation, divorce, and the impact on siblings (Cox, Marshall, Mandleco, & Olsen, 2003; Ho & Kelley, 2003; Martin & Baker, 2001; Singer & Farkas, 1989; Wang et al., 2004). Martin and Baker indicated that most factors contributing to multiple and severe disabilities, including premature birth, genetic and congenital conditions, child abuse, accidents, and childhood illness, occur within the first 3 years of life. In response to a diagnosis of disability, families initially (almost without exception) experience several stages of grief, including shock, disbelief, anger, depression, discouragement, and ultimately, it is hoped, acceptance (Martin & Baker, p. 4). As is evident in Harry's (2010) inspiring book *Melanie, Bird with a Broken Wing*, much depends on the events of any given day and the child's status, as exemplified in the following excerpt. Beth Harry describes an encounter with her young daughter's doctor, who demonstrates the child's severe muscle stiffness by pumping her arms and legs and comparing her movements to the movements of a typically developing infant who is also in the room. Beth observes the marked difference between the two infants' movements and asks the doctor how he interprets this.

> With no hesitation and looking me straight in the eye, he said, "She has suffered brain damage."
>
> I felt something crash inside of me. I was intensely aware of the doctor's and nurse's eyes on my face and knew I could not break now. One more deep breath enabled me to respond.
>
> "You think so?"
>
> With a sinking heart, I heard him reply, "I am sure of it." (pp. 21–22)

The unanticipated responsibilities that come with the birth of a child with severe disabilities affect the predictability of each day and expectations across the lifespan. Professional interactions with families of infants and young children will change from hospital to home to school to later-life accommodations. Early on, families may be involved with medical personnel in life-saving situations in intensive care nurseries. For such children, early intervention and possibly home-based nursing care may become the most important needs. As difficult as the early years may be, many families have indicated that securing appropriate educational and clinical services are much more difficult during children's school years and later. It is infinitely easier for parents to find inclusive educational programs for toddlers and preschool children than for children in the elementary and particularly the adolescent years, when academics are assumed to take priority. Indeed, one of the most painful experiences that families of children with severe disabilities endure is the repeated message that their children cannot or should not be included in activities that are appropriate for their peer group. Accordingly, families and their children are often isolated or excluded from the ordinary pleasures of lifetime activities and interests.

Although findings are inconclusive, some studies have determined that "severity of disability" is a significant predictor of "family satisfaction with quality of life" during the early childhood years, but not uniformly so (Wang et al., 2004). Mothers and fathers indicate different views of how a severe disability affects a family's quality of life, with mothers (who generally assume the greater responsibility for a child's care) reporting less satisfaction and more adverse impact. Wang and colleagues acknowledged that these findings may be less clear-cut than they appear, given differences in levels of intervention and support, two critical considerations in the welfare of families. Some research also seems to indicate that providers themselves may have higher levels of discomfort, when consulting with families of young children with more significant disabilities (Wesley, Buysse, & Keyes, 2000).

Families and service providers understandably may have differing views of the severity of a child's disability, levels of comfort with care and treatment, and perhaps most important, the impact of particular disabilities. Although the specific nature of a child's needs will vary due to his or her disability (Laurvick et al., 2006; Rentinck, Ketelaar, Jongmans, Lindeman, & Gorter, 2009), it is clear that having a child with a disability affects several dimensions of family life, including the decision to have more children, finding affordable and appropriate child care, the decision to return to work, number of working hours, education, living arrangements, social life and recreation, and financial resources (Reichman, Corman, & Noonan, 2008). Although many families with a child who has a severe disability experience chronic sorrow (Olshansky, 1962), certain conditions seem to increase family burdens and warrant particular sensitivity on the part of professionals. Of particular note are families of children with severe behavior challenges and autism (Dabrowska & Pisula, 2010; Estes et al., 2009). In this regard, Wang and colleagues commented,

> A further issue related to understanding the impact of severity relates to the ambiguous nature of the concept of "severity" itself. For example, research has shown that individuals with greater behavior problems could increase their mothers' level of burden and fathers' depressive symptoms . . . and that the impact of young children with autism and behavior problems on their family system and life are "pervasive and often disruptive" (Fox, Benito, & Dunlap, 2002, p. 251).

Given these findings, it is possible that a child with severe and multiple disabilities who has no mobility or language might actually be less challenging to a family than a child who is classified as having mild disabilities because she is highly verbal and mobile but who also experiences high rates of aggressive or other problem behavior. (2004, p. 90)

One parent of a 23-year-old woman with multiple disabilities remarked that she has been able to sleep through the entire night without interruption possibly ten nights since the day she brought her daughter home from the hospital. Her daughter has no consistent means of communication, is unable to roll over, requires total care, and has severe neurological involvement which manifests adversely in response to sound and other aversive stimuli in the home environment. Maintaining some semblance of normalcy while also caring for two healthy adolescents is an ongoing struggle for this single mother, who has devoted her life to her children and to helping other families with exceptional children. Professionals especially supportive to this family have helped during times of family illness and deaths of grandparents, have used restraint in emphasizing the all-too-obvious negatives and have graciously offered kindness and encouragement. And thus for years, these have been the suggestions and recommendations of this mother to students preparing to become future teachers of young children with disabilities; that is, that they, too, refrain from stressing the negative. Echoing this thought, Robert Naseef (the father of a son with autism) has written in a letter to his son:

I've had a lot of practice accepting and loving you as you are. We will continue to face the future with courage while we do our best with what we have. This is so far from what I imagined more than 21 years ago. Nonetheless through acceptance and courage and endurance, the road through hardship has brought peace and love. Thank you for lighting the way. (2001, p. 266)

Less Severe, but Needs Always Present

Stress is also common among parents facing the behavioral problems of young children with disabilities that are considered to be less severe. Attention-deficit/hyperactivity disorder (ADHD), the most common neuropsychiatric condition among school-age children in the United States and one that is chronic, pervasive, and increasing, is one such example (Blanchard, Gurka, & Blackman, 2006; Fewell & Deutscher, 2002; Perrin, Bloom, & Gortmaker, 2007). Spencer, Biederman, and Mick defined ADHD as "an early-onset, highly prevalent neurobehavioral disorder, with genetic, environmental, and biologic etiologies, that persists into adolescence and adulthood in a sizable majority of afflicted children of both sexes" (2007, p. 631). ADHD is commonly indicated by symptoms of inattention, hyperactivity, and impulsivity and it is frequently seen in combination with other learning challenges such as language disabilities.

Prevalence estimates of ADHD in childhood in the United States range from 5% to 8%, a substantial population of children that varies depending on definition and strategies for diagnosis (Spencer et al., 2007). Writing about the etiological classification of ADHD, Millichap commented,

> Genetic factors account for 80% of the etiology of ADHD. . . . Family, twin, and adoption studies support the theory that ADHD is a highly heritable disorder, with the majority of patients having a first- or second-degree relative with a history of ADHD or learning disorder. (2008, p. e359)

As is common with many other learning and behavioral disabilities, boys far outnumber girls identified.

Families have variously described their young children as being always on the go, highly distractible, unable to focus, always getting into things, strong willed, bright but wired differently, up all night, impulsive, irritable, unable to learn from the consequences of their own behavior, unwilling to listen, disorganized, and forgetful. As such behaviors escalate, parents may view their children as noncompliant or defiant, and the behaviors may trigger a vicious cycle of negative responses that increase the level of family stress (Long, Gurka, & Blackman, 2008). This kind of pattern, evidenced in preschool children, often has been noted as a harbinger of continuing adverse behavior and performance throughout the later school years (Long et al., 2008). In particular, in an extensive survey of parents of young children across the United States (based on a population of 27,350 children), "parents who reported behavioral concerns regarding their young children were much more likely to express high levels of stress and difficulty coping" (Long et al., p. 154). Based on these data, these researchers concluded that

> The early identification of language and behavior problems may need to be addressed by a variety of education and healthcare providers, including family doctors and pediatricians, preschool and Head Start teachers, public health nurses, social workers, and child and day care providers, among others. The American Academy of Pediatrics (2006) recommended developmental surveillance of children at the intervals of 9, 18, 24, and 30 months. The families of infants and preschool children should be asked about their own specific concerns regarding their children's comprehension, verbal skills, and behavioral control. Parents should rate their own levels of stress so that service providers can determine the urgency and extent of treatment options. (pp. 154–155)

Because of the potentially disruptive impact of ADHD on families and its possible maladaptive, long-term effects for individuals into adolescence and adulthood, almost every medical and educational research article about this disorder comments about the critical importance of identification and intervention in the earliest years. Addressing these issues, Modesto-Lowe, Danforth, and Brooks concluded,

> Evidence supporting the potential value of behavioral parenting training (BPT) in improving outcomes for children . . . has fostered its increased use in several

countries. . . . In the case of ADHD, early parenting training offers promise in improving parental abilities to cope with the disorder to reduce the risk of CD [compulsive disorders]. (2008, p. 869)

Definitions of ADHD, co-morbid conditions and disabilities, appropriate expected outcomes for individuals, and reasonable interventions are still open to much debate (Stein, 2007). Such disabilities may not be immediately apparent, but they are ever present and the need is clear: to address these issues proactively with coordinated efforts and specific strategies to enhance positive interactions among all family members.

CHRONIC ILLNESSES: LONG HOSPITAL STAYS AND ONGOING TREATMENTS

A family's requirements for professional services for a child with special health care needs will depend on numerous variables. These include the nature and duration of the illness; the child's age and characteristics; the degree of monitoring required; family makeup; support from extended family and friends; the family's income level and individual work schedules; potential consequences of the illness; and the availability of medical, educational, and clinical resources within accessible communities (Johnson, Kastner, & the AAP Committee/Section on Children with Disabilities, 2005). Although there are many chronic illnesses, type 1 diabetes, cancer and blood disorders, and chronic lung diseases are three significant childhood conditions that illustrate the need for multiple, well-coordinated medical, educational, and clinical services. The short- and long-term emotional and psychological effects of these conditions on both families and children have been studied widely because of the vigilance required for monitoring, the potential for negative outcomes, and the pervasiveness and chronic nature of the illnesses.

Type 1 Diabetes

The National Institute of Diabetes and Digestive and Kidney Diseases has reported that 1 child or adolescent in 400–600 has been diagnosed with type 1 diabetes and that approximately 176,500 people younger than 20 years of age are living with the condition (McBroom & Enriquez, 2009). As several authors have pointed out, the management of type 1 diabetes is complex, challenging, and often highly stressful for families (Eugster, Francis, & the Lawson-Wilkins Drug and Therapeutics Committee, 2006; McBroom & Enriquez, 2009;

Patton, Dolan, & Powers, 2008; Piazza-Waggoner et al., 2008; Streisand, Swift, Wickmark, Chen, & Holmes, 2005; Weinzimer et al., 2004). For mothers, who often assume the greater responsibility for a child's care, the risks of developing depression are especially intensified (Driscoll et al., 2010). Families "must quickly learn a rigorous diabetes regimen and integrate it into their daily lives. This includes blood sugar testing, insulin administration, meal planning, and a constant consideration of the interplay among insulin, food [carbohydrates], and activity" (Ginsburg et al., 2005, p. 1095). These authors further commented that

> Because clinicians' effectiveness is mediated by the family, ideally they should con-
> sider how family issues and cultural context might have an impact on the family's
> ability to successfully manage diabetes and use that knowledge to tailor a family-
> specific plan. Such a plan should support the family to understand that although
> diabetes management issues seem pervasive, their primary goal remains to ensure
> that their son or daughter meets the normal developmental tasks of childhood.
> (p. 1095)

From their study of more than 800 families associated with the Diabetes Center of the Children's Hospital of Philadelphia who participated in open focus groups, parent-developed surveys, nominal group technique (NGT) ses-sions, semi-structured interviews, and explanatory focus groups, Ginsburg and colleagues (2005) subsequently offered insight on the factors that seemed to contribute most to "family resilience in successfully adapting to the challenges of living with diabetes" (p. 1103). These included the following:

- A knowledge base needed to manage glucose levels so children can interact with others outside the family (e.g., in child care, at school, and at birthday par-ties), who may not understand the needs of a child with a chronic illness
- Clinicians, physicians, and educators who are sensitive to the perspectives of families raising a child with type 1 diabetes in order to offer optimal care
- Up-to-date information about nutrition and managing meals when eating out
- Information for children about foods that affect blood sugar, maintaining a regular eating and testing schedule, the benefits of good control, and the risks of poor control
- Immediate accessibility to services and supplies
- Assistance in working with insurance companies
- Accessible community supports, such as trained baby sitters for respite care so families can take a break without fear and anxiety (2005, p. 1103)

In conclusion, Ginsburg and colleagues indicated that

> Ultimately, outcomes based research will need to determine whether health care
> teams that respond to the biopsychosocial and contextual needs of families result
> in better metabolic control and children who are emotionally and practically pre-
> pared to incorporate healthy lifestyles to be carried into adulthood. (2005, p. 1103)

Cancer and Blood Disorders

With treatment, the prognosis for children with blood and cancer disorders is much more positive today than 2 or 3 decades ago. Nonetheless, the impact of these disorders on families is profound. Keene wrote,

> The diagnosis of cancer in a child hits families like a nuclear bomb. All parts of life—including school—dramatically change after diagnosis.
>
> One of the first things that the family learns is that the treatment, regardless of the kind of cancer, will probably be brutal and it may take a very long time. Most children with cancer have surgery, chemotherapy and/or radiation. They miss weeks, months and sometimes years of school. There are many reasons for these absences—hospitalizations, illnesses at home, contagious diseases at school, fatigue, low immunity, and many more. In addition, the end of treatment does not always signify the end of difficulties, particularly regarding education. Many children face lasting effects [e.g., body image] of the treatments that saved their lives and these effects may have a significant impact on their education. (2003, p. v)

Stress, anxiety, and depression in families facing such diagnoses and treatments, as well as therapeutic and educational interventions (Burke, Harrison, Kauffmann, & Wong, 2001), have been the focus of much investigation in the related fields of clinical practice, education, and pediatrics (American Academy of Pediatrics Section on Hematology/Oncology/Children's Oncology Group, 2009; Best, Streisand, Catania, & Kazak, 2001; Bjork, Nordstrom, & Hallstrom, 2006; Drotar, 2005; Pao, Ballard, & Rosenstein, 2007; Piersol, Johnson, Wetsel, Holtzer, & Walker, 2008; Tarr & Pickler, 1999; van den Tweel et al., 2008; Wilson, 2005; Zebrack et al., 2002).

Families facing children's treatment and hospitalization need support from several sources, including extended family members, friends, and knowledgeable professionals. Although their coping is ongoing, there will be specific stress points during the course of such illnesses that likely will be especially burdensome. During the various stages of an illness, caring physicians will be invaluable in providing information. Knowledgeable nurses, social workers, and child life specialists can assist in preparing families and children for what to expect during treatments, forming ongoing bonds of support through painful and worrisome procedures; explaining medical procedures that will take place; and offering information about insurance, after-effects of treatment, diet, and so forth. Following treatments, sensitive teachers and educational staff can offer explanations to a child's peers, who will welcome the child through telecommunication classrooms or transitions back to school. The concept of teams working together to coordinate care should be interpreted broadly, extending across medical and educational facilities, so that families are given consistent information and "customized" (Burke et al., 2001, p. 130) supportive services. Depending on the nature of the child's illness, these services need to be available over a considerable period of time, given the prospect of repeated hospitalizations that may prompt "fluctuating stress" points for families (Burke et al., p. 130). Family-focused in-

terventions, created specifically for parents whose infants and young children are facing chronic illnesses and/or repeated hospitalizations, have been found to be effective in helping families develop better coping and problem-solving strategies, at least in the short term. In particular, Burke and colleagues found that

Stress-point intervention [SPIN] by ambulatory clinic nurses was effective in enhancing many parents' coping, in particular coping through maintaining family cooperation and an optimistic definition of the situation in many families. SPIN also acted to improve many parents' satisfaction with how well their family was functioning from before the hospitalization to 3 months after the hospitalization. SPIN was particularly effective in enhancing satisfaction with family interactions with friends, neighbors, and relatives who worked in helping with family tasks. (2001, p. 150)

Consider the words of one parent (Keene, 2003) regarding her daughter's re-entry into preschool:

Elizabeth was in preschool at the time of her diagnosis. The manager did a wonderful job of integrating her back into the fold. All of the other children at the school were taught what was happening to Elizabeth and what would be happening (such as hair loss). They learned that they had to be gentle with her when playing. The manager was a former home health nurse, so I was very confident that she would be able to take care of my daughter in the event of an emergency. She was already familiar with central lines and side effects from chemotherapy. She was a gem! (p. 52)

Chronic Lung Diseases

Chronic lung diseases often cause infants and young children to be hospitalized repeatedly, require ongoing medical treatments, result in frequent absences from school, and ultimately result in increased anxiety and stress for parents. Like type 1 diabetes, cancer, and blood disorders, chronic lung diseases have a large impact on families.

In his insightful editorial entitled *Small is beautiful: but may be breathless,* Bush (2004) summarized trends and needs in the field and among families who daily care for children affected by chronic respiratory diseases. He indicated that

• The 0 to 5 year age group is of particular concern because of the diversity of diseases at this time.

• Chronic lung disease of prematurity (bronchopulmonary dysplasia) is the product of the success of neonatal intensive care. . . . Now, babies weighing less than 500 grams at birth and 23 weeks of gestation are surviving, and often go home on oxygen for many months and years. . . . They have respiratory morbidity, including repeated readmission to the hospital well into the mid-childhood years.

- Respiratory syncytial virus wreaks respiratory havoc every winter, with many infants being admitted to hospitals and requiring intensive care.

- There are sinister long-term sequelae of childhood viral infections; adenovirus obliterative bronchiolitis is making an unwelcome come-back, causing severe prolonged respiratory distress and oxygen dependency.

- Added to the litany noted above are the problems of chronic suppurative lung disease such as cystic fibrosis [which can be diagnosed at an early age with newborn screening] and primary ciliary dyskinesia, neuromuscular and large airway problems, which may require noninvasive or even tracheostomy ventilation, and the various aspiration syndromes (Bush, 2004, p. 181).

- Asthma—which affects nearly 6% of children, or 3.7 million, in the United States and is the most common chronic disease of childhood—recently has shown an especially dramatic increase among children between the ages of 1 and 4 years of age (Brown et al., 2002).

Not surprisingly, medical care for all of these chronic conditions is exacting, constant, and with contemporary technologies often managed largely in the home rather than the hospital. Families, bearing the burden of in-home care, are likely to face numerous stress points in their daily lives with airway clearance techniques (Dodd & Prasad, 2005; Gayer & Ganong, 2006), nebulizer treatments, in-home ventilation, the administration of an array of medications, and special diets and feeding regimens. All of these responsibilities require considerable knowledge and careful monitoring for signs of impending illness or worsening conditions. The care is challenging, raises anxiety in families, and poses extraordinary burdens and responsibilities for primary caregivers. As with parents of children with varying degrees of disability and other chronic illnesses, parents of children with chronic lung diseases may have reduced opportunities to work and to maintain social relationships outside the home, and experience a major impact on their quality of life.

The needs are likewise considerable for professionals working with such families, as is spelled out in an official statement from the American Thoracic Society in 2005:

Parents of MFTD [medically fragile and technology-dependent] children expect nurses and physicians to work respectfully and collaboratively with the family, and to allow parents to direct the care of their child. They expect nurses and physicians to provide safe, competent, skillful care, delivered with the same level of attention and care that parents themselves use. Parents view home care for increasing the ability of family members and respite care providers to provide quality care through education and training. Parents also want nurses to educate the family about available resources, and to help secure these resources through advocacy. Communication among nurses, physicians, and family, and recognition of professional boundaries and respect for the family unit, are highly valued. (p. 1448)

Home-based education and intervention programs (Brown et al., 2002) that focus on helping caregivers maintain family routines (Markson & Fiese, 2000) have been found to be effective in lowering parent anxiety and increasing their knowledge base. In discussing the common features of successful interventions for the control of asthma in children, Clark, Mitchell, and Rand identified the following factors:

1. Recognition of the multiple factors affecting childhood asthma
2. Careful assessment of participants' risk factors and needs
3. Tailoring of program elements to address participants' risk factors and needs
4. Consideration of both physical and social environments
5. Use of sound learning and change theories
6. Family involvement
7. Focus on children with the most serious disease
8. Selection of delivery venues at which learning can be optimized (2009, p. 5185)

BENEFICIAL OUTCOMES: FINDING PEACE AND JOY IN ADVERSITY

This chapter opened with a question: What difference does a difference make in a child? The various disabilities and chronic illnesses that affect infants and young children have unique characteristics. To deny that these distinctions do make a difference in the lives of families would be naïve. However, there are also similarities in what family members feel and in their need to regain a sense of well-being, joy, and peace. It is typical for families to pass through periods of grief, sadness, anxiety, anger, and depression when they learn that their child has a disability or chronic illness. Professionals are in a position to empower families along the pathway to recovery and to help them regain stability and peace after the diagnosis of a child's disability or chronic illness. Children with disabilities and chronic illnesses take their families to different places in the journeys of their lives, and some of these children do not survive. Families who are faced with such challenges can develop a resilience that sustains and teaches as no other lessons of life do. Most assuredly, William David's (Ensher et al., 2009) and Melanie's families (Harry, 2010) were forever changed as a result of their relationships with these children. And although the families were enormously saddened by the eventual loss of their children, they were able to take the lessons they had learned into the future, without question having become more sensitive, compassionate, and loving parents because of what they had experienced.

Thinking It Through: Questions for Discussion

1. How do professionals alter their strategies for developing relationships with families, depending on the families' stages of first learning about, coping with, grief about, and acceptance of a child's disability or illness?

2. How do professionals alter their strategies in working with families, depending on different family circumstances such as their levels of education, work schedules, their support system of family and friends, and other key resources?

3. How do professionals alter their strategies in working with parents, depending on the nature of a child's particular disability or illness; for example, its chronicity, the complexity of treatment, accessible programs?

REFERENCES

American Academy of Pediatrics Section on Hematology/Oncology/Children's Oncology Group. (2009). Long-term follow-up care for pediatric cancer survivors. *Pediatrics, 123*(3), 906–915.

American Thoracic Society. (2005). Statement on home care for patients with respiratory disorders. *American Journal of Critical Care Medicine, 171,* 1443–1464.

Best, M., Streisand, R., Catania, L., & Kazak, A.E. (2001). Parental distress during pediatric leukemia and posttraumatic stress symptoms (PTSS) after treatment ends. *Journal of Pediatric Psychology, 26*(5), 299–307.

Bjork, M., Nordstrom, B., & Hallstrom, I. (2006). Needs of young children with cancer during their initial hospitalization: An observational study. *Journal of Pediatric Oncology Nursing, 23*(4), 210–219.

Blanchard, L.T., Gurka, M.J., & Blackman, J.A. (2006). Emotional, developmental, and behavioral health of American children and their families: A report from the 2003 national survey of children's health. *Pediatrics, 117*(6), e1202–e1212.

Brown, J.V., Bakeman, R., Celano, M.P., Demi, A.S., Kobrynski, L., & Wilson, S.R. (2002). Home-based asthma education of young low-income children and their families. *Journal of Pediatric Psychology, 27*(8), 677–688.

Burke, S.O., Harrison, M.B., Kauffmann, E., & Wong, C. (2001). Effects of stress-point intervention with families of repeatedly hospitalized children. *Journal of Family Nursing, 7*(2), 128–158.

Bush, A. (2004). Small is beautiful: but may be breathless. *Chronic Respiratory Disease, 1,* 181–182.

Clark, N.M., Mitchell, H.E., & Rand, C.S. (2009). Effectiveness of educational and behavioral asthma interventions. *Pediatrics, 123*(Suppl.), 5185–5192.

Cox, A.M., Marshall, E.S., Mandleco, B., & Olsen, S.F. (2003). Coping responses to daily life stressors of children who have a sibling with a disability. *Journal of Family Nursing, 9*(4), 397–413.

Dabrowska, A., & Pisula, E. (2010). Parenting stress and coping styles in mothers and fathers of pre-school children with autism and Down syndrome. *Journal of Intellectual Disability Research, 54*(3), 266–280.

Dodd, M.E., & Prasad, S.A. (2005). Physiotherapy management of cystic fibrosis. *Chronic Respiratory Disease, 2,* 139–149.

Driscoll, K.A., Johnson, S.B., Barker, D., Quittner, A.L., Deeb, L.C., Geller, D.E., et al. (2010). Risk factors associated with depressive symptoms in caregivers of children with type 1 diabetes or cystic fibrosis. *Journal of Pediatric Psychology, 35*(8), 814–822.

Drotar, D. (2005). Commentary: Involving families in psychological interventions in pediatric psychology: Critical needs and dilemmas. *Journal of Pediatric Psychology, 30*(8), 689–693.

Ensher, G.L., Clark, D.A., & Songer, N.S. (2008). Dedication to WD. *Families, infants, and young children at risk: Pathways to best practice* (p. xviii). Baltimore: Paul H. Brookes Publishing Co.

Estes, A., Munson, J., Dawson, G, Koehler, E., Zhou, X-H, & Abbott, R. (2009). Parenting stress and psychological functioning among mothers of preschool children with autism and developmental delay. *Autism, 13*(4), 375–387.

Eugster, E.A., Francis, G., & the Lawson-Wilkins Drug and Therapeutics Committee. (2006). Position statement: Continuous subcutaneous insulin infusion in very young children with type 1 diabetes. *Pediatrics, 118*(4), e1244–e1249.

Fewell, R.R., & Deutscher, B. (2002). Attention deficit hyperactivity disorder in very young children: Early signs and interventions. *Infants & Young Children, 14*(3), 24–32.

Gayer, D., & Ganong, L. (2006). Family structure and mothers' caregiving of children with cystic fibrosis. *Journal of Family Nursing, 12*(4), 390–412.

Ginsburg, K.R., Howe, C.J., Jawad, A.F., Buzby, M., Ayala, J.M., Tuttle, A., et al. (2005). Parents' perceptions of factors that affect successful diabetes management for their children. *Pediatrics, 116*(5), 1095–1104.

Harry, B. (2010). *Melanie, bird with a broken wing: A mother's story.* Baltimore: Paul H. Brookes Publishing Co.

Ho, K.M., & Kelley, M.K. (2003). Dealing with denial: A systems approach for family professionals working with parents of individuals with multiple disabilities. *The Family Journal: Counseling and Therapy for Couples and Families, 11*(3), 239–247.

Johnson, C.P., Kastner, T.A., & the AAP Committee/Section on Children with Disabilities. (2005). Helping families raise children with special health care needs at home. *Pediatrics, 115*(2), 507–511.

Keene, N. (Ed.). (2003). *Educating the child with cancer: A guide for parents and teachers.* Kensington, MD: Candlelighters Childhood Cancer Foundation.

Laurvick, C.L., Msall, M.E., Silburn, S., Bower, C., de Klerk, M., & Leonard, H. (2006). Physical and mental health of mothers caring for a child with Rett syndrome. *Pediatrics, 118*(4), e1152–e1164.

Long, C.E., Gurka, M.J., & Blackman, J.A. (2008). Family stress and children's language and behavior problems. *Topics in Early Childhood Special Education, 28*(3), 148–157.

Markson, S., & Fiese, B.H. (2000). Family rituals as a protective factor for children with asthma. *Journal of Pediatric Psychology, 25*(7), 471–479.

Martin, S.S., & Baker, D.C. (2001). *Families and children with severe disabilities: Daily lives, systems, and concerns.* Paper presented at the meeting of the American Association of Behavioral and Social Sciences (AABSS), Las Vegas, NV.

McBroom, L.A., & Enriquez, M. (2009). Review of family-centered interventions to enhance the health outcomes of children with type 1 diabetes. *The Diabetes Educator, 35*(3), 428–438.

Millichap, J.G. (2008). Etiologic classification of attention-deficit/hyperactivity disorder. *Pediatrics, 121*(2), e358–e365.

Modesto-Lowe, V., Danforth, J.S., & Brooks, D. (2008). ADHD: Does parenting style matter? *Clinical Pediatrics, 47*(9), 865–872.

Naseef, R.A. (2001). *Special children, challenged parents: The struggles and rewards of raising a child with a disability* (Rev. ed.). Baltimore: Paul H. Brookes Publishing Co.

Olshansky, S. (1962). Chronic sorrow: A response to having a mentally defective child. *Social Casework, 43,* 191–194.

Pao, M., Ballard, E.D., & Rosenstein, D.L. (2007). Growing up in the hospital. *Journal of the American Medical Association, 297*(24), 2752–2755.

Patton, S.R., Dolan, L.M., & Powers, S.W. (2008). Differences in family mealtime interactions between young children with type 1 diabetes and controls: Implications for behavioral intervention. *Journal of Pediatric Psychology, 33*(8), 885–893.

Perrin, J.M., Bloom, S.R., & Gortmaker, S.L. (2007). The increase of childhood chronic conditions in the United States. *Journal of the American Medical Association (JAMA), 297*(24), 2755–2759.

Piazza-Waggoner, C., Modi, A.C., Powers, S.W., Williams, L.B., Dolan, L.M., & Patton, S.R. (2008). Observational assessment of family functioning in families with children who have type 1 diabetes mellitus. *Journal of Developmental & Behavioral Pediatrics, 29*(2), 101–105.

Piersol, L.W., Johnson, A., Wetsel, A., Holtzer, K., & Walker, C. (2008). Decreasing psychological distress during the diagnosis and treatment of pediatric leukemia. *Journal of Pediatric Oncology Nursing, 25*(6), 323–330.

Reichman, N.E., Corman, H., & Noonan, K. (2008). Impact of child disability on the family. *Maternal Child Health Journal, 12,* 679–683.

Rentinck, I., Ketelaar, M., Jongmans, M., Lindeman, E., & Gorter, J.W. (2009). Parental reactions following the diagnosis of cerebral palsy in their young child. *Journal of Pediatric Psychology, 34*(6), 671–676.

Singer, L., & Farkas, K.J. (1989). The impact of infant disabilities on maternal perception of stress. *Family Relations, 38*(4), 444–449.

Spencer, T.J., Biederman, J., & Mick, E. (2007). Attention-deficit/hyperactivity disorder: Diagnosis, lifespan, co-morbidities, and neurobiology. *Journal of Pediatric Psychology, 32*(6), 631–642.

Stein, R.E.K. (2007). Measurement of ADHD outcomes: Implications for the future. *Journal of Pediatric Psychology, 7*(2, Suppl.), 1–4.

Streisand, R., Swift, E., Wickmark, T., Chen, R., & Holmes, C.S. (2005). Pediatric parenting stress among parents of children with type 1 diabetes: The role of self-efficacy, responsibility, and fear. *Journal of Pediatric Psychology, 30*(6), 513–521.

Tarr, J., & Pickler, R.H. (1999). Becoming a cancer patient: A study of families of children with acute lymphocytic leukemia. *Journal of Pediatric Oncology Nursing, 16*(1), 44–50.

van den Tweel, X.W., Hatzmann, J., Ensink, E., van der Lee, J.H., Peters, M., Fijnvandraat, K., et al. (2008). Quality of life of female caregivers of children with sickle cell disease: A survey. *Haematologica, 93*(4), 588–593.

Wang, M., Turnbull, A.P., Summers, J.A., Little, T.D., Poston, D.J., Mannan, H., et al. (2004). Severity of disability and income as predictors of parents' satisfaction with their family quality of life during early childhood years. *Research & Practice for Persons with Severe Disabilities, 29*(2), 82–94.

Weinzimer, S.A., Ahern, J.H., Doyle, E.A., Vincent, M.R., Dziura, J., Steffen, A.T., et al. (2004). Persistence of benefits of continuous subcutaneous insulin infusion in very young children with type 1 diabetes: A follow-up report. *Pediatrics, 114*(6), 1601–1605.

Wesley, P.W., Buysse, V., & Keyes, L. (2000). Comfort zone revisited: Child characteristics and professional comfort with consultation. *Journal of Early Intervention, 23*(2), 106–115.

Wilson, K. (2005). The evolution of the role of nurses: The history of nurse practitioners in pediatric oncology. *Journal of Pediatric Oncology Nursing, 22*(5), 250–253.

Zebrack, B.J., Zeltzer, L.K., Whitton, J., Mertens, A.C., Odom, L., Berkow, R., et al. (2002). Psychological outcomes in long-term survivors of childhood leukemia, Hodgkin's disease, and non-Hodgkin's lymphoma: A report from the childhood cancer study. *Pediatrics, 110,* 42–52.

8

A Child with Ongoing Special Needs

Gail L. Ensher and David A. Clark

CHAPTER HIGHLIGHTS

At the conclusion of this chapter, the reader will

- Understand stages of grief and acceptance typically experienced by families upon learning a child's diagnosis

- Understand specific challenges that confront families upon learning a diagnosis

- Understand guidelines for giving families helpful advice

- Understand strategies for assisting families in making transitions to new programs and settings

WELCOME TO HOLLAND: AN AUTISM PARABLE

When you're going to have a baby, it's like you're planning a vacation to Italy. You're all excited. You get a whole bunch of guidebooks, you learn a few phrases in Italian so you can get around, and when it comes time you pack your bags and head for the airport—for Italy!

Only when you land, the stewardess says, "Welcome to Holland." You look at one another in disbelief and shock, saying "Holland? What are you talking about? I signed up for Italy!"

But they explain there's been a change of plans, and you've landed in Holland and there you must stay. "But I don't know anything about Holland! I don't want to stay!" you say . . . .

You go out and buy some new guidebooks, learn some new phrases . . . you begin to discover that Holland has windmills. Holland has tulips; Holland has Rembrandts.

But everyone else you know is busy coming and going from Italy. They're all bragging about what a great time they had there; and for the rest of your life, you will say, "Yes, that's where I was going. That's what I had planned." The pain of that will never, ever go away.

You have to accept that pain, because the loss of that dream . . . is a very, very significant loss. But if you spend your life mourning the fact that you didn't get to Italy, you will never be free to enjoy the very special, the very lovely things about Holland. (Turkington, 2009, p. 14)

DIAGNOSIS THE FIRST TIME: FEARING, GRIEVING, DOUBTING, AND LOVING AGAIN

Many parents who have written about learning that their child has a disability have echoed Turkington's sentiments. Robert Naseef (a psychologist and father

of a son diagnosed with autism) chronicled his own experience in his book *Special Children, Challenged Parents* (Naseef, 2001).

Another parent (Notbohm, 2007) has drawn this analogy:

We've all done it: let ourselves slip into wondering what our lives would be like if our child didn't have autism. It's hard not to think about the "typical" experiences that are bypassing our family. But life isn't some hand of five-card stud where we can throw back a few of our cards in hopes of drawing something better. Nor is it a first draft that we can edit until we get the nuances just right. We play out the hand we drew in real time. Don't let if-onlys or what-I-could-have-done-differentlys thieve precious bits of your life away. (p. 40)

Although diagnoses are difficult for families to hear, the most difficult aspect may be all of the unknowns. In the words of one mother,

> It is frightening to be in charge of a ship that you do not know how to sail. We had no diagnosis for Jack, no plan, and no team of professionals to run the boat. We needed a plan, and since a plan is only as good as the people who work on it, the first step was to get the right professionals. . . .
>
> A whole new world was presented to us. Its existence shattered dreams we have not yet had the joy of defining. Predictions about what life would be like down the road devastated us. The unknown of the situation was frightening. (Addison, 2003, p. 10)

During the times of uncertainty, there are days of painful recognition, artfully described by McDonnell:

> Over the next year, between Paul's first and second birthday, we felt more and more anxious. His pediatrician suggested that I was "doing too much for him, not giving him a chance to ask for things for himself." So one day I withheld a banana from him as he sat in his high chair. I knew he was hungry. I held the banana just out of reach, saying clearly over and over, "Banana, banana," then adapting and playing with baby sounds, "Ba, ba ba, ba ba, ba."
>
> I thought, if I get any kind of sound out of you, I'll give it to you. Just open your mouth. Say something. Anything! Paul became more and more agitated, squirming in his chair, bouncing up and down, reaching for the banana, watching my mouth, trying to say something, struggling to speak.
>
> Finally he burst into tears. He fell back in the chair and sobbed. He sobbed in the most abandoned tones I had ever heard from him. Feeling guilty about my own behavior and angry at the doctor, I picked him up and held him close against my shoulder. I gave him the banana and swore I would never, ever try this particular experiment again. It seemed so clear to me at that moment that he was trying to speak, trying to give me what I wanted. It was also crystal clear that he couldn't. (1993, p. 4)

As Addison describes, there is some relief in assigning a name or label to behaviors:

> When you have a name to put to all the things that have baffled you, you realize two things. One, the behaviors are not your child's fault. And two, his behaviors are not a reflection of your parenting style. Sure it may be something in the genetic code of your family or your spouse's family, but that's hardly your fault. Hearing the diagnosis should take the blame off you, your spouse, and your child. You can then move on. (2003, p. 20)

Parents *do* move on—through the initial shock and disbelief, the sadness that never totally evaporates but that dims with time, the adjustments, and eventually acceptance and a new perspective about their life. The particular journey will differ from family to family, but the patterns toward resolution often are very

similar—and in the process, it is hoped that families will learn to appreciate all of the lovely things about "Holland."

As we discussed in prior chapters of this text, professionals entering relationships with families who are somewhere along the continuum of acceptance are more likely to adopt "collaborative-resource perspectives" (Ho & Kelley, 2003, p. 242) than deficit models of interpretation. Ho and Kelley offer some helpful advice to professionals:

- Validating the pain parents initially feel when learning the diagnosis of a disability is an important beginning point in developing a meaningful relationship with families. How families receive that diagnosis and respond will depend, in large part, on their emotional state and the way in which this information is delivered.

- Families are connected. What affects one member of the family [system] ultimately affects the others. Consequently, "intervention with the entire family is more effective than treating one individual within the system" (p. 243).

- Professionals can be helpful in guiding parents from *naïve optimism* toward more realistic *constructive optimism* (p. 245), which can facilitate problem-solving and alternative courses of action within the context of their own culture-specific community.

Professionals must think carefully about how best to approach families who are making their way through confusion to acceptance.

SHARING A DIAGNOSIS WITH THE OUTSIDE WORLD

Sharing with relatives, friends, and the outside world the discovery that their child has a disability is an extraordinarily difficult undertaking for parents. Doing so validates the reality of the delay, impairment, illness, and/or atypical behavior that families may have been reluctant to acknowledge. People may ask questions that have no easy answers—Will she ever talk? When will he begin to walk? Why does she act that way? Why did this happen to our family? In addition, extended family members and friends may discount parents' concerns, telling them that

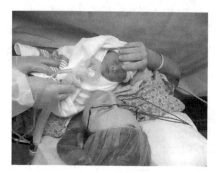

there really is no problem or that the child will grow out of the delay. Relating to this issue, Harry wrote,

I felt it necessary to accept as a fact that Melanie had experienced brain damage, as the evidence seemed indisputable. As always, an essential part of acceptance for me was being able to speak the fact, to hear myself say it, and to experience the reassurance of

knowing that the words were acceptable to my own ears and to the ears of my listener. One of the most unsupportive things a listener could do, therefore, was to
disagree with what I was saying. Thus any well-intentioned friend or acquaintance
who made the mistake of trying to reassure me by expressing disagreement about
Melanie's condition would immediately fall into the category of unsupportive. To
say, "But isn't the doctor jumping to conclusions?" or "Surely it's too soon to diag-
nose brain damage," or worst of all "Oh! There's nothing wrong with the baby,
she's just weak" (or small or dysmature, or whatever) was to alienate me immediately. No doubt such comments were intended to be supportive, but I felt that they
arose from what would turn out to be an unacceptable attitude to such a problem;
that is, if people felt the need to deny the likelihood of Melanie's having brain
damage, it was because the idea was unacceptable, perhaps even repugnant to
them. (2010, pp. 47–48)

Although it perhaps sounds simplistic, professionals need to choose their
comments carefully when speaking with families. Parents may not know the name
of particular disabilities or conditions, but many understand that their child is
not developing typically often long before professionals confirm this. Many families are relieved when a condition is identified because they finally have an explanation for the behavior, delay, or impairment that has been long evident to
them. Under such circumstances, what parents are most looking for is information that is sensitively delivered, with some guidance on what to expect.

MEETING THE NEEDS OF EVERYONE IN THE FAMILY

In speaking about families of infants and young children with disabilities, Ann
Turnbull (1996) described the family unit as a mobile and emphasized the importance of keeping families in balance. If all attention is focused on the child
with a disability, according to Turnbull, family interactions may become skewed
and other family members feel neglected. Parents and partners need time for
themselves, and other children need to have
their parents' attention and feel valued and included. Clearly, in times of crisis, such as the
birth of a severely premature infant or hospitalization for a chronic illness, parent attention will be focused more heavily on the child
with special needs. Medical appointments and
educational activities for the child with a disability, however, should not be all-consuming
to the neglect of other family activities. (Chapter 9 will address the topic of siblings of children
with disabilities or chronic illness in depth.)

Professionals should be mindful not to
make requests of parents that involve unreasonable time frames. Families may feel that expectations for attending meetings and therapy
sessions are taking precedence over spending

time with their children. This kind of situation does not align with a family-centered, relationship-based approach.

SOMEONE ALWAYS IN THE HOME: PRIVACY ISSUES

Typically, parents are grateful for the expertise and assistance offered by home visiting professionals. It is important to recognize, however, the effects of frequent home visits on a family's privacy. One family, for example, described a situation in which the mother was taking a shower while her daughter watched her young son in a playpen downstairs in their home. Much to the mother's surprise, when she finished her shower and returned to her children, she discovered that the early intervention provider had let herself into their home and had started to work with her child without apology or explanation. The family felt violated, and the service provider's actions demonstrated her lack of respect and sensitivity. Not surprisingly, the relationship that the provider presumed she had established with the family ended abruptly.

For more than 2 decades, educators and medical professionals have studied and emphasized the benefits of delivering professional services for families of infants and young children in natural environments (i.e., within homes) (AAP Council on Child and Adolescent Health, 1998; AAP Council on Children with Disabilities, 2007; Dunst, Hamby, Trivette, Raab, & Bruder, 2000; Guillett, 2002; Klass, 2008; Raab & Dunst, 2004). For many families, the home setting is the only option if their child has a medical or disabling condition that requires constant care. Home is also where parents and children generally feel the most comfortable. Providers across disciplines can work together as a team, offering consistent information to families. At home, family members can be involved in the education and caregiving processes with the child so that all of the responsibility does not rest with one individual (often the mother). Similarly, extended family members can be invited to participate if they are serving in caregiving roles, a strategy that can be educational for them as well. In addition, visiting families' homes creates an opportunity for professionals to learn about family traditions, routines, and patterns of interaction that otherwise might not surface until much later in the relationship-building processes.

However, having non–family members in the home or having to depend on respite or in-home nursing care can be stressful. Discussions and disagreements are open for everyone to hear; relatively few situations are confidential. Also, if a child has special health care needs and cannot be left with individuals who are not trained, families may be at a disadvantage if the service provider cannot visit. Although some families are fortunate to have consistent home visiting professionals, some families may encounter a revolving group of people who all need to be introduced to the child's and family's needs and routines.

To help minimize intrusions on a family's home life, professionals can use several strategies:

- Before visits begin, schedule an appointment with the family to learn about priorities, routines, and special considerations.

- Explain the goals for visits so the family understands expectations.
- Bring activities for siblings to help them feel included.
- Know your own limits in terms of offering help and giving advice. If you are not the appropriate person to assist, be willing to suggest someone you trust who can offer the necessary expertise.
- Offer the family choices, and respect their preferences.
- Try to accommodate the family's schedule and needs.
- Prioritize goals. Focusing on the most important goals will be more effective than taking on too many at one time.
- Always leave families with next-visit expectations and with a positive comment.
- Be open with families, and involve them in problem-solving processes.
- Remove yourself when it is clear that your presence is an impediment.

ADVICE: WHEN HELP IS HELPFUL—AND NOT

Advice on medical matters for families must be given clearly, without hesitation, and directly to families. Dunst and his colleagues have written widely about help-giving strategies within the framework of family-centered best practices (Dunst, 2000; Dunst, Boyd, Trivette, & Hamby, 2002; Dunst, Trivette, & Hamby, 2007). According to Dempsey and Keen,

> A growing body of evidence has validated many of the theoretical links between the help-giving practices of staff and desirable outcomes for families with a child with a disability. However, it is clear from the research to date that the relationship between the provision of family-centered services and the achievement of positive outcomes for children and their parents is complex and is yet to be fully understood. (2008, p. 42)

The following guidelines for offering help-giving advice are based on our more than 3 decades of experience working with families. To the extent possible,

- Advice should take into account all family members
- Advice should be connected to positive outcomes or actions; otherwise, words are empty, do not enhance parent competence, and fail to empower families
- Advice must be made within a meaningful and attainable context; if advice is not realistic, families likely will not act on it
- Families need to understand the reasons help-giving advice is being offered
- Advice needs to be consistent with the demands of the hour/day, parent competency, and be sustainable in terms of positive family outcomes (Turnbull, Summers, Lee, & Kyzar, 2007)
- Help-giving advice should offer the potential for leaving families in a better place when professionals no longer provide services

CONNECTIONS: PREPARING THE
FAMILY AND CHILD FOR WHAT IS TO FOLLOW

There is some truth to the adage that it is better to live with knowledge of what is ahead than to struggle with the fear of future unknowns. Under the best of circumstances, transitions are difficult. As we discussed in *Families, Infants, and Young Children at Risk: Pathways to Best Practice* (Ensher, Clark, & Songer, 2009),

> transitions are one of the most challenging periods or stages during the life cycle that parents face. . . . Families of children with and without special needs often feel an array of emotions as they send their sons and daughters to kindergarten for the first time, ranging from excitement and enthusiasm to fear and concern about the future. For children with a disability, as they transition from age level to age level, there can be significant issues of continuity between home and school and between school- and service-based programs. Valuable relationships formed in the earliest years, which for many families have become a foundation of security, will change. Regulations and requirements for eligibility from infancy and the toddler years necessarily differ as children advance into kindergarten and the early primary years of school. Whether appropriate or not, families may find that the supports they were offered at the pre-K stages of programming will lessen, often dramatically as their children grow older, and despite the best intent of transition and annual conferences, services may become less connected, minimally aligned, and less collaborative. However, there are positives to balance the sense of uncertainty and the unknown. For example, the comfort zone of known relationships will expand for parents and children, and new friendships will emerge. The challenges of reality hopefully will open wider doors to the development of maturity, problem solving, and new experiences. (p. 343)

Clearly, there are unpredictable situations for which there are few ways of knowing what is ahead. Among those most challenging for families are the birth of a multiply impaired child who is admitted to a neonatal intensive care unit and a child born with serious health conditions. Professionals can help ease or facilitate processes for families with these strategies:

- Connecting families with new settings, programs, and staff before transitions occur

- Developing child/family portfolios to assist with transitions to new settings

- Preparing families for possible outcomes and next steps

- Making sure that parents (especially single parents) are not alone when receiving essential information

- Making sure that essential pieces of information are written down for families for future reference

- Giving families telephone numbers of knowledgeable persons to call if they have questions or need clarification

As Bryden and Ensher stated,

> In the case of most families, we are meeting them at one of the most fragile times in their lives. Families live through the hopes and dreams for their children, and when a part of that is taken away or tarnished, their lives are never the same. Through relationships with caring and helpful individuals, they are able to move on to refurbished hopes and dreams with renewed strength and energy.
>
> This does not mean that the pathways will be easy. This does not mean that the burdens and responsibilities are lifted from their own, rightfully placed shoulders. This does mean, though, that professionals will be honest and straightforward and offer the best advice known at the time. They will support and hold back, as necessary, so that when they must leave, families are able to sustain their own lives and provide the love and caregiving so necessary to realize the potentials of their children. (2009, p. 348)

BENEFICIAL OUTCOMES: APPRECIATING EXTRAORDINARY MOMENTS IN ORDINARY DAYS

In the lives of most parents of infants and young children, there are those extraordinary moments in ordinary days that that they will never forget: when their child first rolled over, smiled, sat up unassisted for the first time, took a first step, said a first word, wrote her name, said *I love you,* got on the school bus for the first time, and so many others. For parents of infants and young children with special health care needs or disabilities, such milestones are no less precious—indeed, because they are sometimes so long awaited, they may be even more so. Professionals can and should celebrate these extraordinary moments with parents. Many parents of young children with disabilities feel that, after the birth of their child with special needs, they never again will take anything for granted. These families have heard so much of the negative—what's wrong with your child, he never will do this, she's behind—that it is important for professionals to reaffirm a family's strength in these extraordinary moments and accomplishments.

Thinking It Through:
Questions for Discussion

1. If parents disagree with medical professionals about life-saving treatments for their infant, what strategies might be used to reach common ground with the family?

2. As a professional, how can you determine whether or not advice is helpful to families?

3. Other than by word, in what ways can professionals celebrate children's extraordinary moments and milestones to set a different tone and perspective for parents?

REFERENCES

Addison, A. (2003). *One small starfish: A mother's everyday advice, survival tactics & wisdom for rais-ing a special needs child.* Arlington, TX: Future Horizons.

American Academy of Pediatrics Council on Child and Adolescent Health. (1998). The role of home-visitation programs in improving health outcomes for children and families. *Pedi-atrics, 101*(3), 486–489.

American Academy of Pediatrics Council on Children with Disabilities. (2007). Role of the medical home in family-centered early intervention services. *Pediatrics, 120*(5), 1153–1158.

Bryden, D.A., & Ensher, G.L. (2009). Home and school programs for infants and young chil-dren with special needs. In G.L. Ensher, D.A. Clark, & N.S. Songer (Eds.), *Families, infants, and young children at risk: Pathways to best practice* (pp. 335–352). Baltimore: Paul H. Brookes Publishing Co.

Dempsey, I., & Keen, D. (2008). A review of processes and outcomes in family-centered ser-vices for children with a disability. *Topics in Early Childhood Special Education, 28*(1), 42–52.

Dunst, C.J. (2000). Revisiting "rethinking early intervention." *Topics in Early Childhood Special Education, 20*(2), 95–104.

Dunst, C.J., Boyd, K., Trivette, C.M., & Hamby, D.W. (2002). Family-oriented program mod-els and professional help-giving practices. *Family Relations, 51*(3), 221–229.

Dunst, C.J., Hamby, D., Trivette, C.M., Raab, M., & Bruder, M.B. (2000). Everyday family and community life and children's naturally occurring learning opportunities. *Journal of Early Intervention, 23*(3), 151–164.

Dunst, C.J., Trivette, C.M., & Hamby, D.W. (2007). Meta-analysis of family-centered help-giving practices research. *Mental Retardation and Developmental Disabilities Research Reviews, 13,* 370–378.

Ensher, G.L., Clark, D.A., & Songer, N.S. (Eds.). (2009). *Families, infants, and young children at risk: Pathways to best practice* (pp. 335–352). Baltimore: Paul H. Brookes Publishing Co.

Guillett, S.E. (2002). Preparing student nurses to provide home care for children with disabil-ities: A strengths-based approach. *Home Health Care Management Practice, 15*(1), 47–58.

Harry, B. (2010). *Melanie, bird with a broken wing: A mother's story.* Baltimore: Paul H. Brookes Publishing Co.

Ho, K.M., & Kelley, M.K. (2003). Dealing with denial: A systems approach for family profes-sionals working with parents of individuals with multiple disabilities. *The Family Journal, 11*(3), 239–247.

Klass, C.S. (2008). *The home visitor's guidebook: Promoting optimal parent and child development* (3rd ed.). Baltimore: Paul H. Brookes Publishing Co.

McDonnell, J.T. (1993). *News from the border: A memoir.* Northfield, MA: Black Willow Press.

Naseef, R.A. (2001). *Special children—challenged parents: The struggles and rewards of raising a child with a disability* (Rev. ed.). Baltimore: Paul H. Brookes Publishing Co.

Notbohm, E. (2007). *The autism trail guide: Postcards from the road less traveled.* Arlington, TX: Future Horizons.

Raab, M., & Dunst, C.J. (2004). Early intervention practitioner approaches to natural environ-ment interventions. *Journal of Early Intervention, 27*(1), 15–26.

Turkington, C. (2009). Welcome to Holland. In Autism Society of Washington and Autism Connection, *Southeastern Washington Resource Guide.* Southeastern, WA: Autism Society of WA and Autism Connection of Eastern WA.

Turnball, A.P. (1996). *Families, professionals, and exeptionality: A special partnership* (3rd ed.). New York: Prentice Hall.

Turnbull, A.P., Summers, J.A., Lee, S-H., & Kyzar, K. (2007). Conceptualization and measure-ment of family outcomes associated with families of individuals with intellectual disabilities. *Mental Retardation and Developmental Disabilities Research Reviews, 13,* 346–356.

9

Brothers and Sisters

The Family Includes Everyone

Gail L. Ensher and David A. Clark

CHAPTER HIGHLIGHTS

At the conclusion of this chapter, the reader will

- Understand the impact of a child's disability or chronic illness on siblings

- Understand siblings' questions and concerns about a child's disability or chronic illness

- Understand ways in which professionals can assist parents in addressing siblings' concerns

- Understand how sibling responses to chronic illness and disability change over time

- Understand some strategies that can assist with siblings' adjustment to a child's disability or chronic illness

Rett syndrome is characterized by typical development for the first 6–9 months of age followed by a progressive decline in skills, "loss of purposeful hand use and with characteristic hand wringing," and the onset of associated autistic-like behaviors (Gordon, 2007, p. 690). A mother of a child with Rett syndrome recounted a discussion (Vargo, 2010) with her younger, typically developing daughter about what the word *handicapped* meant:

> One day my youngest daughter and I were riding a bus, and we saw a sign marked "handicapped" next to one of the seats. I explained what the sign meant and then, interested in what she would say, asked: Mary, do you know anyone who is handicapped? Her response was: No, Mom, I do not know anyone who is handicapped!

Some siblings, however, exhibit a different response toward a child's disability. Ingman wrote:

> Parents and other adults often assume that the other children in the family may not be aware of their sibling's illness or are not impacted by it. They may even be reluctant to share information about the illness in an effort to "protect" their other children. But the reality is that even very young children will be aware that something serious is happening and will notice that their family has changed.
>
> Siblings of children with cancer often worry about their brother or sister's health. They may be afraid that the ill child will die. They may also worry about their own health, thinking that they too might "catch" cancer. In addition, children worry about how their parents are coping or whether their family will ever get back to normal. They might not talk about their fears in an effort to protect their parents or other family members from further stress. (2003, p. 271)

FAMILY: THE PRIMARY CONTEXT FOR SIBLING UNDERSTANDING AND WELL-BEING

Given the widely accepted systems approach to studying families, there has been much interest over the past 3 decades concerning the adjustment and resilience of siblings of infants and young children with special health care needs and disabilities (Burke, 2009; Cox, Marshall, Mandleco, & Olsen, 2003; Hastings, 2007; Kresak, Gallagher, & Rhodes, 2009; Lobato & Kao, 2002; Mandleco, Olsen, Dyches, & Marshall, 2003; Meyer & Vadasy, 2008; Petalas, Hastings, Nash, Lloyd, & Dowey, 2009; Pilowsky, Yirmiya, Doppelt, Gross-Tsur, & Shalev, 2004; Sharpe & Rossiter, 2002; Shudy et al., 2006; Van Riper, 2000). Research investigations and vignettes such as the ones at the beginning of this chapter indicate a range of responses from siblings toward a child with special needs. Some findings indicate that brothers and sisters of chil-

dren with special needs are more sensitive, compassionate, and understanding
of illness and disability than siblings
within the population of same-age peers
at-large. Other researchers have hypoth-
esized that having a young child with disabilities or special health care needs
adds stress to the family and that these
increased demands may affect siblings'
well-being and behavior. Given such con-

trasts, it is clear that professionals need to pay attention to siblings' needs, as
"the relationships among siblings is one of the most important, dynamic, influ-
ential, and long lasting of all human relationships" (Cox et al., 2003, p. 398).

At the very least, when a child with special health care needs or a disability
is born into a family there are significant changes to the family's routines, such
as visits to the hospital and increased caregiving and medical needs. Demands
will vary with time, sometimes easing and sometimes increasing. Researchers
who have examined the impact of illness and disability on siblings have looked
at a number of questions, including the following:

Does birth order affect siblings' responses to a brother or sister with a disability or illness?

There is considerable reason to assume that if child with special needs is the
firstborn, other children in the family grow up with a sense that this is the
way that life has always been. This was reflected in the vignette at the beginning of this chapter, in which the younger sister, as well as another sister not
mentioned in the vignette, had never known life without their older sister
with Rett syndrome and to this day believe that she has greatly enriched all
of their lives. Although it is impossible to know what their chosen vocations
might have been had they not had a sister with a disability, both younger
daughters chose the medical and clinical health care professions as adults
and consider their sister a central part of their lives.

Is sibling adjustment affected by either the gender of the child with special needs or the gender of the sibling?

As siblings become adults, caretaking for individuals with a disability largely
becomes the responsibility of female siblings, thus the gender of the sibling
with no disability can make a difference. However, this question has no
simple answer and does vary with family circumstances and individual family responsibilities.

Does the nature of a child's health condition or disability influence siblings' adjustment?

Responses to this question vary a great deal, and depend on a number of factors. For example, researchers have compared the adjustment of siblings of
children with Down syndrome with that of siblings of children with autism. It

seems reasonable to assume that brothers and sisters of children with behavioral challenges might have more adjustment difficulties due to increased demands upon parents' time and energy, family disruptions, limitations on friends' visits, and restricted family time away from home (e.g., for vacations and recreational activities). Siblings and families may experience periods of instability and restricted mobility due to health care crises, such as newborns' admission to neonatal intensive care units (NICUs), and chronic illnesses that require frequent hospitalizations. Studies, however, seem to support the finding that despite periods of added stress, families are amazingly resilient, cohesive, and adaptive (Hastings, 2007; Pilowsky et al., 2004) if they have adequate resources and support. In fact, living with a sibling can be a "positive, growth producing experience" (Van Riper, 2000, p. 279).

Does sibling age at the time of diagnosis or onset of illness have an impact on siblings' adjustment and well-being?

The age of siblings at the time of diagnosis or onset of illness of a brother or sister can be an advantage or a disadvantage, depending on the nature of family interactions and the responsibilities placed on siblings by parents. For example, Burke (2009) and Sharpe and Rossiter (2002) made reference to the caregiving tasks assumed by older siblings. Such responsibilities can enhance sibling perceptions of brothers and sisters with special needs; however, if these responsibilities become burdensome and overwhelming, they may result in negative interactions and adjustment outcomes.

Most likely, the dynamics within individual families will ultimately determine how siblings respond to having a brother or sister with a disability or illness.

QUESTIONS, QUESTIONS, QUESTIONS

When a child is born with a disability or becomes ill, siblings may raise questions that are especially troubling to parents because they are often the very questions parents have asked themselves and for which they have found no answers. Addressing this issue, Kresak and colleagues wrote,

Negative effects on siblings can be ameliorated by increased openness about the child with disabilities. . . . Parents may sometimes be at a loss with how to answer siblings' questions, but siblings need and want honest, direct, and comprehensible information regarding the child with disabilities. . . . By including siblings and giving them information about their sibling's disability, parents can help ensure that the siblings become better adjusted to living with a child with disabilities. (2009, p. 143)

In a survey of parents with young children with disabilities (birth to 3 years of age) in a southeastern state's Part C early intervention program, parents were given a sibling questionnaire (Kresak et al., 2009). Among the questions was the following: "What questions do brothers/sisters ask about your child in [early intervention]?" Parents responded with the following:

- Why is she like that?
- Can't the doctor take away the extra chromosome?
- Why does she have therapy?
- Why doesn't she walk like me?
- Why can't he talk?
- Is she going to be able to go to regular school?
- Will he be able to get married and have children? (2009, pp. 148–149)

Questions came from siblings from a wide age range—21 months to 17–20 years. Kresak and her colleagues added that an overwhelming number of responses to the question "As a parent, what do you need to know to ensure that your children are comfortable with their sibling's special needs?" focused on "explaining the disability to the siblings" (2009, p. 149).

The sibling survey study (Kresak et al., 2009) is further instructive to professionals in the qualitative findings that

helped define how siblings are included in early intervention routines by providers, such as having the sibling in exercise/therapy with the child with special needs, educating the sibling on how to play or interact with the child with special needs, and asking and answering questions with the sibling. (p. 149)

Information resources for siblings should change with their age and abilities, as well as those of their brothers and sisters with a disability or chronic illness. Play and reading easily understood books offer appropriate avenues of explanation for younger siblings, as well as communication about challenging behavior, delays in development, or ongoing hospitalizations. For older siblings, the Internet, age-appropriate books, and workshops specifically designed for siblings (e.g., *Sibshops,* which are discussed later in this chapter) are viable resources.

FRIENDS AND FAMILY OUTINGS

Although family is the primary context for facilitating sibling understanding of a child's disability or chronic illness, children interact in other settings, and having a brother or sister with special needs often does cause restrictions for siblings. Burke wrote,

> Siblings are aware of the condition that disability imposes on their brothers or sisters, plus the restrictions placed on their own lives. . . . [They] do express their views, sometimes frustrations, to their parents and, despite providing support and assistance within the family, which mirrors reactions within many families, these are not the same as the experience of their peers due to the additional expectations placed upon them. (2009, pp. 12–13)

When peers and friends become aware of the disability or chronic illness, uncomfortable issues often arise for siblings:

- Friends may ask difficult questions.
- Siblings may feel embarrassed to invite peers to their homes or feel embarrassed about their brother's or sister's behavior.
- Siblings may be excluded from invitations to the homes of others because peers are fearful that the brother or sister also may be present.
- Family times at home, in the community, and on vacation with friends may be limited because of medical restrictions or demands on parents, which again may be a source of embarrassment for siblings.

Challenges such as these are very real and may not be readily solved, although professionals can offer assistance such as providing information, taking time with siblings on home or hospital visits, and helping parents with appropriate explanations. Professionals can also talk to siblings when problems with peers arise, visit schools to address questions (e.g., about cancer and treatment for diabetes), and connect siblings with groups of children who are experiencing similar circumstances. Most important, siblings should not be left on their own as they struggle with concerns but should receive support and guidance.

LATER QUESTIONS

As children grow older, parents struggle with concerns about who will provide for their son or daughter with a disability or chronic illness when they are no longer able to do so. Will this responsibility fall to siblings? As discussed in Chapter 6, in some cultures it is almost assumed that a family member—a brother, sister, or other relative—will act as caregiver.

A parent of a young adult with autism has shared her concerns for her son's future (Autism Speaks, 2010):

> For years we fought side by side, battling for the right school, therapy, job coach, and lately housing. Now, as he moves toward greater independence as an adult, the number one concern my husband and I have for our son is his growing isolation.

The supreme dread for us, and for every middle-aged parent of a special needs adult, the singular ache that dries the mouth and races the heart at 3 a.m. is loneliness: Who will offer my child a healthy, loving touch when I am no longer there? Who will care if he has not made it home by the end of the day? And if there is no one, will there be a safe shelter for him somewhere?

Although professionals cannot eradicate such concerns, as Burke wrote,

Helping siblings through professional intervention is possible. . . . Parents need to talk to their children about future plans . . . so that siblings feel included and understand parental intentions. . . . The need of siblings is to reduce a sense of isolation and difference to others while enabling a sharing of experiences with those who might learn to understand the needs of disabled children and their families. (2009, p. 15)

BENEFICIAL OUTCOMES: IMPLICATIONS FOR FAMILY-BASED INTERVENTIONS

Several family-based interventions have been developed to assist siblings of children with a chronic illness or disability (Lobato & Kao, 2005; Meyer & Vadasy, 2008; Munch & Levick, 2001). For example, *Sibshops* was initially published in 1994 in recognition that a sibling is the "family member most likely to have the longest lasting relationship with the person with special needs" (Meyer & Vadasy, 1994, p. 1). *Sibshops* was designed to offer opportunities for brothers and sisters of children with special health and developmental needs to "obtain peer support and education within a recreational context" (1994, p. 1). The model assumes "a wellness approach" and was designed for school-age children, although it addresses issues across the developmental age spectrum and includes programs for adult siblings. In both the initial publication (1994) and revised edition (2008), Meyer and Vadasy offer a wealth of games, activities, and information for parents and professionals who are attempting to address the challenges facing siblings. Munch and Levick (2001) developed a program entitled SibNight that is focused on intervention with siblings 3–16 years of age who have a brother or sister in NICU. The program provides information about NICUs using art, pictures, and coloring books for instructional activities. Lobato and Kao (2002) developed and evaluated an integrated group intervention, SibLink, for siblings (8- to 13-year-olds) and parents of children with chronic illness and developmental disabilities. The intervention focused on

Improving sibling knowledge, sibling adjustment to [chronic illness or developmental disability] and siblings' sense of connectedness to other children in similar family circumstances [i.e., "sibling connectedness"]. . . . The SibLink intervention consisted of six 90-minute group sessions, conducted over a 6–8 week period and . . . targeted improving sibling knowledge and identifying and managing sibling emotions with problem-solving around challenging situations and focused on balancing siblings' individual needs . . . .By intervening jointly with siblings and parents, the SibLink model emphasized the family as a primary context for sibling understanding and adjustment to a child's illness or disability. This introduce[d] a shift from previous sibling group interventions that have targeted siblings only as individuals with needs for information and peer support. (2002, pp. 711–715)

Interventions with siblings of children with chronic illness and developmental disabilities are best carried out within a natural, family-based context rather than in isolation. In support of this approach, Lobato and Kao (2005) found that sibling "knowledge of the child's disorder and sibling connectedness increased significantly from pre- to post-treatment for both boys and girls, regardless of the nature of the brother or sister's condition" (p. 678). With reference to psychosocial interventions for childhood cancer, Meyler, Guerin, Kiernan, and Breatnach (2010) reached a similar conclusion. Accordingly, it is our hope that family-centered, relationship-based approaches will open more opportunities for meaningful learning by all family members and will be beneficial across a variety of hospital, home, school, and community settings.

Thinking It Through: Questions for Discussion

1. In preparing specific activities and opportunities for siblings to learn about their brother's or sister's illness or disability, what modifications would you make for younger siblings? for school-age siblings? for adolescents?

2. What resources might you recommend to families of children experiencing negative reactions toward their brother's or sister's illness or disability?

3. What strategies might you suggest to families when parent time for siblings is severely limited by caregiving responsibilities?

REFERENCES

Autism Speaks. (2010, April 8). *In their own words: What happens when I am no longer here?* Retrieved February 27, 2010, from http://blog.autismspeaks.org/2010/04/08/itow-finland/

Burke, P. (2009, August). Brothers and sisters of disabled children: The experience of disability by association. *British Journal of Social Work, 6,* 1–19.

Cox, A.H., Marshall, E.S., Mandleco, M., & Olsen, S.F. (2003). Coping responses to daily life stressors of children who have a sibling with a disability. *Journal of Family Nursing, 9*(4), 397–413.

Gordon, E.S. (2007). Syndromes and inborn errors of metabolism. In M.L. Batshaw, L. Pellegrino, & N.J. Roizen (Eds.), *Children with disabilities* (6th ed., pp. 690–697). Baltimore: Paul H. Brookes Publishing Co.

Hastings, R.P. (2007). Longitudinal relationships between sibling behavioral adjustment and behavior problems of children with developmental disabilities. *Journal of Autism and Developmental Disorders, 37,* 1485–1492.

Ingman, K.A. (2003). Helping siblings in the classroom. In N. Keene (Ed.), *Educating the child with cancer* (pp. 271–277). Kensington, MD: Candlelighters Childhood Cancer Foundation.

Kresak, K., Gallagher, P., & Rhodes, C. (2009). Siblings of infants and toddlers with disabilities in early intervention. *Topics in Early Childhood Special Education, 29*(3), 141–154.

Lobato, D.J., & Kao, B.T. (2002). Integrated sibling-parent group intervention to improve sibling knowledge and adjustment to chronic illness and disability. *Journal of Pediatric Psychology, 27*(8), 711–716.

Lobato, D.J., & Kao, B.T. (2005). Brief report: Family-based group intervention for young siblings of children with chronic illness and developmental disability. *Journal of Pediatric Psychology, 30*(8), 678–682.

Mandleco, B., Olsen, S.F., Dyches, T., & Marshall, E. (2003). The relationship between family and sibling functioning in families raising a child with a disability. *Journal of Family Nursing, 9*(4), 365–396.

Meyer, D.J., & Vadasy, P.F. (1994). *Sibshops: Workshops for siblings of children with special needs.* Baltimore: Paul H. Brookes Publishing Co.

Meyer, D.J., & Vadasy, P.F. (2008). *Sibshops: Workshops for siblings of children with special needs* (Rev. ed.). Baltimore: Paul H. Brookes Publishing Co.

Meyler, E., Guerin, S., Kiernan, G., & Breatnach, F. (2010). Review of family-based psychosocial interventions for childhood cancer. *Journal of Pediatric Psychology,* 1–17.

Munch, S., & Levick, J. (2001). "I'm special, too": Promoting sibling adjustment in the neonatal intensive care unit. *Health and Social Work, 26*(1), 58–64.

Petalas, M.A., Hastings, R.P., Nash, S., Lloyd, T., & Dowey, A. (2009). Emotional and behavioural adjustment in siblings of children with intellectual disability with and without autism. *Autism, 13*(5), 471–483.

Pilowsky, T., Yirmiya, N., Doppelt, O., Gross-Tsur, V., & Shalev, R.S. (2004). Social and emotional adjustment of siblings of children with autism. *Journal of Child Psychology and Psychiatry, 45*(4), 855–865.

Sharpe, D., & Rossiter, L. (2002). Siblings of children with a chronic illness: A meta-analysis. *Journal of Pediatric Psychology, 27*(8), 699–710.

Shudy, M., de Almeida, M.L., Ly, S., Landon, C., Groft, S., Jenkins, T.L., et al. (2006). Impact of pediatric critical illness and injury on families: A systematic literature review. *Pediatrics, 118*(Suppl. 3), S203–S218.

Van Riper, M. (2000). Family variables associated with well-being in siblings of children with Down syndrome. *Journal of Family Nursing, 6*(3), 267–286.

Vargo, R. (2010). Personal stories shared in Families of Infants and Young Children with Disabilities course. Syracuse, NY: Syracuse University.

10

The Ills of Substance Abuse and Child Abuse and Neglect

Gail L. Ensher and David A. Clark

CHAPTER HIGHLIGHTS

At the conclusion of Chapter 10, the reader will

- Understand the cycles of substance abuse and child abuse in families

- Understand the connection between substance abuse and child abuse

- Understand how substance abuse and child abuse affect everyone in a family

- Understand some warning signs of substance abuse and child abuse

- Understand strategies to address substance abuse and child abuse in families

We never knew her family, her mother or her father. She and her natural-born family lived in a distant land—likely without enough to clothe or feed themselves, and surely not enough resources to take care of a malnourished infant, born 6 weeks early in a country of hardships. What did become clear, however, as her adoptive family entered the teenage years and beyond was that there must have been patterns of substance abuse that then followed their daughter, like an overarching shadow, that changed her behavior with a heavy handprint of challenge over a multitude of life's tasks and responsibilities. (Anonymous, 2010)

THE MAGNITUDE OF ABUSE AND NEGLECT IN THE UNITED STATES

The focus of this chapter—working with families in which there is substance abuse and child abuse and neglect—is one of the most pressing areas of intervention to address. It is evident to practitioners and well documented by researchers that substance abuse is a major risk factor for the abuse and neglect of infants and young children (Barth, 2009; Dawe, Harnett, & Frye, 2008; Kerwin, 2005; Staudt & Cherry, 2009). Barth wrote,

> Researchers have identified four common occurring parental risk factors—substance abuse, mental illness, domestic violence, and child conduct problems—that lead to child maltreatment. The extent to which maltreatment prevention programs must directly address these risk factors to improve responsiveness to parenting programs or can directly focus on improving parenting skills . . . remain uncertain . . .
>
> Substance abuse by a child's parent or guardian is commonly considered to be responsible for a substantial proportion of child maltreatment reported to the child welfare services. Studies examining the prevalence of substance abuse among caregivers who have maltreated their children have found rates ranging from 19 to 79 percent or higher. One widely quoted estimate of the prevalence of substance abuse among caregivers involved in child welfare is 40 to 80 percent. An epidemiological study published in the *American Journal of Public Health* in 1994 found 40 percent of parents who had physically abused their child and 56 percent who neglected their child met lifetime criteria for an alcohol or drug disorder. (2009, pp. 95–96)

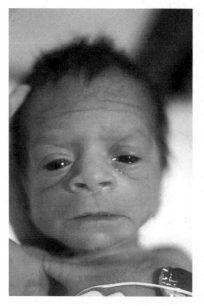

Despite the multitude of technological resources in the United States today, some of the most tenacious, widespread social concerns yet to be adequately resolved are those of child abuse and neglect and parental substance abuse. McGuinness and Schneider (2007) noted that "unfortunately, some indicators suggest that the mental health of U.S children will grow worse: Even as our country's wealth has increased, overall access to mental health care has decreased, and the few existing services for children have declined to a disproportionately greater degree" (2009, p. 296).

THE ECOLOGICAL CONTEXT OF SUBSTANCE AND CHILD ABUSE

Children grow up in families within an ecological context. Ideally, family members are interdependent and thrive in healthy relationships with one other and with individuals outside the family. But when parents become entwined in the web of substance abuse, children are likely to suffer, and these vicious cycles are apt to repeat themselves across generations (Ensher & Clark, 2009; Young, Boles, & Otero, 2007). Such problems have existed within families for decades, as noted by Young et al.:

> Studies have suggested that a sizable majority of the families involved in child welfare services (CWS) are affected by parental substance use disorders (SUDs). However, the information systems that routinely collect and store data in the CWS and substance abuse treatment systems—the Statewide Automated Child Welfare Information System (SACWIS) and the Treatment Episode Data Systems (TEDS)—do not require states to collect specific data elements that would allow policy makers to monitor three critical populations: families in CWS who are affected by SUDs, the children of parents who enter substance abuse treatment and may be at increased risk of child abuse or neglect, and children who come to the attention of CWS because they are prenatally exposed to alcohol or drugs. (2007, p. 137)

The problems related to substance abuse and child neglect and abuse are significant, and estimates do not capture the magnitude of the reality of occurrence (Dawe et. al., 2008; University of New Hampshire, 2009; Whitaker, Lutzker, & Shelley, 2005). Although studies on the impact of prenatal drug exposure have reported mixed results (Smith, Johnson, Pears, Fisher, & DeGarmo, 2007), the consequences of living in often chaotic and violent environments created by parents who are substance abusing are clearly seen in children's poor emotional, social, and developmental outcomes (Baldwin, Songer, & Ensher, 2009; Ensher & Clark, 2009).

The myriad factors associated with substance abuse and child abuse and neglect are well known and have been documented for years. These include but are not limited to poverty, social isolation, lower levels of education, parental histories of violence and neglect, lack of resources and parenting skills, poor parental mental health and depression, violent communities, adolescent pregnancies, limited parental intellect, and selected populations of children (e.g., preterm infants and children with disabilities) (Accornero, Morrow, Bandstra, Johnson, & Anthony, 2002; Ensher & Clark, 2009). Such variables often combine to erupt into volatile situations and/or neglect in families and profoundly affect the youngest victims (Landy & Menna, 2006; Smith et al., 2007); that is, children 5 years of age or younger (Ensher & Clark, 2009).

IN HARM'S WAY: THE ILLS HURT EVERYONE

When a parent abuses drugs and/or alcohol and that abuse leads to multiple forms of child maltreatment and neglect, the family becomes the client, and the family must be the focus of intervention. All members of the family are in harm's way, and the effects are long lasting and require both immediate and long-term intervention (Jordan & Sketchley, 2009).

Research findings point to the long-term developmental and emotional effects of child abuse and neglect. Ensher and Clark wrote,

> Within families with histories of chronic child abuse, neglect, and violence, it is common to find mothers and fathers who suffer from a lack of resources and resilience (Kerr, Black, & Krishnakumar, 2000; Zelenko, Lock, Kraemer, & Steiner, 2000) and who also may struggle with issues of depression or other social-emotional issues (Berger, 2005; Mammen, Kolko, & Pilkonis, 2002). These circumstances place their children at further risk for abuse and neglect. (2009, p. 276)

Moreover, patterns of abuse seem to repeat themselves; that is, children who have grown up in families where they have been the victims of abuse are more likely as adults to abuse their own children.

Consequences of child abuse can be seen in children placed in foster care because of family maltreatment. Of particular concern are the adverse influences on early brain and child development that may accompany "negative environmental conditions including a lack of stimulation, child abuse, and violence" (American Academy of Pediatrics Committee on Early Childhood, Adoption and Dependent Care [AAP Committee], 2000). The AAP Committee emphasized the critical importance of continuity of care, attachment and stability, and a nurturing environment for psychologically healthy infants and young children. The AAP Committee wrote,

> Physical and mental abuse during the first few years of life tends to fix the brain in an acute stress response mode that makes the child respond in a hyper-vigilant, fearful manner. Research demonstrates chemical and electrical evidence for this type of brain response pattern. . . . When an infant is under chronic stress, the response may be apathy, poor feeding, withdrawal, and failure to thrive. When the infant is under acute threat, the typical "fight" response to stress may change from crying (because crying did not elicit a response) to temper tantrums, aggressive behaviors, or inattention and withdrawal. . . . Older children who have been repeatedly traumatized often suffer from posttraumatic stress disorder and automatically freeze when they feel anxious, and therefore are considered oppositional or defiant by those who interact with them. (pp. 1146–1147)

A *ScienceDaily* article (Children's Hospital of the King's Daughters, 2008) highlighted the little-studied problem of children's exposure to parental abuse of siblings and the eventual serious consequences within families. The article noted,

> In many cases, when abusive parents with multiple children target just one child for emotional or physical cruelty, authorities often remove the abused child from the home and return the non-abused siblings.

> But brothers and sisters of abused children can suffer lifelong emotional scars from helping parents conceal the abuse or, in extreme cases, from being forced to participate in torturing their siblings, according to a study published in the current issue of the *Journal of Emotional Abuse*. (p. 1)

As noted previously, abusive relationships in one generation can lead children, later as parents themselves, to be abusive in turn, despite the benefits of intervention (Ensher & Clark, 2009; Schuler, Nair, & Black, 2002).

As evident in the vignette at the beginning of this chapter, possible prenatal exposure to drugs and/or alcohol can be manifested in learning and behavioral challenges in adolescence and adulthood in a number of ways, including attention-deficit/hyperactivity disorder (ADHD), sensory issues, learning disabilities, and mental health concerns. Although this statement should not be interpreted to suggest that there is invariably a direct correlation between maternal substance abuse and these conditions in children, diagnoses of these conditions in the presence of high-risk environments may indicate one point of origin.

WARNING SIGNS OF CHILD MALTREATMENT

As mandated reporters, professionals such as physicians, teachers and child care personnel, school nurses, and social workers must be vigilant about warning signs of child maltreatment (i.e., neglect, physical abuse, sexual abuse, and emotional abuse) (Kellogg and the American Academy of Pediatrics Committee on Child Abuse and Neglect, 2007). Warning signs, which vary with developmental and chronological age, include the following:

- Abrupt changes in behavior
- Withdrawal; aggression or other manifestations of antisocial behavior toward peers
- Inappropriate and/or out-of-character play behavior, suggesting sexual abuse
- Child reports of mother, self, or others at home being hit
- Heightened fears or anxieties toward peers and/or adults
- Excessive fatigue, indicating a chronic lack of sleep
- Frequent absence from school with no reasonable explanation
- Physical marks on the child, burns, or fractures with no reasonable explanation or explanations that are discrepant with age-appropriate accidents
- Chronic unexplained illnesses
- Regression in toileting, language skills, and other developmental milestones
- Social isolation

Moreover, as Ensher and Clark indicated,

> When child maltreatment happens, inevitably there are serious, short-term and long-term effects for young children. Depending on the severity, frequency, age of the child, availability of other significant people to buffer situations, and the type of abuse (i.e., sexual, social-emotional, or physical) or neglect (i.e., social-emotional or physical), the developmental and social-emotional consequences will vary, which

point to diverse needs in intervention and/or remediation treatment programs. (2009, p. 279)

HOW TO BRING ABOUT CHANGE AND WHO CAN HELP

Despite the fact that the prevention of child abuse and intervention with multi-risk families constitute a high-priority agenda with the American Academy of Pediatrics (AAP Committee, 2000; Kairys, Johnson, & the American Academy of Pediatrics Committee on Child Abuse and Neglect, 2002), the Centers for Disease Control and Prevention (Whitaker et al., 2005), Child Protective Services, and other national and state organizations, adequately addressing these problems in the United States continues to be a major challenge. Much research over the past 3 decades has focused on identifying risk and protective factors associated with child maltreatment, perpetuation, and victimization (Whitaker et al., 2005). However, these efforts are complicated by the lack of uniform definitions of child maltreatment across states, inconsistencies in reporting, inconsistencies of investigation of suspected cases, lack of a national public health surveillance system, and inadequate understanding of multiple risk factors. Moreover, it is clear that outcomes for children exposed to multirisk environments (especially substance abuse) are extremely varied. Some children are negatively affected by these environments; others appear to be more resilient, with no apparent negative consequences of their past experiences. In this regard, Velleman and Templeton wrote,

> It is easy to see why commentators have been pessimistic about the future of children brought up in such an environment. However, . . . rather different outcomes might be possible. It seems that not all individuals are adversely affected, either as children or as adults. . . . There seem to be factors and processes that can minimize the negative impact of parental drug or alcohol misuse, or protect against them. Thus, some children are resilient and develop no significant problems related to their parents' substance misuse. . . .
>
> Resilience should be conceptualized as a process, rather than a static trait and/or something solely internal to the individual (Glantz & Johnson, 1999; Little et al., 2004; Masten et al., 1990; Rutter, 1987; Werner, 1993). And as a process it is the product of an interaction between the individual and their social context; hence, it is potentially open to influence. (2007, p. 81)

The authors noted several "protective factors," including the following:

- The presence of a stable adult figure
- A close positive bond with at least one adult in a caring role (e.g., parents, older siblings, grandparents)
- A good support network (e.g., friends, neighbors, community resources, teachers)
- Parents' positive caregiving styles and characteristics
- Engagement in a range of activities
- Individual child temperament
- Positive opportunities at times of transition
- Continuing family cohesion and harmony in the face of the misuse and its related effects (p. 83)

Despite heightened awareness of warning signs by professionals and the establishment of numerous intervention programs, most contemporary reports indicate that society still falls short of reaching families before abuse and neglect take place (primary prevention), after documentation of an isolated incident of abuse and neglect (secondary prevention), and after repeated offenses have occurred (tertiary prevention) (Whitaker et al., 2005). A major focus of the Centers for Disease Control and Prevention is primary prevention, because "it may be easier to intervene to prevent abuse or neglect from developing than to intervene to change behaviors that are already well-established" (Whitaker et al., 2005, p. 251). Depending on the occurrence and co-occurrence of events in families, professional intervention may vary in intensity and follow-up as well as in the specific steps taken toward prevention and amelioration.

BENEFICIAL OUTCOMES: THE LONG ROAD TO RECOVERY, RECONCILIATION, AND BEYOND

Because infants, young children, and families spend a significant amount of time with physicians, nurses, teachers, and to a lesser degree social workers, these are the professionals who will most often report suspected instances of abuse and who will intervene in partnership with other community agencies, such as those involved in child welfare. Both medical and educational settings likely will be the most frequent points of contact with families. Professionals must remember that establishing relationships with families is an essential part of both prevention and remediation of child abuse and neglect. As Daro and Dodge (2009) wrote, "By building relationships with families, early care and education programs can recognize signs of stress and strengthen families' protective factors with timely, effective help" (p. 76).

Common Elements of Successful Intervention

Common elements of successful interventions with families have been identified over the past 10 years (Daro & Dodge, 2009). As is evident in the following core of common elements of successful intervention and descriptions of programs of promise, efforts to realize maximum benefits on behalf of children and families will require collaboration across agencies and from multiple partners, including families. Supporting this idea of partnerships and collaboration within the medical community, Foy, Perrin, and the American Academy of Pediatrics Task Force on Mental Health stated,

> Primary care clinicians who are interested in enhancing mental health services in their community will need to form partnerships. Key partners for a community mental health advocacy effort include other primary care clinicians, developmental-behavioral pediatricians, adolescent health specialists, the local public mental health agency, representatives of the mental health care provider community (e.g., psychiatrists, psychologists, social workers, substance abuse counselors, psychiatric nurse practitioners), community mental health activists including parents and youth, school system representatives, early childhood educators, Early-Intervention

(EI) system representatives, representatives of the child protective and juvenile jus-
tice systems, and the local department of public health. (2010, p. S75)

The need to keep children safe in their homes and communities has often
led to interventions that have punished families in order to ameliorate wrong-
doings, and this may be initially unavoidable. However, focusing on reducing
risk factors of abuse and increasing protective factors and resilience are alternative strategies that professionals can pursue—even in difficult circumstances—
that will involve the child, family, and the broader community (Velleman & Templeton, 2007). In particular, Velleman and Templeton suggested two general
strategies for working with families: first, efforts at reducing family discord and
violence, and second, efforts to strengthen protective factors for children outside of and within the family on behalf of the child. Such efforts will not be
achieved quickly because often such adversities reflect longstanding histories of
the parents themselves. However, as we have discussed throughout this book, focusing on cohesion and facilitating positive relationships within families in the
long term are much more likely to result in beneficial outcomes for both children
and their caregivers and parents. These have been some of the highlights of successful strategies in addressing issues of child abuse and neglect within families.

Programs of Promise

Intervention programs designed to address the problems of child abuse and neglect are not new, and an extensive review of these approaches is beyond the
scope of this chapter. However, we have selected three noteworthy programs
that have shown promise for change in families and that reflect newer philoso-
phies of change and adaptation within multirisk families. These programs are a
hospital-based parent education program (Dias et al., 2005), Triple P—Positive
Parenting Program (Barth, 2009), and ECIPs—Early Childhood Intervention
Programs (Asawa, Hansen, & Flood, 2008).

A Hospital-Based Parent Education Program
In December 1998, all
hospitals in an eight-county region of western New York that provided maternity
care participated in a comprehensive regional program that focused on parent
education about violent shaking of infants (Dias et al., 2005). The program was
offered to parents of all newborn infants prior to discharge from the hospital.
Both mothers and fathers (as available) were given information about the dangers of violent shaking of infants and alternative responses to persistent crying;
they subsequently were asked to sign a statement of commitment, indicating their
receipt and understanding of the information. The goals of this program were

1. To provide a universal, consistent education program to parents of all newborn infants in the region
2. To assess parents' knowledge about the dangers of violent infant shaking
3. To track the dissemination of information through the return of commitment
   statements (CSs) signed by one or both parents
4. To assess the impact of the program on the regional incidence of abusive head
   injuries among infants and children <36 months of age (2005, p. e471)

The regional incidence of abusive head injuries was followed prospectively within this population of infants and young children over a 66-month period, from December 1998 through May 2004, and compared with the historical incidence rates of substantiated abusive head trauma in the Commonwealth of Pennsylvania during the years 1996 through 2002.

At the end of the first phase of the study, Dias and his colleagues arrived at the following conclusions:

> During the first 5.5 years of the program, 65,205 CSs were documented, representing 69% of the 94,409 live births in the region during that time; 96% of the CSs were signed by mothers and 76% by fathers/father figures. Follow-up telephone surveys 7 months later suggested that >95% of parents remembered having received the information. The incidence of abusive head injuries decreased by 47%, from 41.5 cases per 100,000 live births during the 6-year control period to 22.2 cases per 100,000 live births during the 5.5-year study period. No comparable decrease was seen in the Commonwealth of Pennsylvania during the years 1996–2002, which bracketed the control and study periods in western New York State.
>
> A coordinated, hospital-based, parent education program, targeting parents of all newborn infants, can reduce significantly the incidence of abusive head injuries among infants and children <36 months of age. (2005, p. e470)

Some of the most promising aspects of this study were that it was comprehensive, prospective, and longitudinal in nature and reached participants with information before abuse or neglect had taken place.

The Triple-P: Positive Parenting Program   The Positive Parenting Program (Triple-P) is a multilevel, evidence-based intervention first developed in Australia by Matthew Sanders and colleagues. Triple-P has received fairly wide recognition and has been used in several countries, including the United States. As described by Barth (2009), the program was designed to include five levels of intervention and was based on five principles of social learning theory integral to teaching positive parenting:

> ensuring a safe and engaging environment, creating a positive learning environment, using assertive discipline, having realistic expectations, and taking care of oneself as a parent. The conceptual underpinning of Triple-P is that the parent must be "self-regulatory," meaning that she believes that she can improve the behavior of her child through her own actions and is confident in making decisions and problem-solving to do so. (pp. 103–104)

At the time of this writing, Triple-P was being piloted in South Carolina in a major study, the Durham Family Initiative, Strong Communities, and Community Partnerships for Protecting Children (CPPC). Modifications targeted adolescent parents and their children, behavioral and emotional problems of children, parents of children with developmental disabilities, and parents considered to be at risk for child abuse. Barth noted the following:

> The results of this first major U.S. Triple-P trial are quite promising. After training more than 600 primary care practitioners in Triple-P, and implementing the uni-

versal media strategies in half of eighteen counties randomly assigned to Triple-P in South Carolina, Ronald Prinz found that administering Triple-P to families in a population of 100,000 children under the age of eight resulted in 340 fewer cases of maltreatment, 240 fewer children being removed from their homes, and 60 fewer injuries from maltreatment requiring medical attention. (2009, p. 104)

This evidence-based program has incorporated some noteworthy dimensions: It is a large-scale study, prospective in nature, and community based, and it has yielded positive results for children and families as well as for service providers.

Early Childhood Intervention Programs The primary goal of Early Childhood Intervention Programs (ECIPs; a broad class of programs rather than one specific program) is "to promote healthy development and prevent negative outcomes for at-risk children" (Asawa et al., 2008, p. 74). The programs, although extremely diverse, share a common theme: Intervention is preventive and begins early in life before more significant problems develop, and it is based on a developmental-ecological framework. The programs are designed "to address multiple problems at multiple levels and across multiple settings, increasing the likelihood that child maltreatment can be prevented" (Asawa et al., p. 75). In particular, ECIPs include programs that "can address child maltreatment through *promotion* of healthy families, *prevention* of maltreatment in high-risk families, and *early intervention* for children who have been identified as maltreated (National Public Health Partnership, 2003)" (Asawa et al., p. 81). Service providers who might be involved in ECIPs include nurses, mental health professionals, paraprofessionals, social workers, teachers, and law enforcement officers. Overall, several of these programs have demonstrated very promising results within the first years of implementation, although not all have shown encouraging long-term findings.

ECIPs include a variety of models in the United States, perhaps the most common being home-based visitation programs. The first statewide visitation program was Hawaii's Healthy Start Program, which focused on the major goal of preventing child maltreatment. The program initially included 234 families in Leeward, Oahu, an impoverished community with high rates of child abuse and neglect (Asawa et al., 2008). Initial findings, based on evaluation of the 3-year demonstration project, were very positive, with statistically significant reductions in family stress and no evidence of child abuse or neglect in any of the families involved in the study. However, results have not been sustained long term in the Healthy Start Program, which has been challenged by low rates of home visiting, differences across participating agencies, and reporting difficulties.

A second home-based ECIP effort is the Nurse-Family Partnership (NFS), also known as the Nurse Home Visitation Program, originally developed by David Olds more than 2 decades ago (Kitzman et al., 2000; Olds et al., 2002, 2007). With the assistance of trained nurses with reduced caseloads, the goals of this home visiting program were improving child health and development and facilitating economic self-sufficiency of families (Asawa et al., 2008). Home visitors offered parent education, connected families to community resources, and strengthened family support networks.

Long-term follow-up of a randomized trial of 743 mothers with infants born at less than 29 weeks of gestation has been promising, with fewer subsequent births and longer-lasting relationships with family partners, thus enhancing family cohesion, and better overall school performance of children in nurse-visited families. Finally, and most important, there was a trend within nurse-visited families of fewer deaths of young children from the ages of birth through 9 years (Olds et al., 2007).

The fact that all of the programs described here were to some degree successful in bringing about changes in family lifestyle, interactions, and relationships is significant. All of the programs were conducted with the recognition that patterns of substance abuse and/or child abuse and neglect are frequently resistant to modification because they represent repeated incidents over generations and are fueled by the violence in families' communities.

To be sure, challenges in addressing these pervasive problems in the United States and other countries remain (Harden, 2010). Still needed are the following:

- Better ways to train school personnel (teachers and school counselors) to recognize and report suspected cases of child abuse and neglect (Hinkelman & Bruno, 2008)
- Better ways to focus efforts on preventive strategies and programs
- Better ways to engage and retain high-risk families throughout the duration of programs
- Better ways to recognize child abuse and neglect in families across all income and educational levels, especially in those families in which incidents are least suspected and usually not identified

Thinking It Through: Questions for Discussion

1. What training strategies might better prepare school personnel to recognize and work with children and families at risk for child abuse and neglect?
2. What strategies might help improve retention of high-risk families in preventive and remediation child abuse and neglect programs?
3. What protective strategies can professionals use to strengthen resilience in young children exposed to violence in their homes and neighborhoods?

REFERENCES

Accornero, V.H., Morrow, C.E., Bandstra, E.S., Johnson, A.L., & Anthony, J.C. (2002). Behavioral outcome of preschoolers exposed prenatally to cocaine: Role of maternal behavioral health. *Journal of Pediatric Psychology, 27*(3), 259–269.

American Academy of Pediatrics Committee on Early Childhood, Adoption, and Dependent Care. (2000). Developmental issues for young children in foster care. *Pediatrics, 106*(5), 1145–1150.

Asawa, L.E., Hansen, D.J., & Flood, M.F. (2008). Early childhood intervention programs: Opportunities and challenges for preventing child maltreatment. *Education and Treatment of Children, 31*(1), 73–110.

Baldwin, H., Songer, N.S., & Ensher, G.L. (2009). The cycle of substance abuse. In G.L. Ensher, D.A. Clark, & N.S. Songer (Eds.), *Families, infants, and young children at risk: Pathways to best practice* (pp. 249–272). Baltimore: Paul H. Brookes Publishing Co.

Barth, R.P. (2009). Preventing child abuse and neglect with parent training: Evidence and opportunities. *The Future of Children, 19*(2), 95–118.

Children's Hospital of the King's Daughters (2008, March 6). Brothers and sisters of abuse victims often help cover up or even commit abuse, study says. *ScienceDaily*. Retrieved June 25, 2010, from http://www.sciencedaily.com/releases/2008/03/080305163224.htm

Dawe, S., Harnett, P., & Frye, S. (2008). Improving outcomes for children living in families with parental substance misuse: What do we know and what should we do. *Child Abuse Prevention Issues, 29*, 1–14.

Daro, D., & Dodge, K.A. (2009). Creating community responsibility for child protection: Possibilities and challenges. *The Future of Children, 19*(2), 67–93.

Dias, M.S., Smith, K., deGuehery, K., Mazur, P., Veetai, L., & Shaffer, M.L. (2005). Preventing abuse head trauma among infants and young children: A hospital-based, parent education program. *Pediatrics, 115*(4), e470–e477.

Ensher, G.L., & Clark, D.A. (2009). The web of family abuse, neglect, and violence. In G.L. Ensher, D.A. Clark, & N.S. Songer (Eds.), *Families, infants, and young children at risk: Pathways to best practice* (pp. 273–286). Baltimore: Paul H. Brookes Publishing Co.

Foy, J.M., Perrin, J., & the American Academy of Pediatrics Task Force on Mental Health. (2010). Enhancing pediatric mental health care: Strategies for preparing a community. *Pediatrics, 125*(Suppl. 3), S75–S86.

Harden, B.J. (2010, July). Home visitation with psychologically vulnerable families: Developments in the profession and in the professional. *Zero to Three*, 44–51.

Hinkelman, L., & Bruno, M. (2008). Identification and reporting of child sexual abuse: The role of elementary school professionals. *The Elementary School Journal, 108*(5), 376–391.

Jordan, B., & Sketchley, R. (2009). A stitch in time saves nine: Preventing and responding to the abuse and neglect of infants. *Child Abuse Prevention Issues, 30*, 1–26.

Kairys, S.W., Johnson, C.F., & American Academy of Pediatrics Committee on Child Abuse and Neglect. (2002). The psychological maltreatment of children—Technical report. *Pediatrics, 109*(4). Retrieved June 25, 2010, from http://www.pediatrics.org/cgi/content/full/109/4/e68

Kellogg, N.D., & the American Academy of Pediatrics Committee on Child Abuse and Neglect. (2007). Evaluation of suspected child physical abuse. *Pediatrics, 119*(6), 1232–1241.

Kerwin, M.E. (2005). Collaboration between child welfare and substance-abuse fields: Combined treatment programs for mothers. *Journal of Pediatric Psychology, 30*(7), 581–597.

Kitzman, H., Olds, D.L., Sidora, K., Henderson, C.R., Jr., Hanks, C., Cole, R., et al. (2000). Enduring effects of nurse home visitation on maternal life course. *Journal of the American Medical Association, 283*(15), 1983–1989.

Landy, S., & Menna, R. (2006). *Early intervention with multi-risk families: An integrative approach.* Baltimore: Paul H. Brookes Publishing Co.

McGuinness, T.M., & Schneider, K. (2007). Poverty, child maltreatment, and foster care. *Journal of the American Psychiatric Nurses Association, 13*(5), 296–303.

Olds, D.L., Kitzman, H., Hanks, C., Cole, R., Anson, E., Sidora-Arcoleo, K., et al. (2007). Effects of nurse home visiting on maternal and child functioning: Age-9 follow-up of a randomized trial. *Pediatrics, 120*(4), e832–e845.

Olds, D.L., Robinson, J., O'Brien, R., Luckey, D.W., Pettitt, L.M., Henderson, C.R., Jr., et al. (2002). Home visiting by paraprofessionals and by nurses: A randomized, controlled trial. *Pediatrics, 110*(3), 486–496.

Schuler, M.E., Nair, P., & Black, M.M. (2002). Ongoing maternal drug use, parenting attitudes, and a home intervention: Effects on mother–child interaction at 18 months. *Developmental and Behavioral Pediatrics, 26,* 87–94.

Smith, D.K., Johnson, A.B., Pears, K.C., Fisher, P.D., & DeGarmo, D.S. (2007). Child maltreatment and foster care: Unpacking the effects of prenatal and postnatal parental substance
use. *Child Maltreatment, 12*(2), 150–160.

Staudt, M., & Cherry, D. (2009). Mental health and substance use problems of parents involved with child welfare: Are services offered and provided? *Psychiatric Services, 60*(1),
56–60.

University of New Hampshire (2009, October 7). High rates of childhood exposure to violence and abuse in the United States, new study finds. *ScienceDaily.* Retrieved June 23, 2010,
from http://www.sciencedaily.com/releases/2009/10/091007081351.htm

Velleman, R., & Templeton, L. (2007). Understanding and modifying the impact of parents'
substance misuse on children. *Advances in Psychiatric Treatment, 13,* 79–89.

Whitaker, D.J., Lutzker, J.R., & Shelley, G.A. (2005). Child maltreatment prevention priorities
at the Centers for Disease Control and Prevention. *Child Maltreatment, 10*(3), 245–259.

Young, N.K., Boles, S.M., & Otero, C. (2007). Parental substance use disorders and child maltreatment: Overlap, gaps, and opportunities. *Child Maltreatment, 12*(2), 137–149.

11

Family Loss, Disasters, and Young Children

Gail L. Ensher and David A. Clark

CHAPTER HIGHLIGHTS

At the conclusion of this chapter, the reader will

- Be aware of the emotions and trauma experienced by families who lose an infant or young child in death

- Understand ways in which professionals can support families through the loss of an infant or young child

- Understand the trauma of losing loved ones in wars and disasters, and learn ways in which professionals can support individuals in the healing process

- Understand ways in which professionals can support families through the trauma of deployment in war and military service

Families experience loss in many different ways—the death of an infant in the neonatal intensive care unit, the death of a child with multiple disabilities and impairments, family loss and displacement as a result of natural disasters, and the temporary or permanent loss of a family member in military service. This chapter will focus on these family tragedies and the strategies professionals can use to support families through bereavement and recovery.

The following scenarios recount the loss of a child from a parent's and professional's viewpoint. Recalling the death of her 5-year-old daughter, Beth Harry wrote,

> I lost all the control that had kept me going through the wonderful years of knowing and loving Melanie . . . and as they lay her on the bed, oxygen mask over her face, and started pumping her chest, I crouched in a corner some 6 feet away and waited, every ounce of belief and disbelief suspended for those few hopeful moments. This was a doctor, he would save her.
>
> Time was frozen for those moments. The doctor stopped, took off his stethoscope, and looked at me, shaking his head. (2010, pp. 198–199)

FAMILY LOSS: DEATH OF A CHILD

The loss of a family member is always catastrophic. When parents lose an infant or a young child, however, they can feel, as Beth Harry did, "frozen in time." The pain is unimaginable, like none other, even when the possibility of death was always present. Worlds are "forever changed" in ways that never could have been imagined before that loss (Forhan, 2010, p. 142).

With advances in technology and pharmacology, the threshold of viability for infants born prematurely has been lowered (Pignotti & Donzelli, 2008; Singh, Lantos, & Meadow, 2004). Controversies about aggressive medical treatments and ethical issues have escalated and require families and medical staff to make heart-wrenching decisions. Even when an extremely preterm infant does survive, the full picture of developmental outcomes and the effects on behavior and learning may not be known for years (Richardson, 2001):

The birth of an extremely preterm infant is invariably a crisis for parents. It is often unexpected, dashing their dreams of a perfect full-term newborn and casting them into a nightmare of prolonged uncertainty and, all too often, of chronic handicap. The toll on parents can be enormous, including depression, marital discord, financial burdens, and potential loss of employment. Often the mothers are not well from the underlying illnesses that precipitated the preterm birth (preeclampsia and chorioamnionitis), from chronic medical conditions (diabetes, hypertension, and collagen vascular diseases), from birth itself (cesarean delivery), or from complications (septicemia, wound infection, and re-tained placental products). Post-partum maternal depression is common even after term births and can be amplified by the sense of failure and guilt in very preterm births. Increasingly, preterm birth is a result of multiple gestation usually resulting from fertility treatments. The emotional bind in these cases may be in-tense, with parents having undergone extensive treatments to overcome infertil-ity—often at advanced maternal age—then facing wrenching decisions about fetal reduction [parents making decisions to have selective abortions of one or more fe-tuses]. (pp. 1499–1500)

Although professionals can never recover the child who has died, they can help families through palliative care and during the bereavement processes (Engler et al., 2004; Macdonald et al., 2005; Pierucci, Kirby, & Leuthner, 2001). Nurses and physicians, in particular, are likely to be engaged with families in end-of-life care and the family's time of grieving. In this regard, Engler and col-leagues (2004) emphasized the need for cultural sensitivity and more education for nurses regarding their "crucial effect on a family's response to their infant's death" (p. 490). Following are some ways hospital, school, and clinical staff can help families after the death of an infant or a young child:

- Having the family hold the child in the hospital or at home

- Making a memory box of footprints, pictures, and hair for the family in the hospital (Forhan, 2010)

- Taking photos of the child (some families have returned to claim photos years after the death of their newborn) (Ohlson, 2010)

- Follow-up phone calls and visits with family to communicate the continuing importance of the relationship professionals had with the child and family

- Attending individual and collective memorial or funeral services with the family

- Holding pediatric memorial services in the hospital (Penson, Green, Chabner, & Lynch, 2002)

- Sending sympathy cards and cards on the child's birthday or anniversary of the child's death

- Making commemorative books with illustra-tions to celebrate the child's life

- Facilitating connections with other families who have lost children

- Connecting the family with a bereavement counselor, if requested, to facilitate the tran-sition to another professional who can be available on a more regular basis

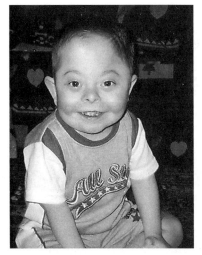

Macdonald and colleagues noted parents' appreciation of staff members' efforts to commemorate a child's life:

> Efforts to support families and to commemorate deceased children are appreciated by bereaved parents. Staff members' absences at commemorative events and a lack of supportive acts are noticed and regretted by families. Staff members and program administrators should attempt to arrange workloads to ensure meaningful contact between staff members and parents during the bereavement period. . . .
>
> The memorial service is particularly significant for parents. Although a collective service cannot give focused attention to individual children, listing each child by name and lighting a candle in his or her memory is meaningful for parents and. . . . siblings. The service fosters community by bringing family members and staff members together and forces a return to the hospital, which, although emotionally difficult, has many positive aspects for families [e.g., the care, compassion, and information that was offered to the infant and family during hospitalization; relationships developed with other families in hospital]. (2005, pp. 884, 889)

To best assist families through the bereavement process, medical staff and teachers will need guidance relating to self-awareness, therapeutic efficacy, sensitivity to professional boundaries, and healthy coping in their continuing relationships with families.

We have included a discussion of memorial services here because we believe that it is a dimension that remains unaddressed by professionals, particularly in the long term, and that this may cause families to feel isolated and abandoned during their greatest moments of need if an infant or young child has died (Bruce, 2007). Although the ways in which families recover and restructure their lives, attribute understanding, and regain a sense of community and hope following the loss of a child need further study, Macdonald and colleagues (2005) and Truog, Christ, Browning, and Meyer (2006) suggested that families' experiences can be greatly affected by their ongoing relationships with professionals and other families. Even as professionals experience many of the same emotions as family members when a young child dies, they are in a powerful position to facilitate and ensure "a more healthful closure to a sad but normal process of life" (Bruce, 2007, p. ES40).

TRAGEDY ON AMERICAN SOIL AND THE AFTERMATH

The extensive loss of human life and the scope of devastation as a result of the acts of terrorism on September 11, 2001, were unprecedented in the United States. Approximately 3,000 people were killed in the city of New York alone.

Professionals have predicted severe and long-lasting psychological effects on families throughout the country (Galea et al., 2002; Gershoff, Aber, Ware, & Kotler, 2010; Melnyk et al., 2002). Approximately 20% to 25% of children and adolescents directly affected by the attacks encountered some mental health difficulty, including such concerns as how to cope with stressful events in their lives, anxiety, depression, low self-concept, and strained relationships with parents (Melnyk et al., 2002). An associated and very connected side effect of these attacks were the young children and families who witnessed the suffering portrayed daily on their television screens; those observations were not without indirect, adverse effects.

Although time has passed since the events of that day, keen reminders remain:

- Many families were traumatized and fractured by the loss of friends, mothers, fathers, children, grandparents, and other close relatives. In particular, as a result of direct exposure to terrorism or indirectly as a result of the impact of terrorism on their mother's psychological functioning (i.e., mothers with both depression and posttraumatic stress disorder [PTSD]), preschool children were found to be more likely to develop "clinically significant behavioral problems" (Chemtob et al., 2010, p. 1129).

- Family members of those deployed or lost to the ravages of war struggle with feelings of vulnerability (Butz & Pulsifer, 2002).

- Global media coverage daily enters homes with keen reminders of terrorism and the threat of war, as noted previously (Ryan-Wenger, 2002; Villalba & Lewis, 2007).

- The proposed building of a mosque near the site of Ground Zero has heightened bias toward Muslim families (Foxman, 2010), with young children inadvertently becoming the innocent targets of such prejudices.

Parents, teachers, physicians, nurses, social workers, the clergy, and other professionals find themselves at the forefront of dealing with the impact of natural and human-made disasters on the development and mental health of young children and adolescents (Leavitt, 2002). As Veenema and Schroeder-Bruce (2002) pointed out, "the resultant war in Afghanistan and the current situation in the Middle East have focused on our need to understand the aftermath of disasters and other acts of violence and their impact on children" (p. 235). The July/August 2010 issue of *Child Development* was devoted to the effect of disasters on children, including two longitudinal studies that examined the effects of the September 11, 2001, terrorist attacks on New York City on children and their families (Masten & Osofsky, 2010). The authors wrote,

> With the rise in international terrorism, concerns about the flu pandemic, an alarming sequence of natural and human-designed disasters around the world, and globalization of media coverage, there is increasing attention to the consequences of disaster for children and youth. (p. 1029)

It is impossible to evaluate the true impact of a disaster on families and young children and their long-term needs. As Masten and Osofsky (2010) pointed out, the complexities of carrying out meaningful, longitudinal research are extensive. Although the shadows of terrorism were evident before September 11, 2001, this kind of attack on American soil was inconceivable to most. However, disasters like this teach important lessons.

The lessons for preventive intervention from the growing body of research on disasters and children in terms of developmental guidelines can be summarized as follows:

1. Protect and restore the secure base of attachment relationships as soon as feasible. Prepare for evacuations and relocations that include keeping children together with their caregivers. Reunite children and adults who have attachment bonds if they have to be separated. Provide nurturing caregivers for children who have lost their caregivers.
2. Train first responders in the range of developmental responses to trauma that can be expected for children of different ages.
3. Remember that first responders for children include parents, teachers, and daycare providers in addition to physicians, nurses, and emergency responders.
4. Support normalizing routines, activities, and contexts for children after disasters, including opportunities for them to play and learn, and the restoration of functional schools and other community organizations that serve children and their families.
5. Attend to community resilience and the function of cultural and community practices that support families and their children, including support for spiritual practices.
6. Support and restore meaningful relationships and opportunities to be effective in play, school, work, or recovery activities. (Masten & Osofsky, 2010, p. 1037)

The lessons for preventive intervention relate not only to the aftermath of September 11 but also to the losses suffered by families during times of continuing war and natural disasters. Although there is no single solution for protecting children and promoting resilience through overwhelming adversity, these guidelines emphasize the importance of maintaining children's connections to caregivers with whom they have significant relationships.

FAMILY LOSS: TIMES OF WAR AND MILITARY SERVICE

The threat of war or loss of a family member in war overshadowed the closing decades of the 20th century and ushered in the first years of the 21st century as U.S. troops were deployed to Afghanistan, the Middle East, and other locations. Ryan-Wenger posed key questions relating to families with young children:

Since 1990, the number of military personnel deployed for war and operations other than war has never been higher. . . . But how prepared for war are the 3.36 million *children* of military parents? What is it like for children who have parents who could be deployed at any moment? To what extent does living with the threat of war cause fear, anxiety, or other emotional responses in children? Are military

health care providers overlooking a need for anticipatory guidance or intervention
for military families? (2002, p. 245)

Researchers and practitioners are becoming increasingly aware of changes
that take place in families when family members are deployed for extended periods of time or are killed in military duties. For instance,

- There is a higher incidence of child abuse and neglect when family members
  are deployed, particularly by female civilian and non-Hispanic white parents
  (Gibbs, Martin, Kupper, & Johnson, 2007; Levin, 2007). Respite care, child
  care, and home visits are three possible supports that may help relieve some
  of the stress experienced by family members in the absence of a partner or
  spouse.

- Young children in military families appear to experience more emotional
  and behavioral challenges (i.e., higher levels of anxiety) as parent deployments are extended (Chandra et al., 2010; Chartrand, Frank, White, & Shope,
  2008; *ScienceDaily*, 2009).

- Prolonged deployment of U.S. Army husbands or partners is associated with
  elevated mental health diagnoses, such as depressive disorders, among wives
  or partners (Mansfield et al., 2010). Such issues may be related to separation
  and return of spouses, disruption of family life, managing of family households as single parents, and fear for the safety of loved ones deployed. Young
  children affected by parental mental health issues need to develop new coping strategies. The absence of needed support from school and community
  may "lead to conflict and risk of poor educational outcomes" for children
  (Fitzsimons & Krause-Parello, 2009). Fitzsimons and Krause-Parello elaborated further:

Evidence of a child's failure to cope may be seen in emotional and somatic symptoms. Military children may feel emotional symptoms of stress such as loneliness,
depression, and anxiety. . . . Feelings such as loneliness may be lessened through
the use of coping strategies, which can include relationships with friends and other
significant attachment figures as these relationships are important to a child's social development.

- Children of military families may face isolation or exclusion if they are forced
  to move from neighborhood schools closer to relatives due to the deployment
  of one parent or both. In the event that a parent is killed, they may be overwhelmed with bereavement (Lamberg, 2004).

- Studies seem to indicate that "parental combat deployment has a cumulative effect on children that remains even after the deployed parent returns home"
  (Lester et al., 2010, p. 206) [e.g., long-term feelings of depression, loneliness,
  even abandonment].

Professionals can provide support proactively to children of military families with whom they have relationships. Frequently, these professionals will be
teachers and physicians who have regular or intermittent contact with children

and their families and have network connections with other professionals who •
can be called upon when needed for counseling, play and recreational groups,
and possibly play therapy opportunities, as needed.

NATURAL DISASTERS

> Hurricane Katrina has been described as one of the worst natural disasters in U.S.
> history (Knabb, Rhome, & Brown, 2006).
>
> Immediately after Katrina struck the Gulf Coast on August 29, 2005, both
> physical and psychological recovery began, and now years later, it has continued to
> affect residents and communities in Louisiana.
>
> Of particular interest to child development is the occurrence of large-scale
> traumas, such as Hurricane Katrina, which affect both the microsystems and ex-
> osystems in which children develop (Bronfenbrenner, 1986; Masten & Obradovic,
> 2008). For many children of Katrina, their once-thriving neighborhoods, grocery
> stores, and playgrounds are no longer functional; many children experienced
> multiple moves and changes in schools as well as parental unemployment. . . . The
> outcomes for these children are still under question. (Kronenberg et al., 2010, p.
> 1241)

Almost without exception, families that have endured the ravages of natural disasters such as Hurricane Katrina, tornadoes, earthquakes, and tsunamis
are forever changed. With widespread devastation followed by weeks, months,
and years of rebuilding, recovery processes influence outcomes for young children in many ways. Such outcomes have been the focus of keen interest among
child development scholars and specialists (Broughton, Allen, Hannemann, &
Petrikin, 2006; Kilmer & Gil-Rivas, 2010; Kronenberg et al., 2010; Masten & Osofsky, 2010; Mills, Edmondson, & Park, 2007; Osofsky, Osofsky, Kronenberg,
Brennan, & Hansel, 2009; Roussos et al., 2005; Scaramella, Sohr-Preston, Callahan, & Mirabile, 2008; Scheeringa & Zeanah, 2008; Sprung, 2008; Thienkrua et
al., 2006; Weems & Overstreet, 2008).

Among the questions asked by researchers, with clear implications for practitioners, are the following:

1. Are there age and gender differences in outcomes among children and adolescents, depending upon whether they are younger or older at the time
   that they are exposed to natural disasters?
2. Do adverse effects on children vary with parents' mental health state? In particular, does the primary caregiver's well-being help protect children from
   more long-term and devastating mental health problems, such as posttraumatic disorders and depression?
3. When children manifest mental health or behavioral problems in the aftermath of disasters, are these typically short or long term?
4. What qualities serve as protective factors? What variables seem to heighten
   children's psychological or physical vulnerability, such as an already existing
   disability?

Such questions can best be answered as researchers, educators, clinicians, and physicians examine both the ecology of natural disaster devastation and individual family member recovery patterns. In so doing, as described by Masten and Osofsky (2010), communities might then better prepare themselves for natural disasters. Such preparation perhaps is more easily achieved in global locations previously affected by

hurricanes, tsunamis, tornadoes, or earthquakes. However, the reality of natural disasters is that they often happen without warning and in resource-poor countries and communities with widespread poverty. This has been especially true in the first years of the 21st century in which economies have been stagnant and families across the globe have been living with heightened levels of stress. Schools and medical homes have become especially important in wide-scale recovery processes (Masten & Osofsky, 2010) and will undoubtedly play a significant role in future preparedness endeavors. These authors noted that "prompt reestablishment of schooling was one of the most highly endorsed best practices emerging from the consensus study based on the expertise of humanitarian agency leaders with extensive disaster experience" (p. 1035). This has also been emphasized for children who have been exposed to other disaster situations such as war (Masten & Osofsky, 2010).

In light of findings regarding elevated prevalence of serious emotional disturbance (SED) among youth several years after exposure to the devastation of Hurricane Katrina (McLaughlin et al., 2010), proactive mental health intervention by professionals who work with families and young children is warranted. McLaughlin and colleagues concluded,

> The results are quite clear in showing that the prevalence of SED among youths who lived through Hurricane Katrina continues to be substantially elevated several years post-hurricane. . . .This finding points to the importance of expanding public health interventions to focus on the most highly exposed youths in an effort to reduce the burden of psychiatric problems. (2010, p. 999)

BENEFICIAL OUTCOMES: RECOVERY, REBUILDING, AND RESILIENCE

In the best of circumstances, recovery, rebuilding, and resilience among families exposed to human-made and natural disasters are extraordinarily challenging. Despite such challenges, lessons learned during recovery can yield strategies for the future. Professionals across multiple disciplines have suggested several strategies to "enhance mental health services" in communities (Foy, Perrin, &

the American Academy of Pediatrics Task Force on Mental Health, 2010, p. S75). These include the following:

- Understand the mental health needs of children, adolescents, and their families, focusing in particular on those protective factors that foster resilience. Foy and colleagues (2010) noted the importance of such variables as effective schools, including high-quality preschools; clear standards for behavior; recognition of achievement and positive self-esteem; positive bonds with schools; strong family relationships and networks; and structured and caring parenting (p. S77).

- Develop partnerships among mental health, medical, and educational advocates and resources in communities. The authors stated that "care-coordination mechanisms are critically important to child and family well-being" (p. S78). They suggest that the National Registry of Evidence-Based Programs and Practices is an excellent resource for child and adolescent psychosocial intervention programs.

- Develop a "community protocol for psychiatric emergencies" to address issues of trauma in human-made and natural disasters, such as "overcrowding, exposure to stressful sights and sounds, and long delays" (p. S81).

- Focus on groups of children with known higher needs, such as those with disabilities and special health care needs, those living in especially high-risk neighborhoods, and those who are in the child welfare system.

- Develop mental health, medical, and educational strategies that are culturally sensitive to populations residing in local communities and cities.

- Integrate and share knowledge across disciplines from studies of children and families who have lived through natural and human-made disasters.

Thinking It Through: Questions for Discussion

1. What community mechanisms could be used to facilitate closer partnerships among professionals in educational and allied health disciplines in planning for disaster relief?

2. In light of research findings showing gender differences (i.e., increased vulnerability to depression among females) and age differences (i.e., increased vulnerability to mental health problems among younger children) in response to human-made and natural disasters, what strategies might be incorporated into school and pediatric services to address such issues?

3. Given that family relationships and networks are crucial to the well-being of children and adolescents in disaster situations, what preventive strategies might be developed to strengthen family ties, especially in times of vulnerability, such as when one or both parents are deployed in military service?

REFERENCES

Aldridge, M.D. (2005). Decreasing parental stress in the pediatric intensive care unit: One unit's experience. *Critical Care Nurse, 25*(6), 40–50.

Broughton, D.D., Allen, E.E., Hannemann, R.E., & Petrikin, J.E. (2006). Getting 5000 families back together: Reuniting fractured families after a disaster: The role of the National Center for Missing & Exploited Children. *Pediatrics, 117*(5), S442–S445.

Bruce, C.A. (2007). Helping patients, families, caregivers, and physicians in the grieving process. *Journal of the Osteopathic Association, 107*(12, Suppl. 7), ES33–ES40.

Butz, A., & Pulsifer, M. (2002). Research on the impact of the threat of war on children in military families: Where do we go from here? *Journal of Pediatric Health Care, 16,* 262–264.

Chandra, A., Lara-Cinisomo, A., Jaycox, L.H., Tanielian, T., Burns, R.M., Ruder, T., et al. (2010). Children on the homefront: The experience of children from military families. *Pediatrics, 125*(1), 16–25.

Chartrand, M.M., Frank, D.A., White, L.F., & Shope, T.R. (2008). Effect of parents' wartime deployment on the behavior of young children in military families. *Archives of Pediatric and Adolescent Medicine, 162*(11), 1009–1014.

Chemtob, C.M., Nomura, Y., Rajendran, K., Yehuda, R., Schwartz, D., & Abramovitz, R. (2010). Impact of maternal posttraumatic stress disorder and depression following exposure to the September 11 attacks on preschool children's behavior. *Child Development, 81*(4), 1129–1141.

Engler, A.J., Cusson, R.M., Brockett, R.T., Cannon-Heinrich, C., Goldberg, M.A., West, M.G., et al. (2004). Neonatal staff and advanced practice nurses' perceptions of bereavement/end-of-life care of families of critically ill and/or dying infants. *American Journal of Critical Care, 13*(6), 489–498.

Fitzsimons, V.M., & Krause-Parello, C.A. (2009). Military children: When parents are deployed overseas. *Journal of School Nursing, 25*(1), 40–47.

Forhan, M. (2010). Doing, being, and becoming: A family's journey through perinatal loss. *The American Journal of Occupational Therapy, 64*(1), 142–151.

Foxman, A.H. (2010, August 2). *The mosque at Ground Zero.* Retrieved August 24, 2010, from http://www.huffingtonpost.com/abraham-h-foxman/the-mosque-at-ground-zero_b_668020

Foy, J.M., Perrin, J., & the American Academy of Pediatrics Task Force on Mental Health. (2010). Enhancing pediatrics mental health care: Strategies for preparing a community. *Pediatrics, 125*(Suppl. 3), S75–S86.

Galea, S., Ahern, J., Resnick, H., Kilpatrick, D., Bucuvalas, M., Gold, J., et al. (2002). Psychological sequelae of the September 11 terrorist attacks in New York City. *The New England Journal of Medicine, 346*(13), 982–987.

Gershoff, E.T., Aber, J.L., Ware, A., & Kotler, J.A. (2010). Exposure to 9/11 among youth and their mothers in New York City: Enduring associations with mental health and sociopolitical attitudes. *Child Development, 81*(1), 1142–1160.

Gibbs, D.A., Martin, S.L., Kupper, L.L., & Johnson, R.E. (2007). Child maltreatment in enlisted soldiers' families during combat-related deployments. *Journal of the American Medical Association, 298*(5), 528–535.

Harry, B. (2010). *Melanie, bird with a broken wing: A mother's story.* Baltimore: Paul H. Brookes Publishing Co.

Kilmer, R.P., & Gil-Rivas, V. (2010). Exploring posttraumatic growth in children impacted by Hurricane Katrina: Correlates of the phenomenon and developmental considerations. *Child Development, 81*(4), 1211–1227.

Knabb, R.D., Rhome, J.R., & Brown, D.P. (2006). *Tropical cyclone report: Hurricane Katrina.* Retrieved May 11, 2011, from http://nhc.noaa.gov/pdf/TCR-AL12205_Katrina.pdf

Kronenberg, M.E., Cross, T.H., Brennan, A.M., Osofsky, H.J., Osofsky, J.D., & Lawrason, B. (2010). Children of Katrina: Lessons learned about postdisaster symptoms and recovery patterns. *Child Development, 81*(4), 1241–1259.

Lamberg, L. (2004). When military parents are sent to war, children left behind need ample support. *Journal of the American Medical Association, 292*(13), 1541–1542.

Leavitt, L.A. (2002). When terrible things happen: A parent's guide to talking with their children. *Journal of Pediatric Health Care, 16,* 272–274.

Lester, P., Peterson, K., Reeves, M., Knauss, L., Glover, K., Mogil, C., et al. (2010). The long war and parental combat deployment: Effects on military children and at-home spouses. *Journal of the American Academy of Child & Adolescent Psychiatry, 49*(4), 310–320.

Levin, A. (2007, September 7). Military deployment stress tied to child-abuse increase. *Psychiatric News, 42*(17), 8–9.

Macdonald, M.E., Liben, S., Carnevale, F.A., Rennick, J.E., Wolf, S.L., Meloche, D., et al. (2005). Parental perspectives on hospital staff members' acts of kindness and commemoration after a child's death. *Pediatrics, 116*(4), 884–890.

Mansfield, A.J., Kaufman, J.S., Marshall, S.W., Gaynes, B.N., Morrissey, J.P., & Engel, C.C. (2010). Deployment and the use of mental health services among U.S. Army wives. *The New England Journal of Medicine, 362*(2), 101–109.

Masten, A.S., & Osofsky, J.D. (2010). Disasters and their impact on child development: Introduction to the special section. *Child Development, 81*(4), 1029–1039.

McLaughlin, K.A., Fairbank, J.A., Gruber, M.J., Jones, R.T., Osofsky, J.D., Pfefferbaum, B., et al. (2010). Trends in serious emotional disturbance among youths exposed to Hurricane Katrina. *Journal of the American Academy of Child & Adolescent Psychiatry, 49*(10), 990–1000.e2.

Melnyk, B.M., Feinstein, N.F., Tuttle, J., Moldenhauer, Z., Herendeen, P., Veenema, T.H., et al. (2002). Mental health worries, communication, and needs in the year of the U.S. terrorist attack: National KySS Survey findings. *Journal of Pediatric Health Care, 16,* 222–234.

Mills, M.A., Edmondson, D., & Park, C.L. (2007). Trauma and stress response among Hurricane Katrina evacuees. *American Journal of Public Health, 97*(S1), S116–S123.

Ohlson, K. (2010, July 9). Just a memory before you sleep forever. Retrieved August 2, 2010, from http://www.miller-mccune.com/culture/just-a-memory-before-you-sleep-forever17742/

Osofsky, H.J., Osofsky, J.D., Kronenberg, M., Brennan, A., & Hansel, T.C. (2009). Posttraumatic stress symptoms in children after Hurricane Katrina: Predicting the need for mental health services. *American Journal of Orthopsychiatry, 79*(2), 212–220.

Penson, R.T., Green, K.M., Chabner, B.A., & Lynch, T.J., Jr., (2002). When does the responsibility of our care end: Bereavement. *The Oncologist, 7,* 251–258.

Pierucci, R.I., Kirby, R.S., & Leuthner, S.R. (2001). End-of-life care for neonates and infants: The experience and effects of a palliative care consultation service. *Pediatrics, 108*(3), 653–660.

Pignotti, M.S., & Donzelli, G. (2008). Perinatal care at the threshold of viability: An international comparison of practical guidelines for the treatment of extremely preterm births. *Pediatrics, 121*(1), e193–e198.

Richardson, D.K. (2001). A woman with an extremely premature newborn. *Journal of the American Medical Association (JAMA), 286*(12), 1498–1505.

Roussos, A., Goenjian, A.K., Steinberg, A.M., Sotiropoulou, C., Kakaki, M., Kabakos, C., et al. (2005). Posttraumatic stress and depressive reactions among children and adolescents after the 1999 earthquake in Ano Liosia, Greece. *American Journal of Psychiatry, 162*(3), 530–537.

Ryan-Wenger, N.A. (2002). Impact of the threat of war on children in military families. *Journal of Pediatric Health Care, 16,* 245–252.

Scaramella, L.V., Sohr-Preston, S.L., Callahan, K.L., & Mirabile, S.P. (2008). A test of the family stress model on toddler-aged children's adjustment among Hurricane Katrina impacted and nonimpacted low-income families. *Journal of Clinical Child & Adolescent Psychology, 37*(3), 530–541.

Scheeringa, M.S., & Zeanah, C.H. (2008). Reconsideration of harm's way: Onsets and comorbidity patterns of disorders in preschool children and their caregivers following Hurricane Katrina. *Journal of Clinical Child & Adolescent Psychology, 37*(3), 508–518.

ScienceDaily (2009, December 7). Military children face more emotional challenges as parental deployments grow longer, study finds. Retrieved July 21, 2010, from http://www.sciencedaily.com/releases/2009/12/091207095503.htm

Singh, J., Lantos, J., & Meadow, W. (2004). End-of-life after birth: Death and dying in a neonatal intensive care unit. *Pediatrics, 114*(6), 1620–1626.

Sprung, M. (2008). Unwanted intrusive thoughts and cognitive functioning in kindergarten and young elementary school-age children following Hurricane Katrina. *Journal of Clinical Child & Adolescent Psychology, 37*(3), 575–587.

Thienkrua, W., Cardozo, B.L., Chakkraband, M.I.S., Guadamuz, T.E., Pengjuntr, W., Tantipiwatanaskul, P., et al. (2006). Symptoms of posttraumatic stress disorder and depression among children in tsunami-affected areas in Southern Thailand. *Journal of the American Medical Association, 296*(5), 549–559.

Truog, R.D., Christ, G., Browning, D.M., & Meyer, E.C. (2006). Sudden traumatic death in children—"We did everything, but your child didn't survive." *Journal of the American Medical Association, 295*(22), 2646–2654.

Veenema, T.H., & Schroeder-Bruce, K. (2002). The aftermath of violence: Children, disaster, and posttraumatic stress disorder. *Journal of Pediatric Health Care, 16,* 235–244.

Villalba, J.A., & Lewis, L.D. (2007). Children, adolescents, and isolated traumatic events: Counseling considerations for couples and family counselors. *The Family Journal: Counseling and Therapy for Couples and Families, 15*(1), 30–35.

Weems, C.F., & Overstreet, S. (2008). Child and adolescent mental health research in the context of Hurricane Katrina: An ecological needs-based perspective and introduction to the special section. *Journal of Clinical Child & Adolescent Psychology, 37*(3) 487–494.

12

Homelessness and Young Children

Robin J. Streever, Gail L. Ensher, and David A. Clark

CHAPTER HIGHLIGHTS

At the conclusion of this chapter, the reader will

- Understand some of the factors that lead to homelessness in the United States

- Understand some of the medical, developmental, and educational consequences of homelessness for children

- Be knowledgeable about community-based strategies and educational resources for working with homeless children and their families

 For Jayden's mother, Suzanna—a 25-year-old mother of three at 3, 5, and 7 years of age—homelessness started with abuse. The walls of Jayden's room failed to protect him from the sounds of his father threatening and beating his mother. After 6 years of spousal abuse Suzanna fled with her children, first to a domestic violence shelter and ultimately to a different state.

The family found refuge in an emergency shelter where they shared one room. Soon after arriving, Jayden (7 years) developed an unremitting cough that required several trips to the emergency room. He was ultimately diagnosed with asthma and depression, prescribed medication, and . . . temporary housing for his family was secured. However, the continuing experiences of homelessness took a toll on Jayden's physical and mental health. Asthma triggers pervaded Jayden's environment. His emergency room visits grew more frequent. Coughing and breathing difficulties limited his ability to play, talk, and sleep comfortably. Suzanna's homelessness made it difficult for her to access the services needed to address Jayden's asthma.

Jayden felt excluded from the community where he grew up. Emotionally isolated, he had difficulty connecting with his peers at school. Although Jayden always was aware that the search for a place of safety spurred his family's move, he still longed for the life that he had lost. He blamed himself for his family's presence in the shelter and frequently apologized to his mother for being unable to prevent his father's violence. (Adapted from the National Center on Family Homelessness, 2009, http://www.homelesschildren america.org/pdf/stories/case_studies/cs_impact.pdf)

THE PROBLEM OF HOMELESSNESS

Homelessness has been defined as the lack of a physical dwelling place that can be referred to as *home*, in addition to an unstable set of relationships within the family (Miller et al., 2007). The United States Department of Housing and Urban Development has defined a chronically homeless individual as "an unaccompanied (alone) individual with a disabling condition who either has been continuously homeless for one year or more, or has had, minimally, four episodes of homelessness in the past three years" (Miller et al., 2007, p. 8). The face of homelessness in the United States, however, has changed. It is no longer a condition affecting only individuals with a disabling condition: Families with children are fast becoming the new face of homelessness. In fact, approximately 40% of the homeless population in the United States consists of families with children (Gargiulo, 2006). Whether homeless individuals are young, old, healthy, ill, male, or female, they all have this in common: the challenge to acquire a minimum quality of life in order to meet their basic human needs (Miller et al., 2007).

Causes of Homelessness

There are multiple causes of homelessness, including domestic violence; poverty; war; unemployment; abuse; illiteracy; mental illness; lack of affordable housing; and natural disasters such as hurricanes, tornadoes, earthquakes, and floods (Gargiulo, 2006; Walker-Dalhouse & Risko, 2008). The refugee population has also contributed to the increase in homelessness in the United States (Vostanis, Tischler, Cumella, & Bellerby, 2001).

One cause of the increase in family and child homelessness in the United States is the economic downturn in the early years of the 21st century (Duffield & Lovell, 2008). As a result, America has seen a dramatic growth in unemployment, declines in the stock market, declining home values, and an increase in foreclosures.

Prevalence of Homeless Children and Families

It has been estimated that over 1 million children are homeless in the United States on any given night (Gargiulo, 2006). A study done by Powers-Costello and Swick (2008) revealed that children are the fastest growing group experiencing homelessness. Consistent with these findings, a profile of homeless individuals served by human services agencies in Lansing, Michigan, indicated that women and children represented 1,809 of 3,220 (56.2%) individuals assisted in 2006 (Miller et al., 2007). Similarly, adults and children in family units constituted 1,614 (50.1%) of the homeless population helped by the Greater Lansing human services sector in 2006. Children and youth made up 876 (27.2%) of individuals receiving assistance during this time period. This survey also revealed that female single-parent families represented more than half of all household types served by Lansing-area agencies; nearly one in five two-parent homeless families with children received assistance (Miller et al., 2007).

Furthermore, in the fall of 2008, the National Association for the Education of Homeless Children and First Focus surveyed schools across the United States to determine the extent that school-age children and their families were experiencing homelessness (Duffield & Lovell, 2008). They found the following:

- In the first few months of this school year [2008–2009], 330 school districts identified the same number or more of homeless students than they had identified in the entire previous year [2007–2008].
- In the first few months of this school year [2008–2009], the number of homeless students was half or more of the number from the previous year in 847 school districts.
- From the 2006–2007 school year to 2007–2008, 459 school districts saw an increase of at least 25% in the number of students identified as homeless. (p. 1)

EFFECTS OF HOMELESSNESS ON CHILDREN

As is evident from the vignette about Jayden and his family, children who are homeless face a host of issues. Homelessness means much more for a child than not having a stable home. It can mean mental and emotional stress, problems at school, lack of medical care and attention, and exposure to violence.

Mental Health

Children who are homeless are likely to face mental health difficulties. The reasons for this have been well documented. Homeless youth have been found to experience more stressful life events than their peers who are living in poverty but are not homeless (Buckner, Bassuk, Weinreb, & Brooks, 1999). These events include exposure to violence, history of physical or sexual abuse, placement in foster care, eviction from homes, maternal addiction to drugs or alcohol, extreme maternal stress or mental illness, and parental arrest or incarceration (Buckner et al., 1999; Harpaz-Rotem, Rosenheck, & Desai, 2006).

Buckner and colleagues (1999) found that the condition of being homeless, along with a mother's psychological distress level, correlated significantly with internalizing problem behaviors in children. These internalizing behaviors included depression, self-criticism, somatic complaints, withdrawn behavior, and decreased feelings of self-worth. In this study, 47% of all children who were homeless scored high enough on internalizing behaviors to need clinical referrals, compared with 21% for housed children also experiencing poverty. Maternal incarceration and maternal emotional problems, experienced by many homeless mothers and children, have been found to correlate highly with children's self-esteem and emotional problems (Harpaz-Rotem et al., 2006).

Homeless children worry about where they will sleep, being separated from family (as well as friends and pets), being seen as different, the well-being of their parents and siblings, and their physical safety; these worries contribute to decreased mental health (Hart-Shegos, 1999). Despite children's increased emotional distress and mental illness, less than one third receive professional help (Zima, Wells, & Freeman, 1994). Among children requiring a psychiatric evaluation for depression, only a minority (<33%) had ever received counseling or treatment in their lifetime, and even fewer (19%) had been in special education classes or received special help in school during a prior 12-month period of time (Zima et al., 1994). Children living in a shelter were almost 20 times more likely to have symptoms of depression than prepubescent children in the general population (Zima et al., 1994).

Shelter Living

Although living in a homeless shelter is certainly not ideal, it at least provides children and their families a place to sleep. There is a profound lack of shelter space, however, to address the increase in the number of homeless children. The results of interviews in six diverse homeless shelters in Georgia showed that 75% of such settings did not have spaces available for children, and 10% had only one or two beds unoccupied (Hicks-Coolick, Burnside-Eaton, & Peters, 2003).

Shelters often lack the services families need. There is limited access to developmental, medical, vision, and hearing assessments, a lack of child care for parents seeking work, and a lack of staff knowledge of families' needs (Hicks-Coolick et al., 2003). For example, although the McKinney-Vento Homeless Education Assistance Improvements Act of 2001 (PL 107-110) (discussed in more detail later in this chapter) mandated ways in which children's needs are to be met, less than one half of the key informants in homeless shelters interviewed were familiar with the law (Hicks-Coolick et al., 2003).

Gaps in Education

Children experiencing homelessness face countless difficulties that interfere with their success in school. Little has been done in supporting teachers to effectively meet the needs of students who are homeless or highly mobile (Powers-Costello & Swick, 2008). Homeless children miss more days of school than their peers, and school enrollment among homeless children is significantly lower (Harpaz-Rotem et al., 2006).

Children who are homeless face multiple risks to their educational well-being, including poverty, child maltreatment, low maternal education, and biological birth risks (Rouse & Fantuzzo, 2009). Children's academic performance is frequently hampered by the circumstances of their homelessness, such as constant mobility (Hart-Shegos, 1999). In a second-grade cohort of urban, public school students in a large city in the Northeast, homelessness (in addition to child maltreatment) was found to be related to poor outcomes across all academic and behavioral indicators (Rouse & Fantuzzo, 2009). Controlling for the effects of all other risks, homelessness was one of the strongest indicators for high absenteeism, school suspensions, and poor teacher ratings of children's social skills. Moreover, the study found that with each additional risk, the odds of poor academic and behavioral performance increased, especially in the area of reading proficiency.

Children who are homeless are more likely to score poorly on math, reading, spelling, and vocabulary tests and are more likely to repeat a year in school (Hart-Shegos, 1999). In a study of 18 emergency homeless shelters in Los Angeles, 47% of homeless children scored at or below the 10th percentile in receptive vocabulary, and 39% had a severe delay in reading (Zima et al., 1994).

Children often do not receive the extra help (such as remedial or special education services) they need to succeed in school (Zima, Bussing, Forness, & Benjamin, 1997). Zima and colleagues (1997) found that 20% of children experiencing homelessness had a learning disability, 8% were given a diagnosis of mental retardation, and over 25% had a behavior disorder; however, only 17% of those with a learning disability, 23% of those found to be mentally retarded, and 36% of those with a behavior disorder ever received services. In summary, more than half of children studied needed special education services, but the majority did not receive help. The Los Angeles study (Zima et al., 1994) yielded similar results.

Parental awareness of children's emotional and academic needs may be a contributing factor in whether or not children are evaluated or receive services. For example, among 78% of children with at least one emotional or academic problem, parents of only one third were aware of the problem (Zima et al., 1994). Moreover, of those children identified by a parent as having a problem, only one half had received any type of mental health or academic intervention (Zima et al., 1994).

When homeless students do have the potential to do well academically, frequently teachers view them as deficient in some way (Powers-Costello & Swick, 2008). This perception can become a self-fulfilling prophecy, leading to lowered academic performance. For example, a study in New York City compared the cognitive and academic functioning of children ages 6–11 years who were homeless and living in a shelter with the performance of housed children, controlling for socioeconomic status, age, and sex (Rubin et al., 1996). In reading, 75% of the homeless children scored below grade level, compared with 48% of housed children. In spelling, 72% of the homeless children scored below grade level, compared with 50% of the housed children. In arithmetic, 53% of the homeless children scored below grade level, compared with 21.7% of the housed children. It is imperative to note, however, that although housed children did fare better in academic functioning and achievement, when comparing scores on verbal and nonverbal intelligence tests that measure a student's potential, *there was no statistically significant difference in intelligence or cognitive functioning between housed children and those who were homeless.* Again, this finding may indicate that teachers' lower expectations (in addition to the number of school changes experienced by homeless children) may have more to do with children's academic performance than their actual ability (Rubin et al., 1996).

Exposure to Violence

Exposure to violence is another risk for homeless children, whether it is domestic violence between parents, street violence, violence against children themselves, violence against siblings, or a combination (Swick, 2008). In a study of children who were homeless, more than half said that they worried about their physical safety, especially in regard to violence, guns, and being injured in a fire (Hart-Shegos, 1999). One fourth had witnessed violence in the family. Such experiences may lead to other problems, such as poor parent–child relationships, family isolation (Swick, 2008), and maternal and childhood psychopathology (Vostanis et al., 2001).

Vostanis and colleagues (2001) studied the mental health problems and access to social supports of parents and children who were homeless and had experienced domestic and neighborhood violence. The participants were 93 homeless families from the Birmingham, Alabama, area who self-reported the circumstances of becoming homeless. Half of the sample of children, ages 3–16 years, had become homeless due to domestic violence, 14 families had become homeless due to neighborhood harassment, and 31 families had become homeless for other reasons, such as landlord eviction, overcrowding, refugee status, and natural disasters. Researchers found that families who had experienced neighborhood violence had the highest rates of mental health problems as well as the lowest amount of social support. This finding could be an important touchpoint for professionals looking at ways to alleviate the effects of homelessness and exposure to violence.

Nutrition, Growth, and Development

Families who are homeless often face poverty, which has been linked to lower nutritional levels, malnutrition associated with social withdrawal, delayed motor development, poor brain development, and delayed physical growth (National Center for Children in Poverty, 2009). In addition, children living in poverty are at risk for exposure to nicotine, alcohol, and drugs, as well as elevated lead levels (National Center for Children in Poverty, 2009).

One study found that homeless children had lower height and weight percentiles than housed children, with homeless children from larger families and with single mothers accounting for the lower height percentiles (Fierman et al., 1991). Children experiencing homelessness also exhibited stunting without wasting, a pattern seen in poor children who experience moderate, chronic nutritional stress. Although these characteristics have been identified more frequently among poor children, Fierman and colleagues found that children who were at similar income levels but who were homeless exhibited these problems to a greater degree.

Duffield and Lovell (2008) also found evidence that homeless children are at greater risk than housed children living in poverty in terms of their overall health. The researchers looked at both groups of children in Washington state and found that children who were homeless were 4 times more likely than other comparable groups of children to be in fair or poor health, twice as likely to be in fair or poor health as other children from low-income homes, 2–3 times more likely than their peers who were not homeless to use emergency rooms, and more likely to go without standard immunizations.

Despite these widespread health concerns, homeless children generally lack access to consistent health care, and this lack of health care may increase the severity of illness (Hart-Shegos, 1999). For instance, children who are homeless are at higher risk for infectious diseases; they have 5 times the rate of diarrheal infections, have twice the rate of respiratory infections, and are twice as likely to have a positive skin test indicating exposure to tuberculosis (Hart-Shegos, 1999) or the presence of allergies, as compared with housed children. One third of homeless children have never visited a dentist, and they are more likely to receive poor preventive care and excessive emergency treatment (Hart-Shegos, 1999).

Homelessness can also affect child behavior. Zima and colleagues (1994) compared homeless children with the general population and found that "28% [of the children who were homeless] scored in the borderline clinical range for a serious behavior problem," and "sheltered homeless children were 1.5 times more likely to have symptoms of a behavioral disorder than those children in the measure's large normative general population" (p. 263). As Masten, Miliotis,

Graham-Bermann, Ramirez, and Neemann (1993) noted, these findings may arise in light of the following. Results suggested that

> homeless children have greater stress exposure and fewer resources than low-income children of similar background whose families have housing. . . . Homelessness in children was associated with disrupted friendships and more school changes . . . as we hypothesized, child behavior problems were significantly higher in the home-less sample than in the normative sample, particularly in the domain of antisocial behavior . . . the primary predictors of child behavior problems in this study were parental distress, cumulative risk history, and recent life events . . . the pattern of scores suggest an underlying continuum of risk, with homeless children at greater risk (p. 341).

In addition, Yu, North, LaVesser, Osborne, and Spitznagel (2008) examined behavior disorders among housed children and those who were homeless. The researchers found that "behavior disorders were four times more prevalent in the homeless children than in the housed children" (p. 7). Although another study (Buckner et al., 1999) found no significant differences in behavior problems, Buckner and colleagues did find that "residential instability, out-of-home placement, and histories of physical or sexual abuse were much more common among homeless school-age children, compared to their housed counterparts . . . and the predictor most strongly associated with the internalizing and externalizing scores on the Child Behavior Checklist was the mother's emotional distress" (p. 255).

NEEDED SOLUTIONS

Children's needs and challenges operate in the context of family; thus, whatever the nature of specific solutions adopted, it is crucial that the needs of the entire family be addressed.

Knowledge of Legislation

Educators and other service providers need to be aware of the McKinney-Vento Homeless Education Assistance Improvements Act of 2001. This act ensures that homeless children have the same access to a quality education as do their housed peers. It applies to *all* homeless children, including those who are homeless because they are refugees or victims of natural disasters. Information regarding this act may be found on the U.S. Department of Education's web site (http://www2.ed.gov/programs/homeless/legislation.html). Here, we offer selected information on this legislation. The act states that

1. Each state agency shall ensure that each child of a homeless individual and each homeless youth have equal access to the same free, appropriate public education, including a public preschool education, as provided to other children and youths.
2. In any State that has a compulsory residency requirement as a component of the State's compulsory school attendance laws or other regulations, practices,

or policies that may act as a barrier to the enrollment, attendance, or success in school of homeless children and youths, the State will review and undertake steps to revise such laws, regulations, practices, or policies to ensure that homeless children and youths are afforded the same free, appropriate public education as provided to other children and youths.

3. Homelessness alone is not a sufficient reason to separate students from the mainstream school environment.

4. Homeless children and youths should have access to the education and other services that such children and youths need to ensure that such children and youths have an opportunity to meet the same challenging State student academic achievement standards to which all students are held.

Because this act may pose a financial burden on school districts, the legislation also provides grants for state and local activities for the education of homeless children and youths. The web site provided earlier includes more specific information on these grants, such as application procedures and requirements. The funding is designed to ensure that a district has enough resources so that, for instance, homeless children will not be segregated and that they will receive transportation services, education services, and meals. To receive funding, states must submit a written plan that includes the following:

- A description of programs for school personnel (including principals, attendance officers, teachers, enrollment personnel, and pupil services personnel) to heighten the awareness of such personnel of the specific needs of runaway and homeless youths.
- A description of procedures that ensure that homeless children and youths who meet the relevant eligibility criteria are able to participate in Federal, State, or local food programs.
- Strategies to address other problems with respect to the education of homeless children and youths, including problems resulting from enrollment delays that are caused by
  a. Immunization and medical records requirements
  b. Residency requirements
  c. Lack of birth certificates, school records, or other documentation
  d. Guardianship issues
  e. Uniform or dress code requirements (McKinney-Vento Homeless Education Assistance Improvement Act of 2001).

Another important piece of the legislation deals with how school districts work with children who become homeless during the school year or have to move out of the district because of homelessness:

- IN GENERAL—The local educational agency serving each child or youth to be assisted under this subtitle shall, according to the child's or youth's best interest:
  a. Continue the child's or youth's education in the school of origin for the duration of homelessness—
  b. [Enroll the child] in any case in which a family becomes homeless between academic years or during an academic year; or

    c.   [Enroll the child] for the remainder of the academic year, if the child or youth becomes permanently housed during an academic year; or

    d.   Enroll the child or youth in any public school that non-homeless students who live in the attendance area in which the child or youth is actually living are eligible to attend

- BEST INTEREST—In determining the best interest of the child or youth, the local educational agency shall—

    e.   To the extent feasible, keep a homeless child or youth in the school of origin, except when doing so is contrary to the wishes of the child's or youth's parent or guardian;

    f.   Provide a written explanation, including a statement regarding the right to appeal, to the homeless child's or youth's parent or guardian, if the local educational agency sends such child or youth to a school other than the school of origin or a school requested by the parent or guardian; and

    g.   In the case of an unaccompanied youth, ensure that the homeless liaison assists in placement or enrollment decisions under this subparagraph, considers the views of such unaccompanied youth, and provides notice to such youth of the right to appeal (McKinney-Vento Homeless Education Assistance Improvement Act of 2001)

Under this act, schools cannot turn away homeless students because they do not have medical, academic, residency, or immunization records. A school must enroll the student and immediately refer the student to the district's homeless liaison to assist in obtaining these records.

Implementation of the McKinney-Vento Act currently still remains fragmented in terms of implementation, partially because of the lack of available funding, poor coordination, and a lack of awareness of school personnel. Where the act has been implemented, however, "children and youth are reaping immense rewards. School provides the obvious benefits of intellectual, emotional, and social stimulation, and academic achievement. By offering educational stability and access, the McKinney-Vento Act helps children and youth experiencing homelessness realize these benefits" (Julianelle & Foscarinis, 2003, p. 50). Individual success due to implementation of this legislation has been well documented. Following are some examples.

An after-school program in Arizona, funded by the McKinney-Vento Act and Title I, serves children experiencing homelessness. It provides clothing, showers, health care, counseling, and academic support for the students and their parents. The program makes it a priority to ensure that the students are not isolated or stigmatized due to their housing status, such that most of the students do not even know why they were selected for the supplemental program. They commonly ask if their housed classmates can also attend.

A 5-year-old boy in Colorado who changed schools in January was certain that his mobility and homelessness were his fault. He thought his former classmates and the teacher did not like him and were happy when he changed schools. The Title I coordinator and McKinney-Vento liaison in his new school district contacted his former teacher and asked her to send him a valentine. On Valentine's Day, the boy opened a bag full of valentines from his former classmates and teachers. Words cannot describe the joy, love, and relief the cards brought to the young child.

After finding permanent housing, a mother in Illinois shared that if had not been for the support of the school, she believed her family would still be struggling with mobility and homelessness.

A girl from Louisiana is preparing to apply for college, after receiving after-school tutoring and transportation to her out-of-district school of origin through the McKinney-Vento program. She wrote: "[The McKinney-Vento liaison] made sure all of my school fees were paid for. [She] saw to it that my ACT [American College Testing assessment] fee was paid. I scored a 22 [out of 36] on the ACT test" (Julianelle & Foscarinis, 2003, pp. 51–52).

What Educators and Other Professionals Can Do

Among the strategies suggested by Swick, early childhood professionals seeking to support homeless families should

1. Develop an ecological understanding of family homelessness.
2. Develop responsive and supportive attitudes and behaviors [with parents and families and model positive attitudes and behaviors].
3. Create an inviting center or school culture by [offering immediate access to basic human services, partnering with families in shaping their own family goals, and providing comprehensive services such as literacy education].
4. Engage parents and families in all aspects of their children's learning and development.
5. Empower parents and families through adult education, job enhancement, and related family literacy [by focusing on parent strengths, competence, and confidence]. (2004, pp. 118–119)

As homeless children could be the target of mistreatment or isolation from their schoolmates, Swick recommends that

> an elementary school use a "buddy" program to match children who are new to the school with caring peer mentors. Many of the children in a particular school [implementing this program] are homeless or at-risk, and several of them eventually become mentors themselves. The "buddy" activities focus on helping children feel secure, important, and connected to their new school. Teachers and staff also act as mentors, often in informal ways with the parents. (2004, p. 119)

Parents also need support from mutually responsive relationships with other homeless families (Swick, 2004). Educators can support these relationships by

- Encouraging families to recognize and support each other's strengths
- Complimenting parents on their positive interactions with their children
- Including parent–child social learning activities in every aspect of the program
- Encouraging families to use appropriate conflict resolution strategies
- Nurturing families in the importance of open and continuing communication with each other (p. 119)

In addition, Swick (1996) noted strategies that teachers developed during a professional development course at a university. These strategies focused on finding better ways to respond to the needs of homeless students.

- Establish a liaison for homeless students at each school district.
- Develop close working relationships with area shelters where homeless students and parents are living.
- Provide homeless students with mentors who help them solve problems related to being successful in school.
- Individualize instruction so that learning problems of homeless students are addressed early in the school year.
- Provide homeless students with needed learning materials for doing school-work and homework.
- Develop close relationships with parents through contacts at local shelters, meeting parents at shelters, and providing parents with transportation to school.
- Establish a family-service referral system within the school that is linked to the community's available social and educational services.
- Educate other teachers and staff in each school about the unique needs of homeless students and families. (p. 295)

The educators also made a plan to implement their suggested strategies (Swick, 1996), with distribution of a resource guide for all teachers involved with homeless children and families, development of liaisons to work with homeless shelters, initiation of mentoring/tutoring programs, and school- and district-wide dissemination of information programs for all teachers.

In addition, parents should be involved in these efforts, as well as children. Collaboration is essential among school districts, state departments of education, and other agencies. Supporting children and families who are homeless is a communitywide effort. Teachers, schools, and medical facilities must support such efforts (Swick, 1996).

Fostering Resilience: Solutions that Lead to the Success of Homeless Students

Landsman (2006) said, "Teachers must become bearers of hope in places where there are depression and despair. It is our job to believe in kids above everything else" (p. 27). This hope means that teachers do not lower their expectations for homeless students, but that they are compassionate and flexible. This hope is also built from giving children and families a sense of control and ownership, because they often feel as if they have no influence over their situation. "The best teachers never lose sight of their students' potential" (Landsman, 2006, p. 29) but believe that *all* children can learn. Strategies that teachers in particular can use include creating flexible, inclusive classrooms where interests of children drive the program; individualizing within the curriculum and tailoring to specific child needs; focusing on the strengths of children, as well as their challenges; soliciting community resources and the advice of colleagues to meet material needs of the children; and above all, being respectful of families and children and being willing to listen and learn (Landsman, 2006).

The teacher strategies described previously speak to fostering resilience in children. Resilience research indicates that in the face of adversity, children can still thrive when protective resources are available (Masten, 2000). Although homeless children often are in high-risk situations, some show remarkable resilience if they have competent, caring adults supporting them (Masten, 2000). If this support is not available at home and schools, teachers and other professionals can provide protective factors, which include the following (Masten, 2000):

- Connections to other competent and caring adults
- Self-efficacy
- Talents valued by society and self
- A sense of meaning in life
- Good schools
- Community resources
- Attachment systems
- Pleasure-in-mastery motivational systems
- Community organizational systems (p. 4)

Professionals do not have control over many aspects of a child's family; however, as Landsman (2006) noted, professionals can make home visits to families, establish relationships with them, and help them find resources in the community that address their specific needs and concerns.

BENEFICIAL OUTCOMES:
COMMUNITY-BASED, FAMILY-CENTERED RESOURCES

Head Start and Early Head Start

Early Head Start and Head Start programs are federally funded, free programs open to infants, toddlers, and preschool-age children. The programs assist families experiencing poverty, as well as homeless families. In addition, "[Head Start] programs are required to serve children with special needs, including children with physical disabilities, intellectual disabilities, emotional disturbances, and developmental delays; at least 10% of the spaces in the [Head Start] program must be allocated to children with special needs" (Dicker, 2009, p. 138).

Head Start stresses literacy development through direct and indirect teaching of verbal skills, reading books to children daily, sending home books and other literacy materials for the entire family, and giving children opportunities to practice their writing skills. Moreover, Head Start serves the entire family. The teaching staff and family workers make home visits to establish and maintain relationships with families and to learn about the families' strengths and areas of concern. Children eat a free, nutritional breakfast, lunch, and afternoon snack in the program. Furthermore, if families have nutritional, clothing, medical, or counseling needs, Head Start staff can help them find programs in the community to assist them.

Community-Based, Family-Centered Resources

In addition to school settings, homeless shelters can be a way to help not only children but also the entire family. In Minnesota, nursing students gained experience in a transitional family homeless shelter in Minneapolis (Stevens, 2002). While the school-age children were bused to local public schools, the younger children remained at the shelter. Part of the nursing program involved providing a weekly preschool program for the children not yet attending school. The nursing students made posters and distributed flyers about the class to families, and then carried out the supervision, teaching, and activities. The nursing students developed and implemented health-related fine and gross motor activities, large-group activities, fingerplays, songs, and art projects. In addition, the students provided the parents with a flyer that described the activities and themes in a way that was easily understood. Students also provided health promotion items, such as soap, toothbrushes, and toothpaste.

The outcomes of this program were very positive. A total of 15–20 children participated in each preschool session, and students learned how to identify families' strengths, discovered how to work with people from cultures other than their own, and felt that they were successful in modeling age-appropriate communication for the families. In addition to implementing the preschool program, the nursing students held a health fair in which they made posters regarding lead poisoning, preventing animal bites, preventing ear infections, identifying poisonous and nonpoisonous products, smoking cessation, nutrition, and blood pressure screening. Feedback from those who attended the fair was highly positive.

This type of program could be implemented in other cities across the United States. It is a fairly simple program to start, and it is akin to student teaching. The nursing students were not paid, as it was part of their college program; thus, the cost was minimal. Homeless shelters might offer a setting for other students as well: those in education, for instance, or those in cultural diversity classes, or others interested in working with families in high-risk groups. The experience also could be a required or voluntary internship as part of training in medical schools, social work programs, or counseling programs.

Respite

Programs aimed at alleviating some of the stress felt by parents and children who are homeless can be very beneficial. One such program, held at an outdoor camp setting, offered respite from the stresses of homeless shelter living (Kissman, 1999). The program was designed as follows:

> A total of 118 [homeless] families [attended] weekend or 5-day sessions where parents [participated] in daily group discussions focused around parenting issues. Groups [were] facilitated by skilled therapists, with specific topics of discussion determined within the group. At other times during the day parents [participated] in camp activities, such as crafts, river walks, archery, cook-outs, and swimming. The high staff–family ratio enabled mothers to feel secure in trusting their children to caring staff members who demonstrated their commitment to serving families by initiating extra activities, such as early morning hikes and cookouts for the older children. (p. 242)

Staff noted that this setting helped

> facilitate dialogues where information flowed relatively freely and group norms were established to enable the women to share information about various obstacles they face in moving toward self-sufficiency. Their obstacles were very much related to their abilities to provide for and to nurture their children. (p. 248)

Immediately following their camp experiences, families were interviewed to assess the success of the outdoor camp program. Mothers reported that as a result of the outdoor camp program, they were able to engage in activities together as a family unit, and they learned that keeping children busy and engaged is a way to prevent negative behaviors in the shelter.

This outdoor camp provided a model for other professionals involved with homeless families, offering assistance with employment searches, searches for child care, and other services that homeless families needed. Many of the other programs and strategies described in this chapter could likewise help alleviate some of the stressors facing homeless children and their families. In conclusion, it is hoped that the information and suggestions described in this chapter will provide a starting point for those who desire to help families improve their life outcomes.

Thinking It Through: Questions for Discussion

1. How might professionals coordinate services for homeless families and young children?

2. With the mobility common to homeless families, how can professionals ensure availability and accessibility of services, with consistent staff?

3. How can professionals ensure both confidentiality and accessibility of student records and information as students move from agency to agency, program to program, and school to school?

REFERENCES

Buckner, J.C., Bassuk, E.L., Weinreb, L.F., & Brooks, M.G. (1999). Homelessness and its relation to the mental health and behavior of low-income school-age children. *Developmental Psychology, 35*(1), 246–257.

Dicker, S. (2009). *Reversing the odds: Improving outcomes for babies in the child welfare system.* Baltimore: Paul H. Brookes Publishing Co.

Duffield, B., & Lovell, P. (2008). *The economic crisis hits home: The unfolding increase in child and youth homelessness.* Retrieved December 15, 2010, from http://naehcy.org/dl/TheEconomic CrisisHitsHome.pdf

Fierman, A.H., Dreyer, B.P., Quinn, L., Shulman, S., Courtlandt, C.D., & Guzzo, R. (1991, November). Growth delay in homeless children. *Pediatrics, 88*(5), 918–925.

Gargiulo, R.M. (2006). Homeless and disabled: Rights, responsibilities, and recommendations for serving young children with special needs. *Early Childhood Education Journal, 33*(5), 357–362.

Harpaz-Rotem, I., Rosenheck, R.A., & Desai, R. (2006, October). The mental health of children exposed to maternal mental illness and homelessness. *Community Mental Health Journal, 42*(5), 437–448.

Hart-Shegos, E. (1999). Homelessness and its effects on children. *American Journal of Disabled Child, 145,* 516–519.

Hicks-Coolick, A., Burnside-Eaton, P., & Peters, A. (2003, August). Homeless children: Needs and services. *Child & Youth Care Forum, 32*(4), 197–210.

Julianelle, P.F., & Foscarinis, M. (2003). Responding to the school mobility of children and youth experiencing homelessness: The McKinney-Vento Act and beyond. *The Journal of Negro Education, 72*(1), 39–54.

Kissman, K. (1999). Respite from stress and other service needs of homeless families. *Community Mental Health Journal, 35*(3), 241–249.

Landsman, J. (2006). Bearers of hope. *Educational Leadership, 63*(5), 26–32.

Masten, A.S. (2000). *Children who overcome adversity to succeed in life.* Retrieved May 10, 2010, from the University of Minnesota Extension web site: http://www.extension.umn.edu/distribution/familydevelopment/components/7565_06.html

Masten, A.S., Miliotis, D., Graham-Bermann, M.R., Ramirez, M, & Neemann, J. (1993). Children in homeless families: Risks to mental health and development. *Journal of Consulting and Clinical Psychology, 61*(2), 335–343.

McKinney-Vento Homeless Education Assistance Improvements Act of 2001, PL 107-110, 42 U.S.C. 11431 *et seq.* Retrieved April 5, 2011, from the U.S. Department of Education web site: http://www2.ed.gov/programs/homeless/legislation.html

Miller, J. R., Griffore, R. J., Steinberg, C., Elam, P., Sproles, C., & Hakoyama, M. (2007, September). University and community partnerships: Working together to solve problems related to homelessness. *Journal of Family and Consumer Sciences, 99*(3), 8–14.

National Center for Children in Poverty (2009, June). *Poverty and brain development in early childhood.* Retrieved October 19, 2009, from http://www.nccp.org/publications/pdf/text_398.pdf

National Center on Family Homelessness (2009). *America's youngest outcasts.* Retrieved October 19, 2009, from http://www.homelesschildrenamerica.org/pdf/stories/case_studies/cs_impact/pdf

Powers-Costello, E., & Swick, K.J. (2008). Exploring the dynamics of teacher perceptions of homeless children and families during the early years. *Early Childhood Education Journal, 36,* 241–245.

Rouse, H.L., & Fantuzzo, J.W. (2009). Multiple risks and educational well being: A population-based investigation of threats to early school success. *Early Childhood Research Quarterly, 24,* 1–14.

Rubin, D.H., Erickson, C.J., San Agustin, M., Cleary, S.D., Allen, J.K., & Cohen, P. (1996, March). Cognitive and academic functioning of homeless children compared with housed children. *Pediatrics, 97*(3), 289–294.

Stevens, M.C. (2002). Community-based child health clinical experience in a family homeless shelter. *Journal of Nursing Education, 41*(1), 504–506.

Swick, K.J. (1996). Teacher strategies for supporting homeless students and families. *The Clearing House, 69,* 293–296.

Swick, K.J. (2004). The dynamics of families who are homeless. *Childhood Education, 80*(3), 116–120.

Swick, K.J. (2008). The dynamics of violence and homelessness among young families. *Early Childhood Education Journal, 36,* 81–85.

Vostanis, P., Tischler, S., Cumella, S., & Bellerby, T. (2001). Mental health problems and social supports among homeless mothers and children victims of domestic and community violence. *International Journal of Social Psychiatry, 47*(4), 30–40.

Walker-Dalhouse, D., & Risko, V.J. (2008, September). Homelessness, poverty, and children's literacy development. *The Reading Teacher, 62*(1), 84–86.

Yu, M., North, C.S., LaVesser, P.D., Osborne, V.A., & Spitznagel, E.L. (2008, February). A comparison study of psychiatric and behavior disorders and cognitive ability among homeless and housed children. *Community Mental Health Journal, 44*(1), 1–10.

Zima, B.T., Bussing, R., Forness, S.R., & Benjamin, B. (1997). Sheltered homeless children: Their eligibility and unmet need for special education services. *American Journal of Public Health, 87*(2), 236–240.

Zima, B.T., Wells, K.B., & Freeman, H.E. (1994). Emotional and behavioral problems and severe academic delays among homeless children in Los Angeles County. *American Journal of Public Health, 84*(2), 260–264.

IV

Emerging
and Finding
the Way
Again

13

Professionals and Families

Partners in Care

Laura A. Jenkins and Mary Beth Sullivan

CHAPTER HIGHLIGHTS

At the conclusion of this chapter, the reader will be able to

- Understand various motivators for entering the helping professions and ways that motivators color specific styles of professional help

- Understand why investing time and energy in relationships with parents is an integral part of service to young children

- Understand roles assumed by team members that may result in increased pain and limited functional change among professionals and within families

- Understand strategies for building and maintaining relationships that facilitate equality and genuine collaboration among professionals and families

- Understand the need to care for oneself and the need to encourage others to do so

The day my son was born I was holding him after nursing. He was wide awake, looking at me and focusing on my face. I remember an overwhelming feeling of being completely in love. A nurse walked into the room to check my blood pressure and, while doing so, commented, "Oh, you have one of those!" She did not expand on what she meant, and I remember puzzling over the comment before going back to admire and love my beautiful boy. Little did I realize that the comment would come back to haunt me over and over again through the years. When I was pacing the floor late at night while he screamed in pain, when he refused to eat solid foods, when he was admitted to the early intervention program for unspecified developmental delay, when the kindergarten teacher told me he lacked maturity, when he had difficulty . . . On and on, and in each new situation I could hear her voice saying, "Oh, you have one of those." Did she know something, even when he was only hours old? Did she see something in my baby that I couldn't see? And if she did, what did it mean for the future?

—Mother of now-25-year-old who has a successful
financial career and a family of his own

When I had about 3 years experience as an occupational therapist in the early intervention field, I met Danielle and her family. Danielle had been born at 25 weeks' gestation and was hooked up to a ventilator, fed through a nasogastric tube, was hearing impaired, and had 24-hour nursing care. There were so many issues to address for Danielle and her family. There was a large team in place at home (nursing staff; physical, occupational, and speech therapists; and a teacher of the speech and hearing impaired). The team discussed our concern that this family was not bonding, but we did not know what to do about it so we kept focusing on our individual goals, hoping that making things easier for Danielle, helping her to gain more function, would ease the burden on the whole family.

One day, Danielle's mother called me and told me to stop bringing toys and equipment to the home. She said, "I don't know what to do with her when you're not here because you take the things you are showing her to play with out the door with you." I felt bad and tried to then use the few toys Danielle had at home.

Eight years later I met the family again in a department store. If they had not recognized me and reintroduced themselves, I never would have known them. Danielle was in a wheelchair and still on a ventilator; however, both parents were fluent in sign language, and all three were enthusiastically and functionally communicating with one another. They all had smiles on their faces and were clearly well bonded to each other. I remember feeling so happy for them, but I also remember thinking, *They did it, despite us and our "help."*

—Occupational therapist reflecting on various perspectives
of help and how much she has learned from families

Previous chapters have presented several reasons for establishing close collaboration with parents and caregivers. Here is another vital reason: Children's ongoing relationship with their parents affects their success later in life (Shinn, 1978). If the help given by professionals interferes with that relationship, they are violating one of the oldest tenets of care: Do no harm. Professionals receive hours of training in their field, learning the *what* of their profession, but regardless of how good they are at the *what* they must learn the *how* as well. *How* they deliver the message and offer services is as critical in their provision of service as the knowledge and skills they possess.

DIFFERENT PRIORITIES AND DIVERSE PERSPECTIVES

Passion, in all of its forms, is encountered everywhere in the fields of medicine, education, and mental health. Those who enter the helping professions typically do so with a strong passion for the well-being of children, and parents encountering services possess a fierce passion for their children. If all of this passion were directed along perfectly parallel lines, bent in the same direction, it might be much easier for professionals and parents to work together. But because they are all individuals with differing temperaments, diverse training and backgrounds, and widely varied life experiences, working together is no simple task. Strong passions may be expressed through anger, self-righteousness, withdrawal, and a host of other ways. Often these strong passions cause individuals to play roles they do not consciously choose; they then find themselves wondering about the tangled webs of communication and relationships in which they find themselves. Even worse, they often feel as if there is no way out.

Some of the prevalent roles assumed by both parents and providers are the *victim, rescuer,* and *persecutor.*

The Victim, Rescuer, and Persecutor

The *victim* has feelings of hopelessness, powerlessness, and little or no control over situations. The victim is seen by the persecutor as someone incapable of making decisions for himself and by the rescuer as someone she can fix things for, in the process feeling good about herself. An individual in the victim's role generally acts in the following ways:

- Frequently complains about the way things are and what others do, typically to people not directly involved
- Calls out for help, generally to those who do not have the power to change the situation
- Feels incapable of making choices and living with the consequences
- Eventually begins to identify himself as a victim and is reluctant to let go of that identity because he does not know who he is without it; he sometimes lashes out at those from whom he tried to enlist help and blames others for his becoming a victim
- May find that continuing to play the role of victim becomes useful in gaining information and resources

The *rescuer* has a desire to be needed, and his feelings of self-worth emerge from his attempts to fix things for others. He is seen by the persecutor as an interferer and by the victim as, initially, a shoulder to cry on and then as an interferer or an untrustworthy person, possibly even a liar. A rescuer acts in these ways:

- Tends to jump right in in response to any call for help, even if the situation does not involve him
- Often promises resources he does not control
- Jumps to conclusions about what will help and proceeds to take steps to provide it, whether or not the person needing help has asked him to do so
- Is overwhelmed with surprise and hurt when someone tells him she did not want his help in the first place or that his assistance was not at all helpful
- Is solely focused on obtaining self-worth by fixing the problems of others; therefore, he frequently finds himself in poor health, financial difficulties, or other challenging situations as a result of lack of attention to his own needs
- May come to be viewed by the victim as a persecutor

The *persecutor* feels that he must maintain control over situations or people at all costs; if he is unable to do so, he ultimately will become a victim. The persecutor is seen by both the victim and the rescuer as controlling. A persecutor displays the following behaviors:

- Holds tenaciously to his opinions and plans
- Pushes forward despite obstacles and the pleas of others to do things differently
- Resists the efforts of others to assist him; believes there is room for only one at the top. If others join him there, he will be removed to the side and will thus be unable to meet his own needs
- May feel hurt by others' perceptions of him as a persecutor; change, however, is difficult because he would rather feel safe in his self-sufficiency and control than give up that safety net to change others' view of him
- May engage in abusive behaviors and actions

One interesting aspect of this triangle of relating is that people tend to move from one role to another as they interact. For example, the victim may complain to a rescuer that something was not done well and he is unhappy. The rescuer may then run to the person being complained about (the person the victim perceives as persecuting him), thinking he can smooth the waters and convince the persecutor to do things differently or change the situation. The persecutor may feel like a victim (*Why didn't she tell me herself?*), but then lash out at the victim (*How dare you talk to someone else about this?*) and even the rescuer (*Why are you getting involved in my affairs?*). This triangle of roles is all about perceptions of identity (feelings of powerlessness, a desire to be needed, the need to be in control). In a sense, each role serves as a mechanism for survival, albeit for limited ways of surviving. These interactions among victim, rescuer, and persecutor are depicted in Figure 13.1.

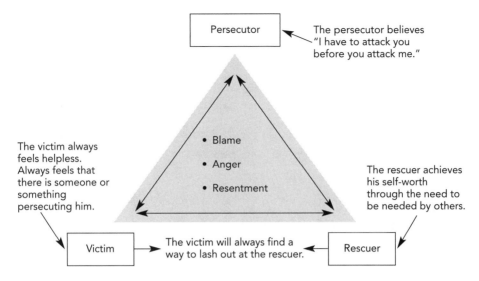

This triangulated relationship is a toxic place to be. It is not productive for self or families.

Figure 13.1.   Triangle of roles: Interactions are shown among victim, rescuer, and persecutor.

The Hero, Guardian, and Martyr

Another triangle of relating, with equally devastating results as the first, includes a different cast of players: the *hero, guardian,* and *martyr.* Unlike the previous roles, which people move into and out of, the roles of hero, guardian, and martyr are often present simultaneously in one person. These roles are shown in Figure 13.2.

The *hero* is that part of an individual that remembers painful life lessons or the sorrowful experiences of others; he has a strong need to protect and wants to save others from going through similar experiences. The hero part of a person causes him to act in the following ways:

- Judges and makes decisions for others, based on his own experiences, perceptions, and religious beliefs
- Responds to complaints from others with the attitude that "I know what is best for you; don't fight me on this; you will thank me in the long run"
- Feels as if all the problems would disappear if only everyone would follow his plans
- Feels hurt by others' perceptions of him as controlling and domineering; thinks, "After all, I am doing this for their own good"
- Responds with "I told you so" if others do not follow his advice and experience pain or failure

The *guardian* includes that part of a person that vows to give up whatever is necessary and to push as hard as needed to protect (e.g., save someone from

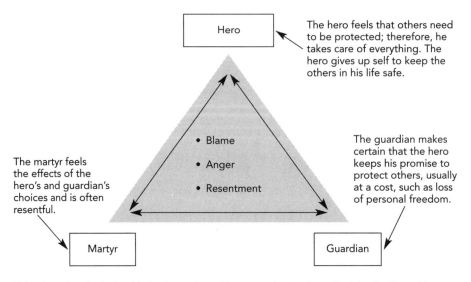

The hero feels that others need to be protected; therefore, he takes care of everything. The hero gives up self to keep the others in his life safe.

The guardian makes certain that the hero keeps his promise to protect others, usually at a cost, such as loss of personal freedom.

The martyr feels the effects of the hero's and guardian's choices and is often resentful.

Hero

- Blame
- Anger
- Resentment

Martyr

Guardian

This triangulated relationship is also toxic and is not productive for self or the families with whom we work.

Figure 13.2.   Relational triangle, with interactions among hero, guardian, and martyr. These roles often are seen in one person.

themselves, save others from pain, change a situation). The guardian part of a person will

- Neglect personal needs to remain on duty
- Accept isolation and lack of companionship as an often necessary side effect of persisting at what he believes is right
- Realize that what he thought were temporary sacrifices have become a long-term way of living, often with devastating effects on personal health and relationships

The *martyr* is that part of a person that feels the effects of playing the roles of hero and guardian: poor health, exhaustion, loneliness. The martyr part of a person will

- Begin to feel resentful for all the sacrifices made
- Feel negatively toward others because of their lack of gratitude for all the martyr has given up and done for them
- Experience high levels of burnout that may result in a change from hero to martyr

Both of these triangle relationships are fueled by feelings of fear, anger, rage, and blame and are often a result of a lack of underlying skills needed to relate to others in different, more constructive ways. The following vignette illustrates how such roles may play out in parent–professional situations, and how these situations are fraught with potential for negative outcomes.

MARIA AND DEY

Maria is the 22-year-old mother of four children (two sons, ages 5 and 3, and two daughters, ages 1½ and 2 months). Her boyfriend and the father of the children, Dey, is in and out of the home with no consistency. He wants to be a part of their lives but often is confused and overwhelmed when he tries. When he is present, he is appalled at the lack of order in the home and frequently responds to the children's misbehavior with spankings and yelling. He consistently complains that Maria needs to discipline the children better and maintain a cleaner, calmer home. Maria feels she might have some chance of success at achieving those things if she could rely on Dey to be available and if they could discuss how to better manage the children's behavior.

Child Protective Services became involved when someone called to report that the 5-year-old had a very large burn on his leg and had walked to the corner grocery store to buy a soft drink. The 18-month-old receives early intervention services from a teacher, physical therapist, and speech therapist to address delays in overall development. In addition, a parent aide was assigned to help Maria cope with parenting her children and managing the household.

Within a month after the first report to Child Protective Services, the oldest child cut his hand with a serrated knife, the second oldest ran into a large window, breaking it and almost falling three stories, and the 18-month-old burned her mouth and hand while trying to drink from her mother's coffee cup when Maria was attending to the baby. When Maria decided that Dey was the cause of all her problems, the parent aide helped her throw his clothes into the street.

Other problems followed. One day the teacher realized that the baby had been in the same diaper for over 14 hours and the children had not had breakfast, so she bought diapers and food for the family. The therapists complained that the household was so chaotic they could not accomplish anything in their sessions with the 18-month-old and that Maria was not interested in learning how to carry over strategies to help this child who had extra needs.

On the day of the children's well-child visit, the parent aide was ill and could not go with the family to the appointment. Maria managed to get all four children on the bus and to the pediatrician's office by herself. While sitting in the waiting room, she congratulated herself on arriving with all of the children on time. She knew the two older ones were being a little wild in the waiting room, but they had been so well behaved on the bus that she felt they needed to be active before going into the exam room.

When they entered the exam room, however, both the nurse and the physician began lecturing Maria. This child needed a bath; Maria needed to learn how to set limits on the children's behavior (someone had almost gotten hurt in the waiting room); the baby would need to come in more frequently for additional weight checks; and, finally, did Maria want to be referred to a parenting class? The small sense of having done something right for a change quickly disappeared, and Maria dealt with her guilt, fear, and diminished sense of self-worth through anger. Her terse questions to the medical staff about how she was going to get back and forth to the office more often, whether they were going to talk to the landlord about fixing the hot water tank so she could bathe the children, and whether anyone was going to provide transportation and child care while she learned how to take care of her children at a parenting class were viewed as excuses and resistance. She even heard one of the staff whisper to someone else just outside the door, "Maybe now she'll finally realize that she shouldn't be having any more children." Since that visit, the home care team noticed Maria withdrawing more and more, and concluded that she just did not care.

Who's Playing Which Roles?

Let's look at who is playing the victim, rescuer, and persecutor in this situation. Maria is certainly feeling like a victim and, accordingly, is placing the blame outside of herself (on her boyfriend, on the staff of the pediatrician's office). She feels hopeless about gaining some semblance of parenting control and skill. She is also playing the persecutor by throwing Dey's belongings out the window. The therapists are feeling like victims of the chaotic household, placing blame on (persecuting) Maria as well as Child Protective Services (*Why don't they do something? People are getting hurt, and the children's needs are not being met*). The parent aide and teacher are jumping into rescuer roles, feeling good about helping the family, but is their help really changing anything? The medical staff [the rescuer] believe that they are helping by giving Maria expert advice and offering her information about other sources of help. However, the effect on Maria is a decreased sense of being able to manage and cope. She sees the therapists and medical staff as persecutors (*How can they possibly think I have the time or ability to do extra things when I can't even keep everyone fed and safe?*), and may in turn persecute the parent aide on her next visit to the home (*"Why did you help me throw Dey's stuff into the street? He was so angry, and the cops ended up here. You're supposed to help me, not get me in more trouble!"*). Dey likely is feeling as if he is a victim of everyone and could easily take on a persecutor role in an attempt to gain some control.

Now let's look at examples of where the hero may be operating, what the guardian might be asking, and how each can end up feeling like a martyr.

The hero in Maria, in an attempt to protect herself and her children (e.g., stop the incriminations, keep the children from being spanked, reserve energy for herself and the children), may choose to sever all ties with Dey. The guardian self-talk may consist of telling herself that she has to give up adult relationships and intimacy in order to keep her children safe and gain some control herself. This perspective might lead her to sever the relationship between the children and their father. In addition, the martyr in Maria may cause her to feel angry with her children because she perceives that she has made great sacrifices for them.

The hero in Dey may try to protect himself and the children by setting stringent limits in the house that others feel are too punishing. The guardian part of him may talk himself into sacrificing a nurturing relationship with his children in order to teach them how to behave so that they will be accepted by others in ways denied to him (i.e., others not accepting him and his views). The martyr part of him may experience significant regret and loneliness as a result of such choices.

The heroes in the therapists are vowing to create some change in this situation, and they are willing to sacrifice (become a guardian) a relationship with the parents to make sure the children are properly cared for. This, however, will likely cause the parents to request different providers, or to refuse any help at all, and the therapists may come to feel like martyrs and strengthen their hero identity.

The hero in the teacher, parent aide, and medical staff initially feels successful, having done something specific that each believes will change things for the better. However, since these individuals responded out of the need to be needed and/or the need to protect and save, rather than from a collaborative plan of care, they will soon find that everything is back to the way it was. The guardian part of them may vow to continue to create change, and the martyr in them will eventually feel unappreciated and unheard.

Why do people fall into these roles? Why do they let them destroy their health and relationships? These are default settings that seem to emerge when individuals are under stress, are afraid, feel they must do something, and are unable to think of anything else to do. Often, the roles most frequently assumed are conditioned initially by a motivation to help, previous life experiences, and habit. Entering the helping professions with certain beliefs can cause professionals to easily fall into default roles such as persecutor, rescuer, victim, hero, guardian, and martyr. A partial list of such beliefs includes the following:

- Children need to be saved.
- Everyone needs to learn everything there is to know about child development.
- Children are victims.
- One's own experiences as children are what every child experiences.
- One's own perceptions of the world are the only view.
- Everyone understands childhood and life like I do.
- Only some parents care about their children.
- Most parents do not know what they are doing.
- There are ways of addressing children's needs that work for every child.

The good news is that no matter what perspective brought providers to their respective fields, they can always expand their perspective to embrace additional beliefs and learn new ways of interacting with others and supporting families—ways that are healthier for themselves, children, and caregivers.

The Ebb and Flow: Acceptance with Possibilities

To move beyond the default roles described in the previous section, professionals must possess essential attitudes that will assist in achieving improved success in collaboration with families. Attitudes of nonjudgment, open-mindedness, and acceptance, accompanied by a willingness to engage in reflective practice regarding interactions with families, are nonnegotiable components of success. We emphasize that this is a responsibility of *professionals* because it is they who have chosen to work on behalf of children's health, safety, development, and growth.

Families come with different levels of experience and from varying cultures. Frequently, they are dealing with stress, grief, a wide range of other emotions, and often extreme levels of fatigue. It is the responsibility of providers to extend respect, acceptance, and caring, whether or not it is reciprocated. In Maria and Dey's situation, trying to convince them to look at where they are lacking in interpersonal skills with professional staff incurs energy that would be better focused on strengthening the parents' skills in relationship with their children. For the most significant changes to occur in this household, Maria and Dey need others to shed light on their *strengths* and how to build on those strengths to feel more competent as parents.

Provider abilities to highlight such parenting skills is not as difficult as it may initially appear. Many professionals are involved in the development of children at some level, and information on best practice for children's growth is prevalent and readily accessible (e.g., *Zero to Three Bulletin*, the National Association for the Education of Young Children, T. Berry Brazelton's Touchpoints approach to working with families and professionals). Best practice involves viewing children with acceptance and unlimited potential. Professionals understand that to gain new skills children have to try them out over and over again, in different settings, and with different people. They can smile at the young child's understanding of the world in concrete ways (*When the toilet is flushed, everything disappears, and I might, too!*) while knowing that, eventually, with loving and caring encouragement to practice, the child will come to a more thorough understanding of how things work. It also frequently happens that while a child is learning one skill, a regression in other skills takes place (Brazelton & Sparrow, 2006). Adults do not look at a child who is struggling to learn how to tie her shoes and breaks down in frustration as having lost all she has gained in regulation and self-control. They understand that frustration and irritability can be part of the growth process. They also do not look at a 5-year-old who is dirty after playing outside and complaining that he is hungry as being unreasonable and obstinate. And yet adults are so much harder on themselves and others. They make snap judgments about others, based on the way they are dressed, their levels of personal hygiene and cleanliness, the words they use in conversation, or how they interact with their children. Adults do not provide themselves and others the kind of patience and time required to deal with grief, pain, anger, and skill acquisition that they provide a child in learning how to tie her shoes!

Why is this so? What makes adults so much harder on one another than on children? Is it possible that the dictates of various societies and cultures that place arbitrary timelines on adulthood cause adults to forget that skills are skills and that learning new skills takes time and differing paths? If adults were to take the same attitude with other adults (including themselves) as best practice recommends with children, they would find themselves more relaxed, much better equipped to focus on the really important things, less likely to take everything personally, and more apt to experience growth and joy in their interactions with one another.

One more triangle (see Figure 13.3) related to interactions can set providers and families on a different path. Instead of sliding into the role of victim, rescuer, persecutor, hero, guardian, or martyr, professionals can choose to state what they are experiencing. Instead of saying, "I am a victim," or "I am a martyr," they can say, "I am having an experience of feeling like a victim," or "I am having an experience of feeling like a martyr." They can say, "I am having an experience, and the experience brings me wisdom. Since wisdom enhances who I am, every experience enhances who I am." This healthier view enables professionals to avoid defining themselves through limiting roles and can assist them in helping parents to define their strengths and face difficult situations when they often feel they do not have the skills to cope with what is happening to them and their children.

Making shifts in perceptions and beliefs can help professionals move to a better place, one with more potential for success. For example, they can

- Shift their focus from child centered (i.e., the child with special needs or even all of the children) to family centeredness, which adds critical team members (parents, other caregivers, colleagues) to the process
- Recognize that every person is doing the best he can in a given moment. For instance, what one is capable of in this moment may be much more or less than what one will be capable of tomorrow, based on levels of stress, past experiences, fatigue, and health. Many factors that affect a person's functional level at any given time are hidden from others and may not be readily under-

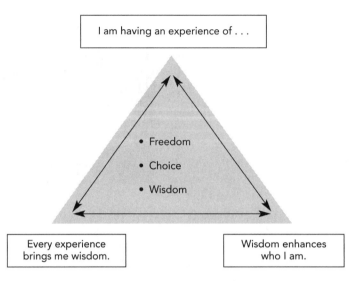

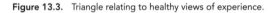

This relationship is the healthiest place to function and can assist self and the families with whom we work to facilitate healthy relationships. We keep the wisdom as our learning experience.

Figure 13.3. Triangle relating to healthy views of experience.

stood (e.g., others may not know of a parent's history of abuse, or the news she has received of a close friend's terminal illness, and she may never feel comfortable with some people to share any of that information).

- Approach a situation and each individual involved as having potential rather than serving as road blocks; this opens up possibilities instead of frustrations
- Recognize that one's own past experiences may negatively influence one's perceptions of others; this allows providers to explore the past to understand what may have caused personal hurt. It is natural to push such memories aside, but sometimes doing so can result in their surfacing at the wrong moment.
- Approach diversity in culture, belief system, gender, race, educational background, and past experiences as a positive and as an avenue for increased understanding. Collaboration can have amazing results in developing plans with parents for their family.

Let's look at the situation with Maria and Dey from this new perspective. Approaching the whole family, including Maria and Dey, with compassion and a willingness to understand and support them allows the providers to take time to ask what the experience of parenting is feeling like for them. Assuring them that parenting is difficult, no matter what a person's history or educational background is, can remove some of the pressure on them of feeling like failures. Acknowledging that parents often come to the task with differing ideas and emotions can also help restore a sense of normalcy in an experience that can often feel out of control. Allowing time for discussion about their current approach to parenting can offer insights that help to reach a collaborative approach that feels positive for everyone. Staying open to the possibility of good intent—that everyone is doing the best he or she can in any given moment—and beginning interaction from that point will increase the chances of success.

For example, the following is an interaction between Dey and the teacher. In this exchange, the teacher stepped out of her rescuer role (*At least I'm one person who can come in and give these kids an appropriate playmate*) and entered a collaborative discussion with Dey to find common ground on which to build and explore limit setting and interactive play.

Teacher: Hi, Dey! I hear it's been a frustrating week. Maria says you had to wash John's mouth out with soap. How are you feeling? It can be so hard to discipline.

Dey: I'm at my wits end! I don't want people thinking I teach my kids these words! They also need to learn respect for me. My mother always washed my mouth out with soap if I swore or was disrespectful to her. Believe me, it worked. I hated the taste and stopped doing it to avoid the punishment.

Teacher: Your mother wanted you to respect her. Do you feel having your mouth washed out with soap taught you how to respect her or taught you to avoid doing something that would get you punished?

Dey: I definitely stopped to avoid punishment. I did learn to respect her, though.

Teacher: What do you think taught you to respect her?

Dey: She worked really hard to make sure we had clothes to wear and food to eat. She always said she wanted us to do good and have more opportunities. Lots of times she put herself last and put me and my brother first.

Teacher: It sounds like she was really there for you, that you could depend on her and that you learned to respect her by watching her choices and how she lived.

Dey: Yeah.

Teacher: I hear you say that you want your children to respect you. Based on your own experience as a child, what do you think will really help John learn respect?

Dey: I guess if I'm there for him. When I show him I care about him.

Teacher: I certainly know you care about him. It's not easy to raise four children, and here you are trying your best to do so. Let's look at the last week and count all the ways you've shown John you care about him.

Dey: I don't know. I go to work so he doesn't see me much, and my hours keep changing so sometimes when I'm home I can't spend time with him because I'm tired and need to sleep before my next shift.

Teacher: You're telling me what you're not doing, but I hear a father who cares about providing for his children and working hard to do so. I also know that despite the work hours you did engage in a game of ball with him, showing your willingness to spend time with him when you can.

Dey: I guess, but when I do try to play with him he gets out of control, wild-like, and if the game doesn't go his way, he starts blaming everyone else, yelling and sometimes swearing; and I don't know what to do with him.

Teacher: It's really hard when kids test their limits with adults. Why do you think they do that?

Dey: To find out how much they can get away with!

Teacher: Yeah, I think you're right about that—they really are looking for where those limits are. I think another thing they're looking for is whether someone cares enough to show them where the limits are, and it sounds like you do.

Clearly, an identical conversation would not be successful with every family. The details of content will shift, based on the individuals involved. However, this interaction points out the importance of believing that a parent has potential, looking for the strengths evident in a situation that otherwise could be viewed as very negative, and working together toward a strategy that might help the child gain appropriate social skills. It does not mean that the first strategy tried is necessarily going to be successful or that additional conversations might not be necessary. However, the teacher's experience as a rescuer used to leave her feeling as if she were abandoning the children after each session, especially the child with special needs. By telling herself that she is having an experience and has learned much through the experience, she is able to use the wisdom of the experience to create additional change for the child she serves, the child's family, and even herself.

MAINTAINING NORMALCY IN THE MIDST OF CRISIS AND ADVERSITY

When a child's difficulties cause professionals to enter a family's life, normal living as the family has known it tends to disappear. As a result of the child's issues and the fact that parents have to look to others for advice on how to care for their child, the parent–professional relationship may begin on an unequal footing. From the start, parents are in a position of requiring help and usually look to providers as the experts. It takes conscious effort on the part providers to help parents understand that they, too, come to the relationship with expert knowledge. Their expertise regarding their child is as vital to success as the knowledge and skills other members bring to the team. Pointing out to parents the value of their information and how it guides decision making for the entire team helps to remove the perception of imbalance.

As noted in previous chapters, it is critical to engage parents in decision making as early as possible. Common mistakes frequently made by professionals include giving parents limited information so that they will choose the plan of action the professional feels is best, giving parents too much information so the parent feels completely overwhelmed, using jargon that makes it hard for parents to understand the information, and expecting decisions to be made by parents without adequate time to fully understand all of the information. Because professionals deal with medical, technical, or developmental information on a daily basis and have observed the outcomes of various decisions numerous times, it is easy to forget what it is like to be hearing the information for the first or even the fourth time. Of course, there are times when decisions need to be made very quickly, such as regarding a medical procedure; more often than not, however, the opportunities for giving parents information about choices

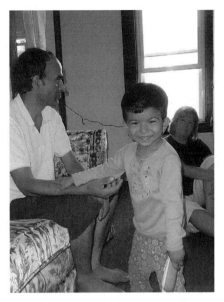

they have and will have in the near future are numerous and can be used as another way to build true collaboration. It is also important to understand that for many parents, previous experiences have caused them to feel they have no options in new situations or are incapable of making good choices. Professionals will need compassion and a great deal of patience as they assist parents in taking the risk to try again, as reflected in the following vignette.

I made so many conscious choices during my pregnancy for health (eating organic foods, eliminating caffeine, refusing certain tests that carried the risk of complications), but despite all that, Angela died and Amy has so many problems. I can't help but think I missed something or made a poor choice. Every time new choices arise, even simple ones, I feel an almost paralyzing fear that I will make a mistake. I know it's silly and so many people have told me none of this was my fault, but when I'm alone, I can't quiet the voice that says maybe I made a mistake somewhere.

—*Mother who carried twins to 32 weeks' gestation and struggled to understand the turn of events with her pregnancy*

Often, professionals are taught to see a child with a disability through the eyes of the disability first and *then* as a child. To reestablish normalcy, professionals must reverse this perspective and view the child as a child first and the disability as an added consideration. Too often professionals cause families grievous pain by forgetting a child's age, stage of development, temperament, and social-emotional or mental health needs when planning therapy or teaching sessions, as seen in the following comments by a mother of a child with autism.

She kept telling me that children with autism need structure, children with autism need consistency, children with autism need to know the routine, children with autism. . . I know she was trying to help, but I just wanted to scream and tell her that I know my beautiful 4-year-old little girl finds safety and reassurance in consistent routines and that our entire family revolves around those routines because we love her so much. We also love her enough to help her find that same safety and reassurance in increasingly complex interactions with others. I did not want to hear what children with autism need. I wanted to hear what my daughter needed and to know that the teacher was with us in the goal of increasing interactions in varying settings and not just improving skills in one-to-one play in our living room.

—Mother of a child with autism, who felt both
her early intervention and preschool team worked on very
isolated, discipline-specific skills rather than on functional life skills

Professionals must make sure that the disability they are focused on eliminating, remediating, or adapting does not become the only or even the major lens for viewing the child. The disability should not negate the possibility for a childhood or exclude opportunities for the development of emotional health and well-being. Many providers, as a result of the widely differing scopes of the professions they are entering, have had only one or two courses in child development, if that. Working with a specialized population after degree completion frequently requires additional coursework or continuing education relating to specific treatment and teaching techniques; however, professionals also need to understand aspects of typical childhood development, a wish expressed by this mother:

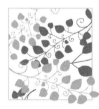

I know that he needs to learn so many skills and that in order to do so he needs someone with him, helping him. I feel so selfish that I also wish he could amuse himself for even 10–15 minutes. It would help so much in preparing a meal or taking a shower.

—Mother of a 2-year-old child with Down syndrome

Professionals often use one-to-one structured time to address a child's needs, which can create issues within the family. What happens when the professionals are not there, and the parent has additional needs to address within the family? Or when, as the mother in the second vignette at the beginning of this chapter expressed, parents do not know how to interact with their child without all the "things" the professional brings to the home? Parents frequently say that some of their greatest issues do not involve the specific motor, speech, or cognitive skills the professionals may be focused on, but how to help their child cope with typical family activities—playing at the park, going to the grocery store, attending their older siblings' ball game, staying in the church nursery, or being a part of family gatherings. Encouraging families to discuss how easy or difficult such routine family activities are, being willing to incorporate these situations into therapy and teaching sessions, and assisting families with functional outcomes is vitally important to the life and well-being of the child and family. Incorporating siblings into sessions so that the

child learns how to interact with them, and working with parents to develop a list of play activities the child can manage independently, can also be very helpful.

THE COURAGE TO BE HUMAN

It is important for professionals to remember that they cannot support parents on a journey to personal empowerment without taking care of their own needs. The various professions entail a great deal of emotional, mental, and many times physical stress with very long hours. Caring for one's own physical, emotional, and mental health is as important a job requirement as anything else in the job description. Professionals spend the majority of their career immersed in situations with people going through crisis, having conversations that involve widely varying philosophical beliefs, and working with individuals of all ages who often tug at their heartstrings. If they do not recognize the fact that such exposure on a daily or weekly basis requires attending to their own needs, they can end up with impaired health, become more entrenched in a victim/hero mentality and interactions, and possibly experience severe levels of burnout.

How do *providers* cope when supporting and working with

- A teen mother trying to deal with the grief over her baby's dying of anencephaly?
- Parents who have just learned that they now have four children diagnosed with autism?
- A family whose child has a disability due to shaken baby syndrome, and whose members are all trying to cope with a history of abuse and neglect and work to put their own family back together again?
- A mother who cries because the provider coaxed the child to eat on the first attempt when the mother has been trying for so long, pouring her heart and soul into it?
- A father who wants to know what the family is doing wrong; the fifth child is now entering early intervention and why don't they ever have a normal child?
- A family who is trying to deal with guilt and create a sense of normal living for their children while pursuing a lawsuit against the caregiver who so severely abused one child as to cause a lifelong disabling condition?

- A family struggling to cope with a child's communication delay when the professional also knows there are signs of much deeper problems than the language delay?
- A family mired in bickering about what is best for their child because they each adjust differently and have different views?
- Parents who, in the process of making the typical transition from a stage of denial to a stage of anger, lash out at the provider?
- A family going through the pain of separation and divorce?

This is the *short* list of the issues providers can face. They are constantly asked to gently insert themselves into a family's experiences and see situations through the family's eyes so that they can better support family members. In doing so, they can experience a roller coaster of emotions if they do not understand what they need in order to maintain balance for themselves. If they allow themselves to take everything personally and allow their hearts to bleed with each family, they quickly become impotent. They are equally ineffective if they maintain the kind of professional distance that does not allow them to understand those they are supporting at a deep enough level to make a difference. Many times professionals find themselves thinking, "If only I could take this child home with me," "Thank God I don't have to take this child home," "If only this parent had more help," or "I could never survive this; how am I going to help them do so?" Each situation raises intense feelings about the child, the parents, the siblings, and themselves. Fear, anger, frustration, guilt, and blame can take over their lives and erase the experiences of extreme joy and satisfaction that can also be found in this field.

So how do providers cope? They need to look at what nourishes them and consciously build time in their life to engage in those activities. If they neglect to do so, they will continually withdraw from their account of personal reserves without adding to it. This does not mean that professionals should not stretch themselves or go the extra mile. It does mean, however, that they reflect on what nourishes them and take the time to do those things. No one can tell anyone else what they need to do! However, when providers are in touch with their needs and take care of themselves, they model how healthy such behavior can be, for their own families, the children and families they serve, and also their col-

leagues. They can be very passionate about their work with children and families, and can do so in a calm and nurturing way or unwisely do so in an intense and unhealthy manner.

Recognizing one's own vulnerabilities and how to cope with them actually facilitates the development of better skills in collaborating with families. Accepting oneself as human, with not only needs but also ongoing potential for growth, helps to perceive others more realistically. Providers then become more patient and compassionate with themselves and others, and their ability to see the strengths and potential for growth in everyone increases as well.

KEEPING CHILDREN SAFE

Keeping children healthy and safe is a challenge in the best of circumstances. With developmental and behavioral challenges, the task becomes even more difficult. Such challenges often wreak havoc with a parent's feelings of competence and can initiate a negative spiral in the parent–child relationship. How do providers approach discipline and behavioral issues with parents and caregivers? When children's safety is at stake, most adults' fears trigger automatic reactions, such as lecturing and scolding parents about their lack of skill in situations rather than supporting their acquisition of new skills. Such responses often result in perpetuating old patterns of behavior.

In his book *Mentoring 101,* John Maxwell (2008) provides strategies for assisting others to reach their best potential. He recommends "treat[ing] others like a 10" (p. 45) and provides the following strategies for doing so:

- See them as who they can become.
- Let them borrow your belief in them.
- Catch them doing something right.
- Believe the best—give others the benefit of the doubt.
- Realize that "10" has many definitions.
- Place people in their strength zones.
- Give them the "10" treatment (pp. 45–56).

Imagine someone truly believing in you, so much so that you start believing you can accomplish something you feared you never could. This person has such confidence in you that you can't help but start believing you can do it. Even when you make mistakes, the person encourages and helps you to understand that mistakes are progress, landmarks on the way to success. This person listens to you so well that he or she knows how to help you make the next step, instead of expecting so much so fast that you end up feeling like a failure. When you are with this person, you never doubt that you have something important to contribute, and you feel great! Imagine that each child *and* each parent feels that with your presence. This is the way to move forward in keeping children healthy, safe, and thriving. It is the path to helping parents build the skills they need to support their children more effectively.

INVOLVING FATHERS

Many cultures across the globe have a deep tradition of women and mothers as the nurturers of children, and men and fathers as the providers as well as disciplinarians. Although many individuals, families, and community groups are

growing beyond these traditional roles, they often find themselves without much support. Many providers in the field have not reflected on how their own relationship with their father and the men in their lives color their beliefs and approaches to working with the fathers of the children in their care. In *Touchpoints—Birth to Three: Your Child's Emotional and Behavioral Development* (2006), Brazelton and Sparrow wrote, "Although stereotypes of male behavior have begun to break down, it may take several generations before they really change. I have had primary caregiving fathers in my practice. They were pioneers who had to work things out for themselves" (p. 426).

Many adults would like to think they carry no prejudices and accept everyone without reservation. As much as that is a worthy goal to work toward, Malcolm Gladwell, in his book *Blink: The Power of Thinking without Thinking,* offers a good deal of evidence that people are often further away from that goal than they would like to believe. He thus encourages them to continue on the journey. Gladwell reports that 25 years ago only 5% of the classical musicians in the United States were women; today the number has reached approximately 50%. What created the change? The change came about with a decision to hold blind auditions, with individuals playing behind screens, and this prevented those evaluating the music from knowing the gender of the musician.

One might think that because women have been discriminated against that women would be less likely to discriminate or hold prejudices against others. However, this is typically not the case. Prejudice and discrimination breed certain underlying fears, concerns, and sensitivities that can be difficult to identify, let alone perceive in one's own interactions. Adding to this is the fact that the fields of child care and early education have been largely dominated by women. Such perceptions are essential to understanding prevailing attitudes toward men and their roles in parenting, understanding ways to collaborate with fathers, and ensuring that services do not interfere with the father–child bond. Brazelton and Sparrow wrote,

> Studies of the effects of the increasing involvement of fathers in their babies' caretaking point to the gains in babies' development. Not only do school-aged children whose fathers were involved with them as infants demonstrate significant gains in their IQ, but they show more sense of humor, longer attention spans, and more eagerness for learning. (2006, p. 427)

This evidence certainly indicates a need for providers (i.e., male or female) of services to young children and their families to reflect on their own experiences with the men in their lives and remain alert to the ways in which these past experiences may color their current interactions.

SETTING LIMITS FOR EVERYONE

To professionals, the term *setting limits* generally brings to mind parents' ability to provide boundaries for their children. They often forget that there is another aspect of setting limits: encouraging families to set limits with providers. This is very important, from the very beginning of the relationship.

As discussed in the section on maintaining normalcy, the relationship between provider and parents frequently starts on an unequal footing. Parents often see the provider as having information and skills that their child needs, which they lack. This perspective can make parents cautious in expressing their own needs and desires because of concerns that they may be judged poorly, feel their needs are selfish in comparison to what their child needs, think that they may offend the experts, or fear they may lose help and support. In reality, professionals can support families much better if families do express their boundaries. The following excerpts from parents illustrate how they felt while receiving services in their homes.

I was told that services were limited, but they would work hard to find someone to work with my son. When the therapist called and asked me if 2:30 on Tuesdays and Thursdays would work, I was so afraid that I would miss my chance at services that I said sure. It took a lot to manage those sessions. Scott usually napped from 1:00 to 4:00, and he was a child very attached to his routines. I had to wake him up early enough so that by the time the therapist arrived he could function during the session, and then the whole family suffered those nights because he was so tired that he fought going to bed for the night and woke crying several times. I was also supporting my mom who was going through chemotherapy, and her sessions were on Thursday afternoons. We could not change her sessions, so a friend took her instead. During every Thursday afternoon session, I was so torn between trying to learn how to help my child and wanting to be with my mom to support her through her own difficult challenge.

Angela is a child who is very sensitive and takes things quite seriously. I knew she needed help with her speech because she was so quiet. I would get encouraged when she laughed because then she would say a couple of words, but she was still way behind on the number of words she would use. Her therapist was very knowledgeable; she always had ideas and left homework for us to do. During sessions Angela hung back and resisted participating. I worked hard to do what the therapist asked, but it didn't seem to help. I sometimes pretended Angela and I had done the homework together. I finally stopped trying and started playing with Angela, trying to get her to laugh more.

Then I would model the words the therapist was trying to get her to say. Angela started to make some progress, and her therapist was pleased. She praised us for our good work. I had very mixed feelings about the whole experience, including guilt about not doing what the therapist said, frustration at how businesslike she was with Angela and the homework she gave us, and finally relief that, despite everything, Angela really was making progress.

 Chase started life with more challenges than many of us will face in a lifetime. He was born at 26 weeks' gestation and was in the hospital for 3 months, hooked up to a variety of machines, and underwent three surgeries. We were surrounded by professionals from the moment he was born, and 7 years later we still are. I am profoundly grateful to the many people who worked to keep Chase alive and help our beautiful boy grow. At the same time, I wish many had taken the time to know us better, be more honest with us, and include us in more decisions. There was the physical therapist who would not look me in the eye or answer any of my questions about Chase's development. I often wondered if she actually thought that ignoring the questions and avoiding me would make me feel any better than honestly confronting the challenges with me. I knew she could not diagnose Chase, but I longed for someone to acknowledge my fears and support me through that difficult time. I wanted to be a part of helping instead of helplessly watching. Then there was the teacher who let me know in many ways (the way she looked at me, the way she kept repeating what she thought) that she disapproved of my discipline choices for Chase. He had been through so much, and I wanted him to enjoy life and find its beauty and fun as well. I really didn't care about time-out; I cared more about what Chase was trying to communicate when he was frustrated and threw something or cried and refused to participate. Another time his team at school ordered him a large, expensive, and complicated communication system without ever asking us what we thought. I admit I know nothing about that kind of technology, but then they expected us to bring it home and use it, too. I was scared to death of breaking the thing!

From the beginning of a relationship with parents, it is essential that providers encourage parents to be honest about their feelings regarding what providers say and do, how providers behave in the home and with their child, and the choices providers are presenting for their child. Opening a discussion with "What are your thoughts about this?" can give parents an opportunity to express their feelings, concerns, and hopes. Some of the most collaborative discussions we have experienced with families have started with that statement. If parents do not want providers to discipline their child or want them to do so in ways the providers are not comfortable with, providers need to ask themselves some tough questions about these limits on their own function in their life. Is the child being harmed or abused by a parent's decisions, or is it just not my personal preference about how to raise a child? Can I legally engage in their method of discipline? Do I feel comfortable in this realm of development, or do I encourage the parent to seek out information for both of us on how to handle the situation (e.g., from a pediatrician, a teacher, a social worker)?

What if abuse is involved? Then honesty is the best policy. Many professionals will read information such as that presented in this chapter and say, "Well, I can see it working for some families but not all." Yet research conducted through programs such as the Touchpoints Site in Napa County, California, have clearly indicated the opposite (Brazelton, 2007). Use of the Touchpoints approach in a setting designed for the most at-risk infants and families in Napa County resulted in no one's losing custody of a child in 34 months of operation.

MOVING FROM ONE PROGRAM TO ANOTHER: LEAVING THE FAMILIAR AND STARTING AGAIN

Transitions are part of life and often are difficult under the best of circumstances. A strong mix of emotions can occur for everyone when families move on to new settings. It can be difficult for parents, who have shared a great deal with providers and watched their children blossom after receiving devastating news of disabling conditions and developmental delays, to face building new relationships with new providers in different settings. Transitions are difficult for providers, too. They may have had a chance only to plant seeds that others will watch sprout and grow, and not surprisingly they have strong attachments to the child and family.

Sometimes the emotions are more complex. Providers may feel relieved to be finished working with a family that was a challenge for them or with a child with whom they did not feel successful. They may have feelings of guilt about ending relationships. Families too may feel guilty at being relieved that their child is transitioning to preschool or school and that he or she will be in someone else's care, providing some respite from the challenges of parenting. While all of these emotions are normal, they often go unacknowledged and can affect both the parting relationships and the new ones that will be developed. In times of transition individuals may fall into any of the roles in the triangles discussed previously. Sometimes professionals are overprotective of a child and family and think that they are being helpful by warning them of the problems that others experienced in dealing with a school district. This kind of information can add fear and worry, and such difficulties may not even surface.

Life is full of challenges, and families of children whose needs require the presence of many professionals in their lives know that better than most. When facing a transition, why not take some time to look at the skills that both child and parents have gained so that they can see how strong and resilient they are? Instead of warning about negative possibilities, share how reluctant you remember they were when you first entered their lives and how strong they were in taking the risk to develop new relationships. Providing specific examples of how they did so can help them focus on their strengths as they enter new settings and relationships. How much more potential there is in preparing everyone for success rather than failure!

SOMEONE ELSE TO TALK TO: INFORMAL FRIENDS CAN MAKE A BIG DIFFERENCE

There are many pressures on professionals and families to create change. Professionals often forget that a strong way to shore up families is to assist them in making wider connections. Extended family members, neighbors, members of community groups (e.g., churches, synagogues, libraries, playgroups, playgrounds, support groups, community centers) can offer vital sources of friendship and support. These more informal supports often develop into deeper emotional bonds than the intermittent relationships involved in help that comes and goes. In fact, some can last a lifetime.

Often these connections require some help to get started. A parent who is embarrassed by his or her child's challenging behaviors when in public needs support in such places to learn strategies for helping their child cope. It is only then that the parent may have the confidence to move into more public settings where the chance for increased friendships and support can occur. Providers need to ask themselves if they are willing to go to the grocery store or the church nursery or the playground with the child and parent to work out and practice strategies for success. Are they willing to work on some independent play skills instead of only activities that require the parent to be a teacher or therapist all the time?

Why is this important? It is difficult for a parent to talk to another person if she has to focus entirely on enhancing her child's skills. If a child has some independent play skills, however, the parent can relax and open up to adult friendships formed in these places. Many parents put this on the bottom of their own priority list, feeling that their child's needs (i.e., therapies) must always come first. In doing so, they fall into the same trap as providers who do not care for their own needs. Taking care of their own needs for friendship and support will help parents to not only survive but also thrive and more fully care for their child. In light of professionals' interest in helping parents experience wider and deeper support, they also need to remember to ask parents whom they would like to be present at sessions and meetings about their child. Are professionals open to a family's inviting their pastor, a neighbor, the babysitter to places typically relegated to the parent(s) and professionals? How do they feel about having equal or greater numbers of family members and friends at the table, along with professionals?

BENEFICIAL OUTCOMES

We realize that this chapter is filled with discussions about simple common sense. We also recognize that relationships are complex, and that collaboration takes a great deal of reflection and ongoing skill development. Effort is required to achieve success. The rewards, however, far outweigh the effort, and what becomes possible for children, families, and providers expands exponentially. Many

providers who have incorporated reflective practice into their professional lives
and honest, open collaboration with all
families they work with have expressed
that they only wish they had known
about and been taught how to grow in
this manner much earlier in their career.
They often look back with regret to failures with some families, but they also remember that every failure is another
step toward success. They would not be
the people they have become without the
total combination of experiences they
have had. Experiences do not tell providers who they are, but they bring wisdom that enhances and expands who
they are and who they can become. In-

corporating reflective practice regarding respectful and effective collaboration
with families into ongoing professional development can become a way of life,
one that has far-reaching, beneficial outcomes.

Thinking It Through: Questions for Discussion

1. What motivated you to choose a helping profession? How do you think
   those motivations affect your style of help?

2. What was your own parenting like when you were a child? What was
   your experience of educational systems and methods? Did they work
   for you? Did you have to find your own way? How have these experiences affected your career choices, your philosophy on child development, and your ideas about parenting? Now, reflect on how they might
   affect your collaborations with parents, other caregivers, and colleagues.

3. Reflect on a past occasion in which you were the provider in a situation
   that was not going well. Look for indicators that you played a hero, rescuer, or victim role. What strategies could you now use to move beyond
   these stereotyped ways of relating?

REFERENCES

Brazelton, T.B. (2007, April). *The Brazelton Touchpoints approach: Description, analysis, and effectiveness.* Unpublished manuscript.
Brazelton, T.B., & Sparrow, J.D. (2006). *Touchpoints—Birth to 3: Your child's emotional and behavioral development* (2nd ed.). Cambridge, MA: Perseus.

Gladwell, M. (2005). *Blink: The power of thinking without thinking.* New York: Back Bay Books, Little, Brown.

Maxwell, J. (2008). *Mentoring 101: What every leader needs to know.* Nashville, TN: Thomas Nelson.

Shinn, M. (1978). Father absence and cognitive development. *Psychological Bulletin, 85,* 295–324.

14

An Epilogue

Climbing to New Heights

Gail L. Ensher and David A. Clark

CHAPTER HIGHLIGHTS

At the conclusion of this chapter, the reader will

- Understand the lessons learned from research, policies, training, and clinical practices about working with families and young children

- Understand some of the most pressing issues for the years ahead that are essential to offering best practice services to families and young children

- Understand the rapidly changing world and developments in research, policy making, education, and direct service that have the potential for formulating more universal best practice

PATHWAYS TRAVELED: LESSONS LEARNED

This book has focused on the vital importance of nurturing relationships—a dimension that transcends every aspect of providers' work with families, infants, and young children. Pathways traveled in years past, especially those through the past decade, have taught those in the field many lessons that need to be integrated into their interactions with families. The following are some of the most noteworthy:

- It is essential for professionals to emphasize the strength-based abilities, resources, and beliefs of families as they seek to build relationships with parents and children. This is a shift in paradigm from the traditional deficit models of many training programs in the health care, medical, clinical, and educational fields. In providing relationship-centered services, professionals empower and validate parents as the genuine experts regarding the needs of their families.

- The service fields have moved beyond an exclusive focus on the child to offer services within the broader context of the family. This change requires all professionals to provide services with an awareness of the larger scope of a family's psychosocial strengths and needs.

- Some of these needs have been incurred as a result of declining financial and employment opportunities in the United States, which have had life-transforming consequences for families. Growing economic instability has affected families' mental health and quality of life, with greater numbers of families living below the poverty line, more rapid return of parents to work following the birth of children, longer working hours, more families in which both parents work, and longer hours of caregiving outside the home from infancy throughout the preschool years.

- Individuals across all of the helping professions must be adaptable and able to problem-solve in an increasingly complex and changing world. Likewise, they need to facilitate adaptability and problem-solving skills among family members so that when professionals leave, parents can carry on their lives with a sense of competence and hopefulness.

- Although much of providers' interaction focuses on infants and young children, understanding how to engage well with other adults, including colleagues and caregivers, is essential. As they work through difficult situations, adults will not always agree on the best course of action. However, working in relationship with others requires that providers sometimes set aside their own agendas and refrain from personalizing conflict. Collaboration is an essential quality of the team process and guides all early childhood programs and health care services.

- Services for families need to be affordable and accessible. Those most in need of medical treatment and early intervention—such as young children in the child welfare system (Dicker, 2009) and homeless children—frequently fail to be identified, enrolled, or retained in programs that could be of significant benefit.

- Families may look very different from decades past—with more single mothers and fathers, grandparents, divorced parents, cohabitating parents, and same-sex parents. Medical care and educational programs must be responsive to a wide range of ethnically, racially, educationally, and economically diverse populations of children and caregivers.

- Professionals cannot neglect the importance of helping families establish informal connections, networks, and friends within their community. Families dealing with disability, addictions, mental health problems, child abuse and neglect, and other challenging situations often find themselves isolated from the vitality of relationships with other humans and even pets (McCardle, McCune, Griffin, Esposito, & Freund, 2011).

Although it is not always possible to circumvent risks and challenging situations, many social problems that continue to plague families and young children—adolescent pregnancies, child abuse and neglect, certain illnesses, chronic violence in communities and neighborhoods, widespread devastation from natural disasters—could be alleviated with more prevention, education, policies, and strategies for preparedness.

ON THE AGENDA: A NEW ERA OF BEST PRACTICE

In the years ahead, professionals will face a new era of unprecedented technology that will save babies who otherwise would not have lived, bring advances in assisted reproductive technology, offer

new solutions to chronic childhood illnesses such as diabetes and cancer, investigate genetics far beyond current comprehension, and make available new augmentative systems in communication for young children with multiple disabilities. All of these developments have the capacity for improving medical and educational interventions for parents and young children.

Still, to achieve best practice in working with families, equal weight needs to be placed on those human qualities that have the potential to make a meaningful difference in their lives. In their summary and conclusions chapter in *From Neurons to Neighborhoods: The Science of Early Childhood Development,* Shonkoff and Phillips wrote that the well-being of children depends on two conditions:

> First is the need for stable and loving relationships with a limited number of adults who provide responsive and reciprocal interaction, protection from harm, encouragement for exploration and learning, and transmission of cultural values. Second is the need for a safe and predictable environment that provides a range of growth-promoting experiences to promote cognitive, linguistic, social, emotional, and moral development. The majority of children in the United States today enjoy the benefits of both. A significant number do not. (2000, p. 413)

The latter statement is as accurate today as it was more than a decade ago. Without minimizing the developments and innovations of the future, we would like to leave our readers with a charge: to tenaciously search for ways to climb to new heights to reach that "significant number" of families and young children who continue to be denied opportunities for well-being—by nurturing healthy relationships in each professional encounter and, in so doing, help families to sustain those critically important relationships throughout their children's earliest years and beyond.

REFERENCES

Dicker, S. (2009). *Reversing the odds: Improving outcomes for babies in the child welfare system.* Baltimore: Paul H. Brookes Publishing Co.

McCardle, P., McCune, S., Griffin, J.A., Esposito, L., & Freund, L.S. (2011). *Animals in our lives: Human–animal interaction in family, community, and therapeutic settings.* Baltimore: Paul H. Brookes Publishing Co.

Shonkoff, J.P., & Phillips, D.A. (Eds.). (2000). *From neurons to neighborhoods: The science of early childhood development.* Washington, DC: National Academies Press.

Index

Page numbers followed by *f* indicate figures and by *t* indicate tables.